Clerical Discourse and Lay Audience in Late Medieval England

FIONA SOMERSET

CAMBRIDGE
UNIVERSITY PRESS

PUBLISHED BY THE PRESS SYNDICATE OF THE UNIVERSITY OF CAMBRIDGE
The Pitt Building, Trumpington Street, Cambridge CB2 1RP, United Kingdom

CAMBRIDGE UNIVERSITY PRESS
The Edinburgh Building, Cambridge CB2 2RU, United Kingdom
40 West 20th Street, New York, NY 10011–4211, USA
10 Stamford Road, Oakleigh, Melbourne 3166, Australia

© Fiona Somerset 1998

First published 1998

Printed in the United Kingdom at the University Press, Cambridge

Typeset in Adobe Garamond 11.5/14pt   [CE]

A catalogue record for this book is available from the British Library

Library of Congress cataloguing in publication data

Somerset, Fiona.
Clerical discourse and lay audience in late medieval England / Fiona Somerset
p.   cm. (Cambridge studies in medieval literature: 37)
Includes bibliographical references and index.
ISBN 0 521 62154 2 (hardback)
1. Christian literature, Latin (Medieval and modern) – Translations into English (Middle) –
History and criticism.   2. Latin Language, Medieval and modern – Translating into
English (Middle).   3. Christian literature, English (Middle) – History and criticism.
4. Learning and scholarship – History – Medieval, 500–1500.
5. Catholic Church – England – Clergy – Intellectual life.
6. Laity – Catholic Church – Books and reading – History.
7. Middle English – books and reading – History.
8. Religious thought – Middle Ages, 600–1500.   9. England – Intellectual life – 1066–1485.
10. Authors and readers – England – History.   I. Title.   II. Series.
PA8030.C47S65   1998
428′.0271′09032–dc21   97-32294   CIP

ISBN 0 521 62154 2 (hardback)

Clerical Discourse and Lay Audience in Late Medieval England

Fiona Somerset investigates the politics of translating learned Latin materials into English between around 1370 and 1410, when such translation was highly controversial. It was thought potentially capable of rendering authoritative intellectual information and methods of argumentation previously available only to educated clerics accessible to a much wider lay audience. The book examines what kinds of academic materials were translated into English, what sorts of audience were projected for this sort of clerical discourse, how writers positioned themselves with respect to potential audiences and opponents, and what dissemination and readership their writings met with. The well-known concerns of authors such as Langland, Trevisa, and Wyclif with clerical corruption and lay education are discussed, and linked to those of more obscure writers in both Latin and English, some only recently edited, several extant only in manuscript. Rather than demarcating orthodox from heretical writers, the book explores their shared attitudes towards lay audience.

FIONA SOMERSET is Assistant Professor of Middle English at the University of Western Ontario; this, her first book, was prepared while she was a research fellow in Medieval English at Lady Margaret Hall, Oxford.

CAMBRIDGE STUDIES IN MEDIEVAL LITERATURE

General editor
Alastair Minnis, *University of York*

Editorial board
Patrick Boyde, *University of Cambridge*
John Burrow, *University of Bristol*
Rita Copeland, *University of Minnesota*
Alan Deyermond, *University of London*
Peter Dronke, *University of Cambridge*
Simon Gaunt, *King's College London*
Nigel Palmer, *University of Oxford*
Winthrop Wetherbee, *Cornell University*

This series of critical books seeks to cover the whole area of literature written in the major medieval languages – the main European vernaculars, and medieval Latin and Greek – during the period c. 1100–1500. Its chief aim is to publish and stimulate fresh scholarship and criticism on medieval literature, special emphasis being placed on understanding major works of poetry, prose, and drama in relation to the contemporary culture and learning which fostered them.

A complete list of titles in the series can be found at the end of the volume.

Contents

Acknowledgements

This book is a revised version of my thesis 'Imaginary Publics: Extraclergial Writers and Vernacular Audience in Late-Medieval England'. I am glad to be able to thank once again all those who helped me in researching, writing, and revising this work. For financial support I thank the Mellon Foundation for a five year PhD fellowship, Cornell University for the Sage Fellowship that supplemented the Mellon and the Clare Hall fellowship that sent me to Clare Hall, Cambridge, and particularly Lady Margaret Hall, which first supported my work by allowing me to attend as a visiting student, and then awarded me the Randall MacIver junior research fellowship, during which I was able to complete this project and begin many others.

For help with my research I thank above all Anne Hudson, who read the thesis in full as I wrote it and offered comments on its argument, suggestions about other possible sources, and practical help in gaining access to them. I'm very grateful also to my thesis committee at Cornell, Winthrop Wetherbee, Andrew Galloway, and Barbara Correll, for supporting my work from the beginning and for their help and suggestions, particularly about plans to revise the thesis and submit it for publication. Other scholars who generously discussed particular topics or shared then unpublished work with me are thanked throughout the book, in the footnotes, but I must thank again Margaret Aston, Helen Barr, David Fowler, Andrew Galloway, Ralph Hanna, Janet Harris, Jill Havens, Andrew Hope, David Howlett, Simon Hunt, Steven Justice, Anne Middleton, Ruth Nissé, Matti Peikola, Larry Scanlon, James Simpson, Paul Strohm, Christina Von Nolcken, Ronald Waldron, and Nicholas Watson. I also thank the two anonymous readers for Cambridge University Press for their very helpful comments.

Acknowledgements

I am grateful to the following for kind permission to publish material from manuscripts in their libraries: the Brno University Library, the Master and Fellows of Gonville & Caius College, Cambridge, the Master and Fellows of Trinity College, Cambridge, Trinity College Library, Dublin, and (many times over) the Bodleian Library, Oxford. My thanks also to the librarians and staff of these libraries, as well as all the others I have visited, for their generous help.

Last, I would like to thank the staff of Cambridge University Press for their help, advice, and efficient work in the production of this book.

PART I

The vernacular oeuvre

I

Introduction

... And so seculer power oweþ and is bounden to ponisshe by just peyne of his swerd, þat is, worldly power, try[u]auntis rebellinge aȝens God and trespassing aȝens man by what kyn trespas; and, þat is more, to chastise his sugetis by peyne or turment of here body. And no drede muche more he may ponisshe hem by takynge awey of here temporaltees, þat is lasse þan bodily peyne. Þerfore seculer lordis don þis riȝtfully, siþ þis is don by comaundement of þe apostoile and by ordinaunce of God. Þerfore it is pleyn of þes resouns and auctoritees; and seculer lordis may levefully and medefully, in mony causes, taken awey temporal godis ȝoven to men of þe Chirche.[1]

When Wyclif, and Wycliffites, appealed to the lay power to disendow the clergy, in one sense their strategy was nothing new. In the late four-teenth century it was not an innovation for argument couched in a high-intellectual idiom and propounded by the highly educated to tell power what it wanted to hear, and the practice has not fallen into disuse since. Around the time of Wyclif in late medieval England, however, this strategy takes on a particularly interesting form: for a short time, in

---

[1] 'A Petition to the King and Parliament', in T. Arnold, ed., *Select English Works of John Wyclif*, 3 vols. (Oxford, 1869–71), iii: 507–23; 516/31–517/4. Arnold has 'n' in place of my reading 'u' in line 2; he does not recognize 'tryuauntis', a term frequently used by Wycliffites to translate *discolos* or *trutannos*. The Latin version of the 'Petition' (I. H. Stein, ed., 'The Latin Text of Wyclif's Complaint', *Speculum* 7 (1932), 87–94; see W. R. Thomson, *The Latin Writings of John Wyclif: An Annotated Catalog* (Toronto, 1983), 258–9 for the title *Peticio ad regem et parliamentum* and a description) uses 'discolos' (91/173), as does the *Testimony of William Thorpe*, where in a paraphrase of I Peter 2:18 and 2:20 Thorpe translates the bible's *discolos* as 'trowantis'. (See A. Hudson, ed., *The Testimony of William Thorpe*, in *Two Wycliffite Texts*, EETS, o.s. 301 (Oxford, 1993), 48/816–49/825.) Thanks to Matti Peikola, who is writing about Wycliffite usage of 'tyrauntis' and 'tryuauntis', for discussion of this point.

between the beginnings of an extensive translation of Latin learning into the vernacular from the mid-fourteenth century onward and the growing legitimation of English as an 'official' written language of government and administration during the reign of Henry V, this strategy of argument requires what is temporarily a highly controversial sort of translation.

The controversy arises because this appeal is written in English, at a point when the written records of legal and government business are still, except in very rare cases, written in French or Latin, and when the deployment of 'resouns and auctoritees' within the structures of academic argument is overwhelmingly restricted – like the texts, commentaries, and treatises on which such argument draws – to Latin, and to clerics trained at university.[2] Though trials and parliaments may have been conducted partly or wholly in English, while certainly proclamations and public sermons would have been delivered in the vernacular, their textual forms in Latin and French were available to a wider audience only through trained intermediaries.[3] And though scholastic

---

[2] J. H. Fisher provides the outline of a history of the transfer of official written language from Latin and French to English briefly in 'A Language Policy for Lancastrian England', *Publications of the Modern Language Association of America* (hereafter *PMLA*) 107 (1992), 1168–80 (where he suggests that the change was a deliberate act of royal policy aimed at widening the Lancastrian base of support), and at rather more length in 'Chancery and the Emergence of Standard Written English in the Fifteenth Century', *Speculum* 52 (1977), 870–99. Very little work has been done on the transfer of academic argument to English, although A. Hudson (*The Premature Reformation: Wycliffite Texts and Lollard History* (Oxford, 1988), 217–24) and M. Aston ('Wycliffe and the Vernacular', in *Faith and Fire: Popular and Unpopular Religion, 1350–1600* (London, 1993), 27–72, especially 66) have briefly discussed Wycliffite usage. On the ways in which intellectual material more generally (and more loosely) was being transferred to English see below, pp. 10–16.

[3] The difficulty in determining the language in which a text was spoken is always of course that the language of record may differ from the language of delivery. For a general introduction to this difficulty (though focused on the period 1066 to 1307) see M. T. Clanchy, *From Memory to Written Record*, 2nd ed. (Oxford, 1993), 197–223. For a judicious practical discussion of difficulties in determining the initial language of Wycliffite works see A. Hudson, 'William Taylor's 1406 Sermon: A Postscript', *Medium Aevum* 64 (1995), 100–6; 101–3. Where English words difficult to translate are interspersed or English sections included in a document, use of English on the occasion it records may safely be deduced. On some occasions, too, it is specified that English was used. Fisher collects together occasions where the language of Parliament or of legal process was clearly English, in 'Chancery and the Emergence of Standard Written English', 879–80. Leaving aside more mundane occasions where English words are

clerics were frequently employed to defend the actions and policies of secular power, as when Wyclif was employed to defend royal officers' breach of sanctuary in a parliament held in Gloucester in 1378,[4] only other educated clerics would be expected to have the ability to evaluate, rather than simply to accept, their arguments.

Whereas if presented in Latin as a justification of the views of the king or certain lords, the passage with which we began would have amounted to no more than an argument for the disendowment of corrupt clergy on which those few to whom it was accessible might or might not choose to act, the English version cast as exhortation carries the potential for a much further reaching redistribution, if not disendowment, of social power. When made available in the vernacular the tract becomes potentially accessible to every person who can read English, and through those readers to an even wider audience of listeners. Along with the monetary disendowment of corrupt clergy that would ensue if lords acted upon its recommendation, this tract itself if presented to unprecedented audiences has the potential to redistribute intellectual capital by teaching lay audiences information previously inaccessible to them. There is even the possibility, if lay people learn from reading this sort of material how to formulate arguments themselves and how to evaluate critically arguments presented to them, that it might accomplish a 'disendowment' of previously exclusively clerical intellectual skills. Further, as the Peasants' Revolt of 1381 was perhaps especially important in bringing to public notice, the presentation of polemic argument in English carries with it by virtue of its possible influence on even the lowest of the laity the potential for a redistribution of secular power as well.[5]

---

probably included for no reason more significant than awkwardness of translation, S. Justice suggests that some clerics include material in English in their Latin writing out of extremes of outrage (*Writing and Rebellion: England in 1381* (Berkeley, CA, 1994), esp. 13–66) or boredom ('Inquisition, Speech, and Writing: A Case from Medieval Norwich', *Representations* 48 (1994), 1–29; reprinted in R. Copeland, ed., *Criticism and Dissent in the Middle Ages* (Cambridge, 1996), 289–322).

4 See, most recently, A. Hudson, *The Premature Reformation*, 64, and the references to contemporary records and scholarly discussions of this incident cited there, nn. 28 and 29. On the sorts of public role clerics might play in political controversy see, most recently, J. Coleman, 'The Science of Politics and Late Medieval Academic Debate', in Copeland, ed., *Criticism and Dissent*, 181–214.

5 On the importance of vernacular writing in the Peasants' Revolt see S. Justice, *Writing*

Reserving for the moment the question of how the writer of this tract, and others like him, confront the potential implications of their unprecedented mode of address, it is worth considering what can be discerned about the actual dissemination of his tract, and the usefully characteristic methodological difficulties that question raises. There are two manuscripts of the English version of the 'Petition'. Cambridge, Corpus Christi College 296 (hereafter C) has the ending of another tract spliced onto it at Arnold's 520/18, whereas its own conclusion has been attached to the end of that other tract.[6] Dublin, Trinity College 244 (hereafter T) breaks off unfinished at Arnold's 520/17.[7] In addition, there is a single copy of a Latin version of the tract in a Florentine manuscript (hereafter F).[8] The English copies have been used as the basis of speculations about Lollard book production that would suggest the work was at minimum circulated amongst an audience of Lollard sympathizers: noting that the 'Petition' was added to the end of

---

and Rebellion; R. F. Green, 'John Ball's Letters: Literary History and Historical Literature', in B. A. Hanawalt, ed., *Chaucer's England: Literature in Historical Context* (Minneapolis, 1992), 176–200; A. Hudson, '*Piers Plowman* and the Peasants' Revolt: A Problem Revisited', *The Yearbook of Langland Studies* 8 (1994), 85–106; S. Crane, 'The Writing Lesson of 1381', in Hanawalt, *Chaucer's England*, 201–21; and P. Strohm, ' "A Revelle!" ': Chronicle Evidence and the Rebel Voice', in *Hochon's Arrow: The Social Imagination of Fourteenth-Century Texts* (Princeton, 1992), 33–56. R. Hanna III suggests in *Pursuing History: Middle English Manuscripts and Their Texts* (Stanford, 1996), 67–8, 239–41, that the possibilities of reaching a broad lay public, rather than a small coterie audience, by writing in the vernacular were first brought home to polemical writers following the Peasants' Revolt. Of course the extent to which writers may consider the potential consequences of vernacular audience continue to vary widely, and are not always congruent with practical possibility: for an object example compare chs. 4 and 5, and for a useful warning about the dangers of universalizing the experiences or perceptions of particular writers (with reference to the Oxford translation debate of the early fifteenth century) see N. Watson, 'Censorship and Cultural Change in Late-Medieval England: Vernacular Theology, the Oxford Translation Debate, and Arundel's Constitutions of 1409', *Speculum* 70 (1995), 822–64; 847.

6 Cambridge, Corpus Christi College 296, ff. 288–297v line 20, continued at 170 line 35–172. The textual accident has been described by both Arnold, *Select English Works of Wyclif*, iii: 507–8, and F. D. Matthew (who prints the other tract involved), *The English Works of Wyclif Hitherto Unprinted*, EETS o.s. 74 (London, 1880), 187. An explanation has been suggested by R. Hanna III, 'Two Lollard Codices and Lollard Book-Production', *Studies in Bibliography* 43 (1990), 49–62; reprinted in R. Hanna III, *Pursuing History*, 48–59.

7 Dublin, Trinity College 244, ff. 141v–148v.

8 Florence, *Bibl. Laurent. Flor. Plut. xix cod. xxxiii*, ff. 23v–26v. For the most recent description see I. H. Stein, 'The Wyclif Manuscript in Florence', *Speculum* 5 (1930), 95–7.

C by a different scribe when the book had been completed, Hanna suggests that the exemplar the T and C scribes both used was made up of booklets at least some of which could be detached for separate circulation, and that the 'Petition' had in fact been separated for copying elsewhere when the main part of C was being copied.[9] The single copy of the Latin version appears, as its editor Stein pointedly mentions, in a manuscript that otherwise consists of what are certainly authentic works of Wyclif.[10] But neither internal evidence within the copies themselves nor annotation in the manuscripts gives us any precise indication of title, occasion, and date, or any ascription to an author.

Which came first, the English or the Latin? Who wrote the original version? Who translated and adapted it? When was each written? What audience did each reach, and does that audience differ from the projected audience addressed from within the tract? Here as so often, the questions that immediately arise require careful evaluation, and may finally be unanswerable.

Although the usual assumption in late medieval European studies is that Latin versions precede vernacular versions, since many Wycliffite texts were exported to Hussites in Europe after composition in England this assumption is never a safe one for Wycliffite works.[11] The evidence available for determining priority of composition among Wycliffite versions is, however, seldom easy to interpret. That the Latin version gives chapter and verse for the authorities it cites while the English merely names them may, for example, show that an English translator was simplifying for an audience that would not have access to the books named, but it might just as well show that a Latin translator was specifying sources for the benefit of a new audience abroad. Nor is Latinate syntax in an English text a reliable indication of clumsy translation from Latin: the language in which educated writers would have been trained in argumentation was invariably Latin, so that any English rendering of such idioms would involve at the very least mental translation. T and C, like most English Wycliffite tracts, include no form of ascription to an author or translator. And the

---

[9] See R. Hanna III, 'Two Lollard Codices', esp. 56–9.
[10] See Stein, ed., 'Wyclif's Complaint'.   [11] See n. 3.

evidence for F is inconclusive: F ends 'Explicit bonus et utilis tractatus secundum magistrum Iohannem <erasure>'; but even if Stein is correct that the erasure removed 'Wiclefum', whether the force of *secundum* is to ascribe the text to Wyclif, to note that it was good and useful according to Wyclif, or to claim its goodness and usefulness are in accord with what Wyclif thought, is unclear.

What it is certainly safe to say is that there is no warrant, external or internal, for the nineteenth century title 'A Petition to King and Parliament', still less for the assertion, repeated by all the work's editors, that Wyclif presented the work to Parliament in 1382. None of the copies has a medieval title, and even C's sixteenth to seventeenth century title 'A complainte to the king and parliament' avoids any suggestion that the work was a petition presented formally in Parliament.[12] There is no record in any chronicle or in the Parliament rolls that Wyclif or anyone else presented any such petition; while the petition if presented and rejected might well be struck out of the official record, the incident would surely be notorious and could scarcely escape being reported somewhere.[13] The tract begins with the address 'Plese it to oure most noble and most worþi King Richard, kyng boþe of Englond and of Fraunce, and to þe noble Duk of Lancastre, and to oþere grete men of þe rewme, boþe to seculers and men of holi Chirche, þat ben gaderid in þe Parlement, to here, assent and meyntene þe fewe articlis or poyntis þat ben seet wiþinne þis writing, and proved boþe by auctorite and resoun . . .', but the tone throughout, and even here, is far more assertive and contentious than that conventionally found in a parliamentary petition. Like the

---

[12] Hanna dates the title written in the margin of C s. xvi to s. xvii ('Two Lollard Codices', 60).

[13] Compare Walsingham's account of a proposal for disendowment put forward by knights of the shire and lords in the 1385 Parliament; Walsingham is pleased to report that Richard rejected the proposal and ordered that it should be destroyed rather than recorded (*Historia Anglicana*, 2 vols., ed. H. T. Riley (London, 1863–4), ii: 139–40). Walsingham and other chroniclers hostile to Lollardy would surely not have missed an opportunity to recount Richard's rejection of a petition by Wyclif: indeed it is surprising, given that there was a written version of a text by Wyclif or a Wycliffite that ostensibly addressed Parliament, that no account of its presentation was manufactured. On Walsingham's account see M. Aston, ' "Caim's Castles": Poverty, Politics, and Disendowment', in *Faith and Fire*, 95–131; 109, and see also 108, where she briefly discusses the 'Petition' and notes its indeterminate dating.

Wycliffite *Twelve Conclusions* of 1395, the 'Petition' seems designed for and perhaps even brought to the attention of Parliament, yet not cast in the accepted supplicatory form of documents officially presented to Parliament.[14] Rather than describing a wrong and seeking a remedy as a parliamentary petition conventionally would, the writer seeks to prove to the king and nobles that they are bound to act as he recommends.

Still, the purpose of recognizing the flimsiness of the nineteeth century assertions made about this tract is not to substitute for them a series of corrosive denials leading to the conclusion that there is no reason to give the tract any further attention. Rather, the aim is to pursue another set of possibilities that previous false certainties have tended to obscure, by giving due attention to the distance between the tract's actual and projected audiences, and to oddities and inconsistencies in its address to its projected audience. The tract's address to the king and influential laity breaks with the conventions of parliamentary petition, and indeed is rather too assertive even for the general designation 'complaint' assigned it by the title in C; further, what we know of its dissemination seems to indicate that it circulated amongst another limited vernacular circle entirely. Even if the gap between the tract's actual and projected audiences can never be accurately measured, acknowledging that it must be there – that even if the audience addressed is identical to the text's first audience, the writer cannot fail to be conscious of the possibilities of writing in the vernacular – opens up a space for us to consider other questions.

Why does the tract use such thoroughly academic language in its attempt to convince this ostensibly parliamentary audience? How does the writer's mode of address function to place the tract, and even its writer, in a novel social position? Why should this writer, or a group of Wycliffites, have chosen *this* tract, with its relatively narrow scope of address, to be disseminated in two languages in connection with what

---

14 On the *Twelve Conclusions* see ch. 4, esp. pp. 103–6. A comprehensive introduction to procedures and formats for parliamentary petitions may be found in J. Roskell, *The History of Parliament: The House of Commons 1386–1421*, 4 vols. (Stroud, 1992), i: 76–102; the proceedings of parliaments held during the reigns of Richard II and Henry IV are edited in J. Strachey, ed., *Rotuli Parliamentorum*, 6 vols. (London, 1767–77), iii.

seems to have been a well organized system for textual distribution and copying? Questions like these – to do with the kinds of academic material imported into English in argumentative contexts and the kinds of audiences explicitly or implicitly projected by writers for that material; with how writers position themselves in relation to their audiences and opponents; and with the conjunction or lack of it between those factors and what we know about the dissemination and readership of a given work – are the ones with which this study will chiefly be concerned.[15]

I locate this study at the point when the transfer of official legal and administrative information from French or Latin to English had scarcely begun, and when the translation into English of any scientific or philosophical material, let alone the academic topics 'extraclergial' writers draw on, was still far from routine. Much interesting work has been done on the larger historical processes amid which I place this study, and much yet remains to be done. While Fisher has traced the emergence of English as the official written language of government in the fifteenth century, and has linked this emergence with the pro-motion of Chaucer as the pre-eminent late medieval English poet that began from about 1400, he ignores entirely the unofficial and even illicit dissemination of controversial material in English before as well as after 1400, and discounts records of lay ownership of English works and translations before 1400.[16] Increasingly, however, it is recognized that the 'official' written language Fisher traces emerged oppositionally: the legitimation of some kinds and contexts of written English tended to suppress or delegitimate others. And we know a great deal more about those other kinds of written English than we did. Evidence for Wycliffite production in English has been extensively studied by Anne Hudson and Margaret Aston.[17] Ralph Hanna, as well as Anne

---

[15] For further discussion of the 'Petition', see ch. 3, pp. 80–1.

[16] See 'A Language Policy', 1170.

[17] See especially Hudson's 'Lollardy: The English Heresy?', *Studies in Church History* 18 (1982), 261–83, reprinted in A. Hudson, *Lollards and Their Books* (London, 1985), 141–63; as well as 'Wyclif and the English Language', in A. Kenny, ed., *Wyclif in his Times* (Oxford, 1986), 85–103; and Aston's 'Lollardy and Sedition, 1381–1431', and 'Lollardy and Literacy', in *Lollards and Reformers: Images and Literacy in Late Medieval Religion* (London, 1984), 1–47 and 193–217, and 'Wycliffe and the Vernacular', in *Faith and Fire*, 27–72.

Hudson, has examined ways in which from the early 1380s onward it became controversial for orthodox as well as heretical writers to use English, while Nicholas Watson has shown how orthodox vernacular devotional writers along with heretics were affected by the repressive measures introduced by Archbishop Thomas Arundel's *Constitutions* in 1409.[18] Bowers's suggestion that the growth of the 'Chaucer tradition' in the early fifteenth century was accompanied by the association with dissidence and perhaps even the active suppression of a 'Langland tradition' is also a step in the right direction.[19]

Little has yet been written in any systematic way about the early translation of philosophical and scientific works: while the editors of individual translations or of collected works of particular translators have attempted to place the works they have studied in context, the field still awaits systematic study.[20] One reason why is not far to seek. The interests and concerns of lay readers were both highly various and on the whole rather different from those currently fashionable at Oxford: 'popular' science seems to have concerned itself with medical recipes, lapidaries, astrology, and alchemy (among other subjects ranging from the thoroughly practical to the wildly speculative), and 'popular' philosophy with advice-to-princes in the *Secretum Secretorum* tradition. The systematic study of these kinds of translations will

18 R. Hanna III, 'The Difficulty of Ricardian Prose Translation: The Case of the Lollards', *Modern Language Quarterly* 51 (1990), 319–40, examines fifteenth as well as fourteenth century works both Lollard and orthodox; see also A. Hudson, 'The Context of Vernacular Wycliffism', ch. 9 of *The Premature Reformation*, 390–445; and N. Watson, 'Censorship and Cultural Change'.

19 J. M. Bowers, '*Piers Plowman* and the Police: Notes Toward a History of the Wycliffite Langland', *The Yearbook of Langland Studies* 6 (1992), 1–50; '*Pearl* in its Royal Setting: Ricardian Poetry Revisited', *Studies in the Age of Chaucer* 17 (1995), 111–55; and '*Piers Plowman*'s William Langland: Editing the Text, Writing the Author's Life', *The Yearbook of Langland Studies* 9 (1995), 65–90.

20 See editions by F. M. Getz (*Healing and Society in Medieval England: A Middle English Translation of the Pharmaceutical Writings of Gilbertus Anglicus* (Madison, WI, 1991)) and G. R. Keiser (*The Middle English 'Boke of Stones': the Southern Version* (Brussels, 1984)), the edited selections from works of astrology, prognostication, medicine, horticulture, and navigation collected in L. M. Matheson, ed., *Popular and Practical Science of Medieval England* (East Lansing, MI, 1994), and editions of and articles about Trevisa's translations cited in ch. 3, nn. 1, 2, 3, 7, 8, 25. Ralph Hanna has been planning to write about forms of informational vernacular prose translation spanning at least the period 1370 to 1413 and perhaps continuing as late as 1500, and has generously shared his ideas about types of informational translation with me.

contribute to a greater attentiveness to the larger context of late medieval learning outside the universities, in which varieties of knowledge based in written materials in the vernacular seem to have proliferated in a way that is now beginning to receive its due.[21] But it has not been of much interest to those writing the history of learning in the universities.

Nor was this sort of popular science and philosophy of great concern to its university-learned contemporaries. These kinds and varieties of popular learning do not mount any direct challenge to university learning: even if, as Hanna and Keiser have pointed out, some medical treatises included highly sophisticated material also of interest to academic students of medicine, recipes for rosemary are, patently, unlikely to bring the kingdom to its knees.[22] Instead this kind of learning seems to be viewed by academics as a largely innocuous distraction for the laity, dangerous only perhaps insofar as some forms of it may mislead those who dabble in them.[23] While they maintain their distance from university idiom, these kinds of writing are no threat to it.

The kind of learned vernacular writing that *is* highly controversial is that which turns the terms, modes of argument, and topics currently of interest to highly educated academics to its own ends, either combining this academic material with better-known popular learning, like Trevisa and Langland, or using it undiluted (even if often allusively rather than in a straightforwardly expository way) as Wycliffite writers often do. The writers of controversial works such as the 'Petition' are far from oblivious to the threat to their own clerical privileges implicit in their unprecedented form of address. Typically, they distance themselves from the institutional clergy they criticize and ally themselves with the laity, yet continue to employ the kinds of sophisticated

21 See for example essays by A. Galloway such as '*Piers Plowman* and the Schools', *The Yearbook of Langland Studies* 6 (1992), 89–107, 'Gower in his Most Learned Role and the Peasants' Revolt of 1381', *Mediaevalia* 16 (1993), 329–47 and – on the backhand, through consideration of Latin materials – 'The Rhetoric of Riddling in Late-Medieval England: The "Oxford" Riddles, the *Secretum philosophorum*, and the Riddles in *Piers Plowman*', *Speculum* 70 (1995), 68–105, as well as the more specialized introductory essays to the editions in Matheson.

22 See Hanna's and Keiser's contributions to Matheson, ed., *Popular and Practical Science of Medieval England*, especially 185–6 and 225.

23 Recall for example Dame Study's rebuke to Will in *Piers Plowman* B x, discussed by Galloway, '*Piers Plowman* and the Schools', 97.

argument that grant them clerical legitimacy. They take up, that is, an extraclergial position – presenting themselves as outside the clergy, yet if anything more ostentatiously learned than the typical clerical writer; 'lewed', or lay, in status or alliance, but possessed of 'clergie', or learning, nonetheless.

This characteristic extraclergial positioning exploits a telling ambiguity in the usage of the terms 'lewed' and 'clergie'. The range of meaning for both *clergie* and *lewed* includes status-linked senses – 'clergy' vs 'laity' – and also senses in which each word designates attributes conventionally linked to the status: 'clergie' is used to mean 'learning' and even 'body or field of knowledge' as well as to refer to persons of clerical status, and 'lewed' means 'uneducated' or 'illiterate' or even 'stupid' as well as 'lay'.[24] Of course the conventional linkage between learning and status did not hold fast in fourteenth century England, if indeed it ever had.[25] 'Clergie'/learning was not the exclusive province of the clergy; practically speaking the paradox of a person 'lewed' and 'clergie' both at once is no paradox at all. Yet still, when the two terms are imagined as mutually exclusive possibilities, 'lewed clergie' presents a conceptual paradox very useful to late medieval English writers. It presumes, then challenges, the conventional model of didactic pastoral interaction whereby clerics are charged with conveying to the laity the essentials of faith necessary for salvation.

There had developed an expectation that the clergy in England should instruct the laity in the essentials of faith; a reasonably effective mechanism for delivering this instruction by means of sermons and penitential examinations; and a growing mass of didactic pastoral writings designed to assist in its delivery. These might be viewed as resulting from the reformative movement in the church that produced the provisions for univeral lay instruction of the Lateran Council of 1215, and within England more particularly as a consequence of the systematic programme of instruction mandated by Pecham's *Ignorantia sacerdotium* of 1281 and the very similar *Lay Folks' Catechism* issued in

---

[24] See H. Kurath *et al.*, eds., *Middle English Dictionary* (Ann Arbor, MI, 1954–), (hereafter *MED*) s.vv. 'clergie', n. and 'lewed', n. and adj.

[25] As Clanchy has shown, even in the thirteenth and early fourteenth century there were any number of illiterate vicars and literate sheriffs (M. T. Clanchy, *From Memory to Written Record*, 224–46).

both Latin and English by Thoresby in 1357, whereby the basics of faith were to be conveyed to the laity by the clergy.[26] But beginning with the very canons and constitutions that prescribed reform and the circulars in which its particulars were detailed, and continuing in pastoral materials that came to be written not only for parish priests, but directly for their parishioners, there also developed a corresponding rhetoric of criticism of the clergy for any failure in their duty of instruction.[27] And the laity were admitted, since it might closely concern their salvation, to have a stake in that criticism.

It is a short step from allowing that criticism of clerical insufficiency concerns the laity, and providing them directly with pastoral materials in the vernacular that acknowledge that fact, to employing this rhetoric of clerical critique to justify writing vernacular tracts capable of conveying far more 'clergie' than the minimum the laity are strictly said to require. Materials and methods of counterargument made accessible to the laity could potentially authorize them to argue, and even act, against the clergy, while information about just how the clergy are abusing their positions might galvanize them to do so. By virtue of its tendency to diverge in all directions into matters of learned 'clergie' previously unexplored in English, the surplus-to-pastoral instruction extraclergial works provide cannot readily be subjected to a schema. Still, certain recurrent topics, kinds of information deployed in pursuing them, and terminology and techniques of argument employed in that pursuit, are worth sketching out before they are treated *ad hoc* as they emerge in the chapters to come.

Most broadly, extraclergial writing aims at criticizing the behaviour of some or all of the clergy. Clerics are blamed for failing to achieve the ideals they themselves espouse, for failing to live up to Christ's example

---

[26] On reforms in the instruction of the laity and the kinds of vernacular literature they produced see the survey by W. A. Pantin, in *The English Church in the Fourteenth Century* (Toronto, 1980 [Cambridge, 1955]), 189–262. Pecham's and Thoresby's Latin constitutions, the English translation of Thoresby, and a Wycliffite adaptation of that translation are all printed in *The Lay Folks' Catechism*, ed. T. F. Simmons and H. E. Nolloth (London, 1901). On instruction of the laity by means of sermons see H. L. Spencer, *English Preaching in the Late Middle Ages* (Oxford, 1993), 196–227.

[27] References to clerical insufficiency in pastoral writings are far too numerous to detail, but for criticism of the clergy in Pecham and Thoresby see Simmons and Nolloth, eds., *Lay Folks' Catechism*, 4–7.

and precepts or to other biblical injunctions, or for encroaching upon the roles or possessions that properly belong to the laity. Sources of authority called upon by extraclergial writers include canon and common law as well as church fathers and the bible. The areas on which controversy centres, as in contemporary Latin polemic writing, are sometimes surprising until it is clear what questions they allow writers to pursue: for example, the precise nature of Christ's poverty is crucial because it can be used to justify or criticize mendicant poverty and clerical possessions, whereas the powers Christ had in keeping with his human as opposed to his divine nature are deeply implicated in controversies over the boundaries of temporal as opposed to spiritual jurisdiction, the division between clerical and lay roles, and the nature of the vicarious rule Christ conferred on Peter – which is in turn the focus of arguments over the supremacy of the pope over secular rulers, or more locally the loyalty clerics owe to the king as opposed to the pope.[28] The kinds of information that are often deployed in arguing these topics similarly often seem surprising, but they are in fact the *lingua franca* of clerics possessed of at least minimal university education in the faculty of arts: arguments may turn on points of grammar, philosophical logic, natural science, or mathematics, as well as theology (the subject most broadly at issue), and frequently employ the terminology of these disciplines as well as the peculiarly specialized techniques of disputation and exposition developed in their academic pursuit.[29]

Academic argument may be deployed in the vernacular largely for purposes of ostentatious display, with no intention that inexpert readers should be able to follow it – though it should be noted that it is not always easy to tell whether a telegraphically cryptic argument is being presented obscurely out of a deliberate attempt to obfuscate, or because its anticipated audience are presumed to know it already.[30] More interesting, though, are the frequent cases where the presentation

---

[28] For treatment of these issues see below ch. 2, pp. 57–60, ch. 3, pp. 82–6, ch. 4, pp. 115–20, and ch. 5, pp. 147–50 and 168–77.

[29] For more extended discussion of how clerical university training shaped the terminology and techniques of academic argument see ch. 6, pp. [191–3], and the references given there.

[30] On cryptic vernacular argument see ch. 6, pp. 200–1, and the references given there.

of vernacular argument is at minimum expositional, clearly laying out the steps in the argument; more expansively exemplary, explaining how the argument works; or even explicitly instructional, laying out general criteria for making and discerning good arguments. Explicitly instructional moments focus around questions of 'lewed' critique (Which clergy are hypocritical or heretical? How may they be discerned?), 'lewed' hermeneutics (How should authorities be interpreted? How may statements by respected authorities be weighed?), and 'lewed' epistemology (What sort of mental attitude (belief, knowledge, supposition) should be maintained toward different propositions, and on what grounds?).[31]

Of course no vernacular tract, however step-by-step its didactic exposition, could possibly substitute for several years of clerical education. A writer cannot truly place his projected lay readers on a par with the clergy; nor, of course, is it likely many, or perhaps any, would really want to. To justify the necessary supposition that the laity could instantly acquire the learning they would need, and make it possible to admit lay persons to the conversation of clerics without taking upon themselves any direct responsibility for the laity learning anything, necessary or not, writers draw on a compensatory biblical authorization of 'clergie' independent of institutional training; one that also supports them in claiming to be learned themselves while leaving their own training and position strategically unclear. Christ's promise to the apostles at Luke 21:12–15 guarantees that regardless of their status and education, his followers will receive whatever learning may be necessary to combat trained, established clerics by means of a special grant of grace.[32]

This study will focus on extraclergial writings that can be dated fairly closely between the mid-1370s and about 1410. Certainly the period *c.* 1373–1410 does not mark the beginning and end of extraclergial writing, much less of the larger processes amid which it is produced. Learned material in English seems to have begun to be produced from the mid-fourteenth century onward, even if it was unusual to find the

[31] For examples of these three types of questions see chs. 4, 5, and 6 respectively.
[32] On authorization through grace see especially ch. 2, pp. 32, 34–5, 42–4, and ch. 6, pp. 184–5 and n. 20.

kinds of learned material that might be perceived as a threat to Latin academic learning translated into English until the 1380s. The composition of the A version of *Piers Plowman*, which as we will see poses the problem of vernacular 'clergie' so insistently at its ending, can probably be dated to the late 1360s.[33] And of course when English began to achieve official legitimacy as a language of administration in the 1410s and 1420s the repression of dissident writings in English did not end, but rather took on new and more refined forms. Nevertheless, on the evidence of the datable texts discussed here, the period *c.* 1373–1410 seems to have been extraclergial writing's most oppositional phase, when transferring the terms, modes, and topics of academic argumentation to English carried a special charge, and claims to write clergially for a wider audience had a kind of untried excitement.

The five chapters that follow chart a phase of experimental ferment in the years between 1370 and 1390, gradually superseded by increasing repression or prevention of the possibilities that first phase had envisaged. Part I examines the experimentation with possibilities of vernacular audience that preceded their more organized repression, focusing on the work of two writers not readily classifiable as 'heretical' or 'revolutionary', William Langland and John Trevisa. Each of these writers presents a vernacular *oeuvre*, a life's work, that drastically exceeds minimal pastoral requirements in an exorbitant tour of unprecedented possibilities for vernacular learning; and each, in a staged literary moment of dialogic challenge, represents his vernacular writing as not fully subject to his own self-motivated control, but rather dependent on external support and inspiration. Following the first phase in which Langland and Trevisa did the bulk of their work, in an increasingly polarized climate hostile to controversial publication in the vernacular, Wycliffites became the most prominent and most

---

[33] The generally accepted date for the manuscript dissemination of the A version is *c.* 1368–74. (See for example G. Kane, 'The Text', in J. A. Alford, ed., *A Companion to 'Piers Plowman'* (Berkeley, CA, 1988), 175–200; 188–9.) R. Hanna III has suggested (*Pursuing History,* 236) that the A text was an early coterie draft of the poem which achieved much wider circulation only after the B text was 'published'; of course this theory need not force us to reconsider when the early sections of the poem were written, but the idea that *Piers Plowman* became especially popular in the late 1370s to 1380s obviously fits well with my chronology.

extreme proponents of the extraclergial stance. Part II focuses on three important examples of Wycliffite extraclergial writing and, in each case, on attempts by the orthodox to meet and defeat Wycliffites on their own ground: these are the *Twelve Conclusions* of 1395 and Dymmok's *Reply*, the *Upland Series* of replies and further rebuttals to *Jack Upland's faux naif* antifraternal questions, and the *Testimony of William Thorpe*, Thorpe's narrative account of his self-defence before Thomas Arundel.

We have no firm evidence about the poet who wrote *Piers Plowman*, and neither the poet *in propria persona* nor his dreamer narrator ever makes any explicit reference to the 'public', or projected audience, for his poem. *Piers Plowman* is extraordinarily oblique in its approach to the issues of authorization and audience that confront extraclergial writers, but despite this, indeed perhaps because of it, undertakes the most searching exploration of them to be found anywhere in late medieval English writings: its discontinuous narrative of multiple subjects recurs again and again to the problem of what it means for the 'lewed' (lay/uneducated/stupid) to have 'clergie' (clergy/learning), and finally its reflections on this point lead the poem as close as it ever gets to reflecting on its own project of disseminating 'clergie' in the vernacular to an unprecedented audience. Chapter two examines the recursive treatment of the problem of 'lewed clergie' as posed by the dreamer at C v, Piers at B vii, Will at A xi, Ymaginatif at B xii/cxiv, Anima at B xv/C xvi-xvii, and the 'lewed vicory' at B xix/cxxi, giving attention to the poem's reception by external audiences as well as to the interchanges between internal clergial and extraclergial speakers and their audiences with which the poem is obsessively – to the exclusion, but also the inclusion, of all external considerations – concerned.

John Trevisa is probably the best documented and was certainly one of the earliest educated clerics to translate a large body of Latin prose directly and as faithfully as he was able into late medieval English. While in a general sense some of the works he translated can be fitted in with current lay interests – the *De Proprietatibus Rerum* contains a great deal of medical information as well as lapidary and horticultural sections, and the *De Regimine Principum* can be classified with the sort of popular philosophy found in works of advice-to-princes in the *Secretum Secretorum* tradition – it remains that even these two works are highly learned examples of their types, of interest to university academics as well as lay readers. Trevisa's interpolated notes, too, often steer his reader toward academic interests, instructing his reader for example about mathematics, grammar, and physics, and employing scholastic argumentative idioms. While Trevisa is not the first translator of scientific and philosophical information into English, then, he might be described as the first extraclergial translator to transfer highly learned argumentative Latin material to a new lay audience. Examining Trevisa's presentation of the clerical translator's role in his two free-standing original prose compositions, the signed notes he interpolates into his translations, the works he chose (or was given) to translate, how he handled their translation, and how and to whom his translations were 'published', Chapter three considers how it was significant for Trevisa to be translating information, even when it is of an apparently uncontroversial sort, to a regionally influential member of the gentry; and why Trevisa, with Berkeley's support or even inspiration, presents this activity of translation as the publishing of beneficial information to the widest possible lay audience.

The *Twelve Conclusions*, if the stories about their posting on the doors of Westminster and St Paul's are true, show the Wycliffites aiming to publish their tendentious arguments to the widest and highest audience they can find. To provide an adequate counteractant Dymmok's *Reply* claims to be just as widely accessible, but does so with the narrowest possible basis in fact: his book, which fills 315 pages in the printed edition and is written in scholastic Latin, was given in an elaborate presentation copy to the king, and what we know of the extremely limited dissemination of the few other copies does not extend its reach much broader or lower. Chapter four shows that Dymmok poses as a royalist Champion in a way that seems designed above all to bolster, and even forward, his own social position: he defends another sort of mixing of 'lewed' and 'clergial' roles than that posed by Trevisa or *Piers Plowman*, arguing against the *Conclusions'* criticisms of clerics in the service of lords or the king and presenting himself in the kind of pastoral advisorial role he says such clerics play. But if Dymmok is, by virtue of his defence of clerical secular service, in a sense an exponent of 'lewed clergie', when in returning to his initial claims of universal accessibility at the end of his text Dymmok numbers among the discerning members of his audience only those who agree with him, it is clear that the exclusivity of his text's dissemination and of its quite uncompromising scholastic Latin idiom is matched by a highly exclusive imagination of its public. That Dymmok claims to present his arguments for universal adjudication despite the ways this pose would seem to compromise his project illustrates especially well, perhaps better than any other extraclergial work discussed here, how the gesture toward universal audience advances other aims than the ostensible one of mass education.

Chapter five places the writing of the *Upland Series* not as Heyworth, editor of *Jack Upland, Friar Daw's Reply and Upland's Rejoinder*, would have it in the mid-fifteenth century, but in the centre of the controversies of 1380–1410; and shows that far from being a tired and ill-informed reiteration of stale stereotypes as Heyworth claims, the *Upland Series* involves itself in the most pressing interclerical controversies at Oxford, and even in royalist polemic of the most contested sort. The 'lewed' clerics who voice these various questions, answers, replies, and rejoinders stage a debate central to the concerns of this study: from a set of naively 'lewed' questions they move to contest who, orthodox or heretic, can successfully take up an extraclergial position without simply being labelled as 'lewed'; who can best claim to support the interests of the laity in general; and who (particularly in the midst of a usurpation of the throne) is a more loyal supporter of the king. Yet despite its provocatively controversial content, the *Upland Series* differs from all the other works examined here in its attitude to its audience: none of the participants ever makes any reference to the possibilities of lay audience. The series could scarcely provide a greater contrast to Dymmok, for example: whereas Dymmok makes much of the implications of explaining oneself to a universal vernacular audience, even though his Latin work is inaccessible to all but a tiny group, the *Upland Series* writers seemingly use English mainly as a way of authorizing their own productions and scoring points against one another, in happy unconsciousness of their potential (and even, as it turns out, actual) wider audience. The whole debate has an oddly interclerical, academic feel, despite the language in which it is presented: there are no explicit appeals to a wider readership, and it is not entirely clear what – other than rhetorical advantage – the writers of these questions and answers hope to gain by writing in English.

The *Testimony of William Thorpe* is quite evidently an exemplary text: through its first person narrative of an examination for heresy it presents its readers with a model of ethical commitment to dissident beliefs. Because William Thorpe himself is an educated cleric, however, the extensive dialogue with Archbishop Arundel and his clerks included in the narrative makes much use of scholastic techniques of argument. Chapter six shows how Thorpe reconciles what would seem to be an elitist, exclusionary mode of argument with an inclusionary insistence on the universal capacity of all members of his audience to act as discerning judges of the superiority of his arguments and even use them themselves. The *Testimony* provides an exemplary model of 'lewed' interpretation and argumentation made possible by grace that places readers on a direct par with the writer as 'lewed' exponents of 'clergie'. Yet it does so in a way that confines its projected lay audience to a particular response even more thoroughly than at one stage it compels Arundel to reply in a way that shows his position has nothing to do with reasoned argument. Thorpe remains a polemicist, not a neutral instructor, and his inclusiveness is in one sense hardly more than the obverse of Dymmok's exclusiveness: only readers who say 'yes' count for Thorpe as virtuous. Still this text does more than any other examined here to render the 'clergie' it presents genuinely accessible to a less educated reader. It is at the historical moment when vernacular publication in England has become more dangerous and difficult than it ever has been – and this is scarcely a coincidence – that such publication offers its yet more restricted readership the greatest possibilities.

2

'Lewed clergie': vernacular authorization in *Piers Plowman*

The poem that provides the most sustained vernacular consideration of the terms and possibilities of 'lewed' and 'clergie' in late medieval England is at the same time extraordinarily circumspect about the position from which it views them.[1] *Piers Plowman* gives us no definite specification of its author's or even its narrator's rank, status as clerical or lay, level and source of education, immediate or projected audience, or source of support during the writing of his poem. Nor does it offer us a clear statement of motives, methods, and objectives, or a straightforward narrative of events. Unlike vernacular scientific, devotional, and pastoral treatises, historical writings, and even romances, the poem lacks a formal prologue of the sort that so often addresses and directs readers; lacks as well the sort of asides and interpolated notes in which writers often reveal their views more directly; and is anything but consecutively systematic in its presentation.[2] Even when compared

---

[1] I use D. Pearsall's edition of C (Berkeley, 1978 [1982]), G. Kane and E. T. Donaldson's edition of B (London, 1988 [1975]), and G. Kane's edition of A (London, 1960) unless otherwise noted; references are to passus and line number. Where I compare Kane/Donaldson's edition of B with A. V. C. Schmidt's (London, 1987 [1978]), I give Schmidt's line numbers in square brackets.

[2] Middleton throws the poem's circumspection about its projected audience, or 'public', into sharp relief by comparing its avoidance of any explicit declaration of intent or remark upon the manner of its self-presentation to an audience with the expository prologues and internal commentary found in contemporary works with similar generic affiliations (A. Middleton, 'The Audience and Public of *Piers Plowman*', in D. Lawton, ed., *Middle English Alliterative Poetry and its Literary Background* (Woodbridge, Suffolk, 1982), 101–23; 111–13). She then explores in depth the oblique indications about the poem's 'public' that its generic affiliations provide, and shows how at the moments where the dreamer/narrator is challenged to explain his way of life the poem hints at the literary status it hopes to gain. Her reflections on challenges to the dreamer/narrator, particularly the one posed at C v, are greatly extended in her

with the generic affiliates this book examines, extraclergial works that employ the tools and topics of clerical argument in the vernacular for polemic ends in which it is normal for writers to leave their position and education unclear, *Piers Plowman*'s determined indeterminacy is rather extreme. The poem's narrator takes on more 'lewed' and more 'clergial' roles depending on the circumstances, and he is not even the only site of the poem's uncertainties about 'clergie': on some occasions he is merely an onlooker at the discussions or disputes of speakers whose positions may be at least as difficult to fix as his own, while on others he modulates into addressing readers directly – in a voice apparently authoritative, but not clearly authorial.[3]

This cumulation of uncertainty has spurred many readers, from the poet's contemporaries to our own, toward some kind of further mediation; toward, that is, more or less respectful redoubling of the poem's project in more accessible terms, and more or less sensitive attempts to 'fix' the authorial voice and its audience.[4] One can scarcely escape these impulses; indeed, they may be regarded as a kind of involvement with its terms that the poem requires of its readers. But the poem's avoidance, in every possible sense, of a singular narrative subject[5] is what enables its extraordinarily detailed and subtle exploration of tensions between learning and status in the late fourteenth century. Tracing the subject of those tensions between 'lewed' and

---

forthcoming paper 'Acts of Vagrancy'. I am grateful to her for allowing me to read this paper in its summer 1995 version, and again in the final publication version; my debt to her searching discussion will be detailed below. On Langland's audience see also J. A. Burrow, 'The Audience of *Piers Plowman*', revd. in *Essays on Medieval Literature* (Oxford, 1984), 102–16, and important new ideas about the versions and dissemination of the poem in R. Hanna III, 'On the Versions of *Piers Plowman*' in *Pursuing History: Middle English Manuscripts and Their Texts* (Stanford, 1996), 203–43; 236–8, 242–3.

3 Hudson's comments on how the poem's multiple voicings make it difficult if not impossible to discern the views of the author are succinct, but very much to the point: see A. Hudson, *The Premature Reformation*, 402–3.

4 On medieval scholars' redoubling of the projects of the poets they study in mediative commentary on their work, see P. Strohm, 'Chaucer's Lollard Joke: History and the Textual Unconscious', *Studies in the Age of Chaucer* 17 (1995), 23–42.

5 The observation that the poem in many senses avoids a single subject is David Lawton's: he discusses a number of these subjects (multiple narrative voices, personas, 'actants' [i.e., participants in the action], discourses, etc.) in 'The Subject of *Piers Plowman*', *The Yearbook of Langland Studies* 1 (1987), 1–30.

'clergie' – the object of this chapter – requires attention to that subject's multiple terms, as well as to the reductive mediations they have provoked.[6]

While avowedly partial – I by no means intend to suggest that tensions between 'lewed' and 'clergie' are the only, or even the principal, subject of the poem – my approach will avoid the more exclusive focus on either audience or narrator of the sometimes highly divergent critical traditions that examine the poem as sociopolitical document on the one hand, or an account of personal spiritual growth on the other.[7] To be sure, critical traditions focusing exclusively on the social or the personal converge in much of the most interesting recent work on Piers: Anne Middleton for example has focused on showing how the writer of *Piers Plowman* in the process of refining and revising his poem over the course of many years produces a life's work that concerns itself with social as well as personal reform.[8] My chapter aims to pursue a narrower question, but through a wider focus: to show how Will, but also other exponents of 'lewed clergie', exemplify through their roles as speakers and audiences a mode of critical questioning that readers themselves, as an audience at one further remove, might emulate in their own speech – all the more so because this mode does not place itself above critique or beyond question.

To whatever extent finding a way to authorize vernacular or 'lewed' writing about 'clergie' and the clergy was Langland's primary concern to begin with, it was a major concern of his readers over the period this book covers, and it became a greater preoccupation for Langland in the later stages of his work. As was discussed in the Introduction, the possibility, or threat, of a broad general vernacular reading public rather than particular limited vernacular coterie audiences was increas-

---

[6] On the range of meaning in Middle English for both *clergie* and its usual opposite *lewed* see ch. 1, p. 13.

[7] For an introduction to the history of criticism of *Piers Plowman* including further bibliography see A. Middleton, 'Introduction: The Critical Heritage', in J. A. Alford, ed., *A Companion to 'Piers Plowman'*, 1–25. Among recent publications that focus largely on one aspect or the other, S. Justice's chapter '*Piers Plowman* in the Rising', in *Writing and Rebellion*, 102–39 is an example of a sociopolitical treatment focusing on audience, and B. J. Harwood, *'Piers Plowman' and the Problem of Belief* (Toronto, 1992) an account of the narrator's spiritual growth.

[8] See the articles cited in n. 2.

ingly brought to the notice of writers in the period on which this book focuses, perhaps especially as a traumatic result of 'lewed' responses to written culture in the Peasants' Revolt.[9] Of course different writers and readers came to recognize new possibilities of audience at different times, and to varying degrees, depending on their circumstances. But for the writer of the work directly cited by the rebels,[10] the perils of vernacular publicity surely became a pressing concern, even if it is debatable at what precise point in the revisions of his poem Langland was forced to confront them. The challenges to its own position that the poem incorporates, increasingly as it goes on, and the extensive revisions and extensions it underwent over the course of the first phase of the time period this book covers, will begin to show us why and how encouraging readers to question became so controversial.

'CLERGIE' AS VOCATION: LANGLAND'S DREAMER

The most fundamental challenge to Langland's dreamer persona is found at the point where the dreamer voices his most extended self-justification: where he is questioned by Reson and Conscience in C v. Awake, but 'romynge in remembraunce' (v 11), Will is interrogated by Reson: Does he know some craft? No, he replies. Does he have lands to live by, or is he crippled, so that he has some good reason not to work? The answer is no, but Will pleads another excuse:

> When y ȝong was, many ȝer hennes,
> My fader and my frendes foende me to scole,
> Tyl y wyste witterly what holy writ menede,
> And what is beste for the body, as the boek telleth,
> And sykerost for þe soule, by so y wol contenue.
> And foend y nere, in fayth, seth my frendes deyede,
> Lyf þat me lykede but in this longe clothes.
> And yf y be labour sholde lyuen and lyflode deseruen,

---

9 See ch. 1, pp. 3–5 and esp. n. 5.
10 On the citation of *Piers Plowman* in letters by the rebels see A. Hudson, '*Piers Plowman* and the Peasants' Revolt', 85–106. Of course it may be that the rebels, like Langland, are drawing on a stock figure of dissent; but if so, that the rebels use the same figure as the erudite writer of *Piers Plowman* underlines all the more strongly the perils of vernacular publicity.

That laboure þat y lerned beste þerwith lyuen y sholde.
In eadem uocatione in quo uocati estis.
(v 35–43)

Will 'professes clergie' in this passage in that he avows his commitment to 'clergie' in the sense of learning, and even to the 'longe clothes' worn by the institutional 'clergie'. But he places himself in a rather shaky position with respect to the clergy, and even to learning, by the very obscurity of his profession. He does not specify the institution, teachers, or curriculum of his study – though his implication that his schooling ended when his 'frendes deyede' may suggest he was supported by the sort of patronage required for work at the university level.[11] And he does not, or cannot, name any position in the ecclesiastical hierarchy that he has subsequently held, or any secure source of clerical livelihood.[12]

---

[11] Various interpretations of what institution 'scole' might designate and what curriculum might be implied by 'what holy writ menede' have been proposed, most not acknowledging the deliberate vagueness of Langland's terms. Hanna, who does acknowledge and thoughtfully explore Langland's imprecision, suggests that the need for the help of 'frendes' implies university study: R. Hanna III, *William Langland* (Aldershot, 1993), 19. Examples where Middle English 'frendes' is used to denote supporters during higher education include Chaucer's clerk, supported in his study at Oxford by the 'frendes' for whom he prays in return (*General Prologue* to *The Canterbury Tales*, in *The Riverside Chaucer*, gen. ed. L. D. Benson, 3rd ed. (Oxford, 1988 [1987]), lines 299–302), John Metham's 'scolerys the qwyche stody in vnyuersyteys at her frendys fyndyng', who cannot conceal the bodily manifestations of their pampered lifestyle (*Physiognomy*, in H. Craig, ed., *The Works of John Metham* (London, 1916), 118–45; 135/31–136/3; quotation from 135/31–3), and William Thorpe's account of support during education by the 'frendes' who wanted him to become a priest (*The Testimony of William Thorpe*, in A. Hudson, ed., *Two Wycliffite Texts*, 37/437–39/498; and see below, ch. 6, p. 184). At A x 66 it is 'þe fadir and þe Frendis' who are responsible for guiding 'fauntis' – but it is even less clear what specific form that guidance might take.

[12] We must await the publication of Hanna's 'more extensive project' for his full presentation of evidence that Will is representing himself as a hermit. For a preview see R. Hanna III, '"Meddling With Makings" and Will's Work', in A. J. Minnis, ed., *Late-Medieval Religious Texts and their Transmission: Essays in Honour of A. I. Doyle* (Woodbridge, Suffolk, 1994), 85–94. M. Godden also suggests that Will is a hermit; see 'Plowmen and Hermits in Langland's *Piers Plowman*', *Review of English Studies* n.s. 35, no. 138 (1984), 129–63, and *The Making of 'Piers Plowman'* (London, 1990). If Will claims to be a hermit, this patently does not confer upon him the legitimacy of an established and recognized status secure from reproach, any more than it fixes him more firmly on one side of the divide between 'lewed' and 'clergie': see N. Watson's

Will's answer is difficult in the same way that Piers's answer to the priest is in B VII:

> 'What!' quod þe preest to Perkyn, 'Peter! as me þynkeþ
> Thow art lettred a litel; who lerned þee on boke?'
> 'Abstynence þe Abesse myn a b c me tauȝte,
> And Conscience cam afte[r] and kenned me [bettre].'
> (B VII 136–9)

In reply to the priest's challenge to the discrepancy between Piers's 'lewed' status and his assumption of a learned role, Piers affirms an ethical commitment rather than giving the information about his education we would need in order to account for the learning he has just displayed. It is easy enough to see why Piers evades the priest's condescending demand that he explain his ability to produce a good argument. But in the circumstances of C v, precision would seem more urgent. Reson is challenging Will to define the status into which he fits and justify his activities as appropriate to that status; his questions are lent authority, and menace, by his use of the juridical language of the Statute of Labourers.[13] It is surprising, then, that Will fails to give precise, institutionally ratified backing for his 'clergie', and, all the more, for the clerical status he is claiming. Nor does his answer satisfy Reson and Conscience: although Will does not carry the bag or bottle that are the conventional signs of voluntary mendicancy, he none-theless – as they soon bring him to acknowledge (82–101) – bears an uncomfortably close resemblance to the voluntary mendicants the poem elsewhere criticizes.[14]

---

nuanced account of Richard Rolle's insecurity-riven self-presentation as hermit in *Richard Rolle and the Invention of Authority* (Cambridge, 1991).

13 On resemblances between Reson's questions and those given in the Statute of Labourers, see L. M. Clopper, 'Need Men and Women Labor? Langland's Wanderer and the Labor Ordinances', in B. A. Hanawalt, ed., *Chaucer's England*, 110–29; Hanna, *William Langland*, 31–2, where excerpts from the 1388 version of the Statute of Labourers are conveniently printed and their resemblances to C v briefly detailed; and Middleton's extensive discussion of the petition and statute versions of the 1388 labour ordinances, the original 1349 Statute of Labourers, and their use in C v, in 'Acts of Vagrancy'.

14 For a crisp history of critical attitudes to the uncomfortable resemblance between Will and voluntary mendicants criticized elsewhere in the poem see W. Scase, *'Piers Plowman' and the New Anticlericalism* (Cambridge, 1989), 137–40; her view is discussed below, 30–2. For criticism of mendicancy elsewhere in the poem see, for

Readers have over the years exhibited some discomfort with Will's insecure position; it has seemed to them incompatible with the capacity to exemplify and/or exhort personal and institutional reform that the poem seems to assume.[15] One solution, of course, is to fix instead upon some other seemingly more secure locus of virtuous 'lewed' authority, such as Piers himself;[16] others are to gloss over the problem

example, the pardon sent by Truth, C IX 98–254; whereas 98–158 might excuse Will, 187–254 seems to implicate him. The tiny portion of this much-extended C passage present in B (VII 90–106; cf. C IX 166–86) also condemns Will's kind of begging, if only by omission from the list of those approved. It is not clear what sort of authority ought to be granted to the lines expounding the pardon: Piers is named as the speaker of them only in part, even if the illicit assumption of a clerical pastoral role they imply appears to be one reason for the priest's challenge of Piers; and (famously) they do not correspond to the written text of the pardon when it is unfolded. J. R. Thorne, 'Piers or Will: Confusion of Identity in the Early Reception of *Piers Plowman*', *Medium Aevum* 60 (1991), 273–84, shows one early reaction to this uncertainty: the scribe of San Marino, Huntingdon Library HM 114 transplants the C IX passage into its passus VI and there attributes it firmly to Piers.

[15] E. T. Donaldson's is the classic attempt to resolve the problem of Will's status – though he does acknowledge the self-description's wilful obscurity (see Donaldson, *The C text and Its Poet* (New Haven, 1949), 218) – arguing the identity of author and narrator and analysing the C V passage together with others where the dreamer describes his social position to conclude that Langland was (in the oft-quoted phrase) a 'married clerk in minor orders' (*The C text and Its Poet*, 220, 202–7, and ch. 7 *passim*). At the opposite extreme, Kane asserts that no lack of similarity between Langland and his narrator requires explanation – absolving himself from any obligation to account for the 'self-descriptive' passages – and suggests that Langland was highly learned and had a learned coterie audience (G. Kane, 'The Autobiographical Fallacy in Chaucer and Langland Studies', R. W. Chambers Memorial Lecture, 1965 (University College, London), printed in G. Kane, *Chaucer and Langland: Historical and Textual Approaches* (London, 1989), 1–14). See also the Introduction in G. Kane and E. T. Donaldson, eds., *Piers Plowman: The B Version* (Berkeley, 1988), 122 and n. 47. Others have speculated that Langland was a Benedictine monk (M. W. Bloomfield, 'Was William Langland a Benedictine Monk?', *Modern Language Quarterly* 4 (1943), 57–61) or 'in all probability a man very much like John Trevisa' (D. C. Fowler, *Piers the Plowman: Literary Relations of the A and B Texts* (Seattle, 1961), 186, and see ch. 7 *passim*). For a persuasive recent account of Langland's possible coterie audience see Hanna, 'The Versions', 236–8.

[16] The 'lewed' vicory of B XIX/C XXI (on whom see further below, pp. 57–60) is perhaps the first to adopt this strategy. On its popularity from the fifteenth century onward and on the tendency even to confuse Piers with the narrator of the poem, see A. Hudson, 'Epilogue: The Legacy of *Piers Plowman*', in J. A. Alford, ed., *A Companion to 'Piers Plowman'* (Berkeley, 1988), 251–66; A. Middleton, 'William Langland's 'Kynde Name': Authorial Signature and Social Identity in Late Fourteenth-Century England', in L. Patterson, ed., *Literary Practice and Social Change in Britain, 1380–1530* (Berkeley, 1990), 15–82; J. R. Thorne, 'Piers or Will'. Piers's 'clergie' is of

by conflating Piers with the narrator of the poem, or else to attribute secure authority to speakers whose views one approves of without regard for the positions of those speakers.[17] What all these solutions fail to do, however – largely because they are so bent on its solution – is confront the deliberate paradoxical incompatibility of Piers's and Will's social position with their learning: how is it possible for them, or indeed anyone else, to be 'lewed' and yet to have 'clergie'?

Of course, as was discussed in the Introduction, the association of learning with clerical status and stupidity or lack of training with the laity did not hold fast in the fourteenth century, if indeed it ever had; literate sheriffs and illiterate parsons might be known to any contemporary reader of *Piers Plowman*.[18] And of course, as we will soon see and as will repeatedly emerge in our examinations of other extraclergial writings, the solution to the question is always through a special grant of God's grace. But what needs attention is why in extraclergial works, and most especially in *Piers Plowman*, the question is made into a problem much harder than it really is; why it is posed so insistently, and so often, and in a form so defiant of logic and quotidian practicality. In *Piers Plowman* as in other extraclergial works, the conventional distinction between the facets of status- and education-descriptive 'lewed' and 'clergie' is under severe strain, as is the presumption that since no writing of any importance is available in English, the only literacy worth worrying about is literacy in Latin. The conceptual paradox of 'lewed clergie' cannot be resolved, in *Piers Plowman* or elsewhere, by ignoring the evidence for either learning or status. Nor should it be dismissed.

Instead, it would be worth inquiring what this combination of 'lewed' and 'clergie' helps the dreamer narrator, or perhaps the writer he screens, to accomplish, and how it draws on newly emergent

---

course subject to question as well, as we have seen, and his status though more readily categorized is not as fixed or as clearly defined as is often assumed; nor is he even an infallible guide to right behaviour, as the range of critical opinion over the interpretation of the pardon tearing episode illustrates. For a quick and informative survey of views on the pardon tearing see the positions summarized in D. Pearsall, *An Annotated Critical Bibliography of Langland* (New York, 1990), 200–6.

17 On these largely outmoded strategies, employed by early editors of the poem, see A. Middleton, 'Introduction: The Critical Heritage', 4–6.

18 See ch. 1, p. 13.

possibilities of 'lewed clergie'. Some scholars have recently been pursuing this line of inquiry. Galloway examines how in the England of *Piers Plowman* the spread of knowledge was creating new sorts of possibilities for the professional employment of learning: a 'new clericalism'.[19] Arguing that the dreamer's status is obscure by design rather than by accident,[20] he attends especially to the non-institutional forms of learning on which the poem intermittently focuses, and claims that they, as well as the C v declaration, 'push the poem's focus in general and its main protagonist in particular beyond any simple ties to institutionalized "scoleiyng", and thus beyond any easy assessment of its author's educational ties or background' (90). Whether or not it accu- rately describes the writer's life, then, the narrator's stance is broadly supportive of the poem's general aims: the C v profession's lack of any clear relation to institutional definitions is in keeping with the poem's interest in new kinds and applications of knowledge that were proliferating at the time. Scase, on the other hand, provides a literary satiric context for the dreamer's stance. Because Will's self-description so closely links him to practices the poem elsewhere deplores, and because there is a well-established tradition of satire against an order or kind of clergy voiced by a fringe or former member of the very group being satirized, she asserts that Will has in fact *no* grounds for his claim to be different than other idlers (139–40). As in earlier satires, where the 'gyrovague' or 'extraregular' (used as target and often as narrative persona as well) shields the satirist by providing a safe target, so in *Piers Plowman* the 'unbeneficed secular cleric' narrator voices what she terms the 'new anticlericalism': a new, more broadly based critique developed in late medieval England which while thoroughly shielding its author from view takes all clerics, even all 'clergie', as its target, and employs for this purpose the polemic weapons, hence the 'clergie', refined in previous intraclerical battles.

While the new possibilities for as-yet undefined forms of 'clergie' that Galloway raises may well help to make possible the obscure and uncommitted position Will and his 'lewed' clergial counterparts take,

[19] A. Galloway, '*Piers Plowman* and the Schools', *The Yearbook of Langland Studies* 6 (1992), 89–107; 98. Galloway derives the phrase from Scase's; see below.
[20] Others who have suggested that the dreamer's self-positioning is calculated rather than accidental include Hanna, Middleton, Clopper, and Scase.

however, it remains that in C v Will does not, cannot, affirm a new sort of 'clergie' explicitly. Only in an ideally pluralistic world where economic and intellectual capital were easily available to all – where the death of Will's 'frendes' and what school he went to would make no difference – would the writer and the poem be able unequivocally to affirm a new kind of lay status and new varieties of lay learning. Instead, Will's position is in tension with the established understandings of 'clergie' and of 'lewed', and has to work with their terms and assumptions. For Scase, conversely, who focuses on those terms and assumptions, in the end Will's espousal of insecurity produces a self-consuming artifact: a text that undermines its own authority by virtue of the way it advances it.[21] But if Will, and the voice that condemns his way of life in C ix/ B vii, are not entirely outside the terms of 'clergie', they are not, either of them, entirely within them either – as Scase herself suggests in her conclusion, in the course of her insightful exploration of the rhetorical breakdowns over the 'lewed/lered' distinction pervasive in the poem (166–8).[22]

Middleton dissects in detail the oddity of Will's alignment between the conventional expectations of 'lewed' and 'clergial' behaviour. She suggests that Langland's 'lewed' clerical position functions as a specific sort of strategic screen: he stages the threat of secular prosecution, which as a cleric he can easily escape, to protect himself from the possibility of ecclesiastical suspicion.[23] I would note that it may be a bit premature in 1382 to fear persecution: there was as yet no active systematic persecution of heretics in the 1380s.[24] Admittedly some limited provisions were implemented during these years, and if Hanna is right that Langland was a legal clerk in London who had associations with the court, it is even possible that he might have been aware of them – though perhaps less likely that he would have fallen victim to them.[25] Still, for Langland as for other extraclergial writers, a sense of

[21] See Scase, *'Piers Plowman' and the New Anticlericalism*, 161–73.

[22] Scase has even Lewte call Will an extraregular (p. 168, referring to B xi 56 where it is in fact Coveitise of Eighes who is speaking within the inner dream, unless she has omitted a reference to another manuscript tradition), but Lewte is (as she also notes, p. 166) one of those figures who characterizes Will as 'lewed', and he authorizes Will's vernacular production on that basis rather than that of his 'clergie'.

[23] Middleton, 'Acts of Vagrancy'.   [24] See below, pp. 51–2 and nn. 71–2.

[25] For Hanna's recent speculations about Langland's status see 'The Versions', 236–8.

personal threat seems far less likely to have motivated his self-positioning than the rhetorical advantage he can gain by distancing himself from the conventions of clerical expression.

The rhetorical purchase of the dreamer's persona in C v, I would suggest, is the ethical commitment that the dreamer's insecurity permits. What distinguishes Langland's dreamer's plea from 'the Confession of the Archpoet, the self-congratulation of Faus Semblant, the bragging of Chaucer's Pardoner',[26] and also, we might add, from the complacent statements of a great many better-established clerics within the poem and even outside it, is the commitment to persevering in 'clergie' which it expresses in 'by so y wol contenue', in Galloway's reading of the phrase as prospective rather than merely retrospective.[27] The dreamer's inability to defend his commitment except as an unshakeable preference – 'foend y nere . . . /Lyf þat me lykede but in this longe clothes' – reinforces rather than detracts from his credibility. Will's profession of constancy is validated by the very necessity of his reliance on grace to turn to profit the insecurity of the circumstances in which its speaker lives and the obscurity of his position. Langland's dreamer is extraclergial, in the sense discussed in the Introduction, because he does not claim membership in any established religious group, and his education, though obviously not inconsiderable, is obscure. But he is also extraclergial in that his searching attitude toward learning rejects conventional answers and uncovers new questions even as – or perhaps especially because – the various figures he encounters repeatedly solicit (*vel sollicitant*) the grounds for his position.

As we have seen, writers who position themselves extraclergially usually also project an unprecedented 'lewed' audience; yet the authenticity of an extraclergial's claim to speak for, or to, that audience does always remain a separate question, largely independent of the question of what authority he gains by making the claim.[28] For Langland, the

---

[26] Scase, *'Piers Plowman' and the New Anticlericalism*, 140.

[27] See Galloway's careful dissection of this phrase, 94; he suggests it could just as well be glossed 'I would (expressing purpose) continue in this manner' as 'provided that I will persevere'.

[28] See ch. 1, pp. 12–16.

question of projected audience in one sense forever remains un-answered, for the dreamer persona, much less any authorial voice, never explicitly projects an audience for its writing.[29] In another sense, however, this question receives more protracted consideration in *Piers Plowman* than in any other extraclergial text: *Piers Plowman* introjects a multitude of 'lewed' audiences, and stages for the reader's benefit their interactions with a variety of clergial and extraclergial figures. The dreamer is far from being the only locus of extraclergial tension in the poem: often his position is, like that of the reader, that of an unacknowledged audience, a bystander observing the interchange between a speaker and his projected and immediate audiences and well placed to perceive where projections and immediate reactions do not meet. By internalizing responses to much of its argument the poem anticipates those gaps between actual and projected audience – between what Middleton has called 'audience' and 'public' – that often gape so wide in works that take an extraclergial stance.[30]

'CLERGIE' IN DISPUTE

We might regard the C v defence as the dreamer's most clergial role: he takes up an obscure position somewhere on the shifting ground between the approbative and negative senses of 'lewed' and 'clergie', in such a way as to profess 'clergie', and defend the value of learning, without in the process affirming any clear stable position in the clerical profession. Before moving on to consider how other extraclergial subjects – Piers, Ymaginatif, Anima, the 'lewed' vicar, and others – display a mixture of 'lewed' and 'clergial' characteristics and as appro-priate take on more 'lewed' and more 'clergial' roles to provide shaky grounds for their vernacular authority, we will need also to examine the dreamer's most 'lewed' role – perhaps in the pejorative as well as the status-bound sense – where in posing the social crisis of how the

---

29 See below, pp. 60–1 and n. 85 for more detailed discussion of this point.
30 Middleton, 'The Audience and Public of *Piers Plowman*'; Middleton is speaking of the actual and projected audiences of the work as a whole, but the distinction adapts itself well to the poem's introjected audiences. See also A. Middleton, 'The Idea of Public Poetry in the Reign of Richard II', *Speculum* 53 (1978), 94–114, on the stance taken with respect to their projected audiences by late medieval English court poets.

'clergie' required for salvation can be made universally available he sharply criticizes the professional clergy, and even their learning.

At the point where the text of the A version ends in many manuscripts,[31] Will affirms common cause with the 'lewed' he was so anxious to dissociate himself from when it was the manner of his own work he was defending: he asserts that the unlearned 'lewed' are more assured of salvation than are learned clerics. The bulk of critical attention to this passage has focused on what Will says about salvation; it has not been remarked that here Will poses once again, and more sharply than ever, the difficulty in reconciling 'lewed' and 'clergie' that we found in Will's and Piers's accounts of their education. The difficulty becomes yet more prominent in revision:

> 'Wh[anne] ȝe ben aposid of princes or of prestis of þe lawe
> For to answere hem haue ȝe no doute,
> For I shal graunte ȝow grace of god þat ȝe seruen,
> Þe help of þe holy gost to answere hem [alle].'
> (A XI 298–301)

> 'Though ye come bifore kynges and clerkes of the lawe,
> Ben noght abasshed, for I shal be in youre mouthes,
> And yyve yow wit and will and konnyng to conclude
> Hem alle that ayeins yow of Cristendom disputen.'[32]
> (B X 451–3 [Schmidt 442–5])

> 'Thogh ȝe come bifore kynges and clerkes of þe lawe
> Beth nat aferd of þat folk for y shal ȝeue ȝow tonge
> And connyng and clergie to conclude suche alle.'
> (C XI 280–2)

By the time we reach the C version (where indeed the lines are attributed to Rechelesnesse rather than Will), the quality by means of which uneducated lay people are to confute 'clerkes' is specified as

---

[31] For full details see below pp. 38–9.

[32] To give a fuller spectrum of revision, since Kane and Donaldson 'correct' to a C reading, I quote Schmidt's edition, the reading of most of the B manuscripts. But I restore the line division between Schmidt's lines 444 and 445 before 'hem' (as it appears in all the manuscripts) rather than after 'hem'; and in line 444 I give and[1] in place of 'at' (which appears in only 3 manuscripts) and and[2] in place of Schmidt's emendation 'with'. The passage lists the human capacities that will be enhanced by grace, emphasizing in particular 'konnyng to conclude', and in my view Schmidt's version obscures this.

'clergie'. But the passage is quoted precisely to show that Christ does not commend 'clergie', and in the subsequent remarks about salvation 'clergie' is the quality that makes the 'clerkes' who have studied it less fit for salvation than the 'lewed' who (as the lines quoted would have it) will employ it against them. While strongly criticizing 'clergie' both in the sense where it designates status and in the sense where it means 'learning', the passage shows the 'lewed' using 'clergie'/learning in the most institutionally rooted and status-bound of ways, flouting, as did Piers and Will, our commonsense understanding that in order to deploy 'clergie' in learned argument one must engage in prolonged academic study.[33] The passage provides, indeed promises, a solution to the problem it poses: it assures us that God's grace overcomes all practical difficulties. However, the fact that God's grace is required demonstrates that the problem admits of no ordinary, everyday solution. The 'lewed' need instruction that they are not getting, and because it seems impossible to ensure that this instruction should be reliably administered to them by the clergy, they must be supernaturally endowed with scholastic disputational skills – more, surely, than the minimum learning required for salvation – so that they will be able to refute incorrect information.

This crisis over the social administration of 'clergie' is Will's longest and most truculent contribution to his discussion with Clergie and Scripture, and it plays a crucial role in the development of the argument of all versions of the poem – but since the manner in which *Piers Plowman* might be said to 'develop' or 'progress', much less the classification and dating of its versions, are subject to widely differing interpretations in criticism of the poem, my discussion had better be preceded by some introduction.

Piers Plowman is a poem beautifully designed to frustrate formalist notions that a text ought to present a readily apprehended unity of design and conception, and a narrative and conceptual progress toward then (subsequently) away from a clearly signposted 'goal' or 'climax'. Indeed, one precipitant of the controversy over whether the poem had one or several authors was the conviction that because of their readily perceived variety in style and allegoric mode, the pieces of *Piers*

---

33 On the semantic range of 'clergie' see ch. I, p. 13.

Plowman B must be the work of a less competent reviser who did not manage to gain control over his diverse materials.[34] Now that that conviction has fallen away, and that the poem has largely ceased to attract those critics of a formalist bent who remain, attempts to find in the whole text a single process and a structural unity are mercifully rare.[35] In this sense as in so many others, the poem's subjects are acknowledged to be multiple. However, if any more than a short isolated passage is to be treated, then the mode of *Piers Plowman's* sustained engagement with the issues it takes up must be considered. Middleton's essay on the narrative of *Piers Plowman* has been seminal in this regard.[36] Attention has come to focus on the smaller unit of the dream, or even the episode within a dream, where Langland can be seen to be engaging with what one might call an allegoric mode, or a genre, or a realm of discourse: the poem's variability in tone and treatment is attributed not to lack of control or multiple authorship, but to a poetic of modulation.[37]

Piers Plowman may be viewed as a series of engagements, in different arenas and using different methods, with certain fundamental issues. A given engagement will devote sustained attention to articulating the

[34] The articles by J. M. Manly, J. J. Jusserand, and R. W. Chambers reprinted in *The Piers Plowman Controversy* (London, 1910) launched the controversy; G. Kane attempted to lay it permanently to rest in *Piers Plowman: The Evidence for Authorship* (London, 1965). See A. Middleton, 'Introduction: The Critical Heritage', for a general guide to the critical history.

[35] Insightful studies that examine the whole text in terms of a single theme are of course still produced: see for example Harwood, *'Piers Plowman' and the Problem of Belief.*

[36] A. Middleton, 'Narration and the Invention of Experience: Episodic Form in *Piers Plowman'*, in L. D. Benson and S. Wenzel, eds., *The Wisdom of Poetry: Essays in Early English Literature in Honor of Morton W. Bloomfield* (Kalamazoo, 1982), 91–122.

[37] Other discussions that attempt to chart these kinds of modulations include J. A. Burrow's 'The Action of Langland's Second Vision', *Essays in Criticism* 15 (1965), 247–68; reprinted in *Essays on Medieval Literature*, 79–101; S. Justice, 'The Genres of *Piers Plowman'*, *Viator* 19 (1988), 291–306; J. Simpson's 'little book' *'Piers Plowman': An Introduction to the B-Text* (London, 1990), which is admirably attentive to variations in discourse and genre throughout the B text; and Middleton's analysis of the generic commitments of the dreamer's defence in C v in 'Acts of Vagrancy'. The poem's generic compendiousness, as we might call it – clearly signalling affiliations to various kinds of writing but remaining comfortably within the bounds of none of them – might be viewed as a feature of Langland's attempt to come to grips with an unprecedented audience. Certainly it is a characteristic displayed by several other extraclergial works; especially perhaps by Dymmok's *Reply*, but also by the *Petition*, the *Twelve Conclusions*, and Thorpe's *Testimony.*

issues it considers, but that need not, does not, prevent them emerging again later in a different form: portions of narrative just as much as argument tend to be disrupted by untimely awakenings or 'lewed' interruptions rather than brought to resolution. Although figures given the same name, like topics, recur, the behaviours and characteristics of a named personification in one dream need not correspond to those of a figure given the same name in another dream: even major figures like Piers and Will appear in different roles, whereas minor figures such as the Pees of passus IV and the Pees of passus XVIII have nothing in common but an association with the concept of peace.[38] The poem is certainly more than merely a string of dissociated modules, but relationships between sections are now rarely analysed in terms of straightforward progression.[39]

Concurrent with the virtual abandonment of attempts to submit the whole poem to a single narrative and thematic progression has been an increase in interest in charting the development of Langland's views, or their expression, across versions of the poem – so that B and/or C might be seen as exploring certain themes much more fully than A, or so that changes between B and C in particular, but also B and A, might be attributed to Langland's reaction to sociopolitical developments such as the Peasants' Revolt, the Despenser Crusade, or the development of and reaction to the Wycliffite movement.[40] Partly as a result of closer attention to topical reference and to development between versions, the dating, order of composition, and differentiation one from the other of the versions have come into question, and while on the whole the demarcation of A from B from C has stood firm – though an initial Z version and an intermediary version between B and C have been suggested, it has recently been argued that A postdates

---

38 Lawton, 'The Subject of *Piers Plowman*', analyses these discontinuities well. The example of Pees is Simpson's. M. Carruthers [Schroeder] 'The Character of Conscience in *Piers Plowman*', *Studies in Philology* 67 (1970), 13–30 analyses different manifestations of Conscience.

39 For the suggestion that the poem acquires or achieves a sort of overall formal design in the final stages of its development, and differing theories about whether or not Langland completed his revisions to the C text, see Middleton, 'Acts of Vagrancy' and Hanna, 'The Versions'.

40 The most recent general overview of previous work on topical reference in all three versions is A. Hudson, '*Piers Plowman* and the Peasants' Revolt: A Problem Revisited'.

both B and C, and the degree to which passus XII of A may be Langland's work has been debated[41] – interest has also come to focus on the versions found in individual manuscripts.[42] Even among those who agree with George Kane that the editor's goal should be to restore as closely as possible the superior expression of artistic genius presented in the A, B, and C texts as Langland actually wrote them, few would accept that all scribal variation from those three ideals is merely accidental, mechanical, or conventional, and should only be regarded as uninteresting debasement.[43] Every manuscript may be viewed as a negotiation of 'lewed clergie'; the record of one or more copyists' – trained or untrained, attentive or inattentive – engagement with this challenging and innovative work.

It is generally the case that episodes or scenes in *Piers Plowman* tend to end at points of crisis for *clergie*; that the poem seemed incomplete or unresolved to its readers at these points is perhaps attested by the frequency with which these points are patched over in manuscripts.[44] All three of the points where the poem frequently ends in manuscripts are such points of crisis: the point in B XX or C XXII at which Conscience cries after grace until the dreamer begins to awaken is the most frequent and the most probably authorial, but the poem also comes to an end near the tearing of the pardon that follows Piers's

---

[41] The newest discussion of the A, B, and C versions is by Hanna, in 'The Versions' and 'MS Bodley 851 and the Dissemination of *Piers Plowman*', *The Yearbook of Langland Studies* 7 (1993), 14–25, reprinted in *Pursuing History*, 195–202. Rigg and Brewer proposed that the Z version predates A (A. G. Rigg and C. Brewer, eds., *Piers Plowman: The Z Version* (Toronto, 1983), esp. 33–4), while Mann suggested that A postdates B (J. Mann, 'The Power of the Alphabet: A Reassessment of the Relation between the A and the B Versions of *Piers Plowman*', *The Yearbook of Langland Studies* 8 (1994), 21–50). Both these suggestions have provoked considerable controversy; see most recently Hanna, 'The Versions'. For an exhaustive discussion of A XII see A. Middleton, 'Making a Good End: John But as a Reader of *Piers Plowman*', in E. D. Kennedy, R. Waldron, and J. S. Wittig, eds., *Middle English Studies Presented to George Kane* (Woodbridge, Suffolk, 1988), 243–66.

[42] See, for example, D. Pearsall, 'The "Ilchester" Manuscript of *Piers Plowman*', *Neuphilologische Mitteilungen* 82 (1981), 181–93; G. H. Russell and V. Nathan, 'A *Piers Plowman* Manuscript in the Huntingdon Library', *Huntingdon Library Quarterly* 26 (1963), 119–30; Hanna, 'MS Bodley 851 and the Dissemination of *Piers Plowman*'.

[43] Kane expresses this view for example in 'The Text', 194. For a lucid general discussion of the history of editing *Piers* see Bowers, '*Piers Plowman*'s William Langland', 65–90.

[44] All the information about manuscripts provided here may be found in Kane, 'The Text', 177–82, but is duplicated here for the reader's convenience.

argument with the priest, in three manuscripts,[45] while two others have a C text continuation patched on.[46] The poem ends with Will's condemnation of 'clergie' in another four manuscripts,[47] while eight have continuations; of those eight, five manuscripts have a C text completion spliced onto their A text opening[48] – one with a small ending verse that 'makes a good end'[49] – and three have part or all of a passus XII.[50]

Whether it is held that Langland deliberately issued his poem in a version that ends with Will's 'lewed' condemnation of 'clergie', or that the wide distribution of the A version is merely an accidental result of a considerable pause for reflection in Langland's composition of the poem,[51] while for the majority of A text manuscripts Will's speech is a point of irresolute conclusion, in the B and C texts it provokes extensive efforts (even if not success) at resolution. In the B text the speech, and the scorn with which Scripture responds, precipitate the formal innovation of a dream within a dream in which Will's conclusions are tested against extended experience; this dream appears in the middle of the third dream, which began in passus VIII after Will awoke from watching Piers confront the priest and tear the pardon and had his waking encounter with the complacent friars, and will end in passus XII after Will's encounter with Ymaginatif, the poem's most committed spokesman for 'clergie' in the conventional status-bound sense. In the C text the third dream again begins after Will meets the friars (X 66) and ends with Ymaginatif (XIV 217); however, Scripture's scorn for Will

---

45 London, British Library, Harley 875 (ends VIII 142), London, Lincoln's Inn 150 (ends VIII 185), Dublin, Trinity College D.4.12 (ends VII 213).

46 Oxford, Bodleian Library, Bodley 851 (A to VIII 192 plus C XI–XXII. Also known as the Z version; but the important point here is where the C continuation is spliced on), Aberystwyth, National Library of Wales 733B (A I 176 to VIII 184).

47 Oxford, Bodleian Library, Ashmole 1468, Oxford, Bodleian Library, Douce 323; Oxford, Bodleian Library, English Poetry a.I (to XI 183); London, Society of Antiquaries 687.

48 Oxford, Bodleian Library, Digby 145; London, British Library, Harley 6041; Liverpool University Library F.4.8; Cambridge, Trinity College R.3.14; and see n. 46.

49 The Westminster Manuscript: see Kane, 'The Text', 182, for a transcription; see also Middleton, 'Making a Good End'.

50 Oxford, Bodleian Library, Rawlinson Poet. 137; New York, Pierpont Morgan Library M 818 (to XII 88), Oxford, University College 45 (to XII 19).

51 The first is the generally accepted theory, presented for example in Kane, 'The Text', 183–6; the second is Hanna's suggestion, in 'The Versions', 232–8.

does not require the prompt of his 'lewed' condemnation of 'clergie', but itself causes Will to fall into the inner dream (XI 163); the 'lewed' condemnation is assigned to Rechelesnesse within the inner dream, and folded into what in the B version was Rechelesness's short speech encouraging Will to ignore his need for repentance (XI 34–41/XI 197–311).

Whether Ymaginatif resolves the problems Will or Rechelesness has raised in B or C is a matter of some controversy even among recent critics who have abandoned the attempt to discern any simple overall form or narrative in the poem.[52] While this preoccupation might be regarded as a holdover from an older style of thematic criticism, the question does still have some importance to a more modulated mode of analysis. For at the end of the third dream, the expectations that its generic affiliations and mode of procedure have raised come into conflict with the poem's persistent posing of the question of 'lewed clergie'. Ymaginatif's defence proves incapable of justifying 'clergie' on its own terms; what he reveals, almost despite himself, is the impossibility of any defence that might attempt to confine 'clergie' to the conventional sense whereby learning and clerical status are bound together. No more than any other speaker in the poem (and rather less than some) is Ymaginatif a reliable authoritative guide.

Particularly in the B version, but also in C, the third dream has for a long time been acknowledged as the most 'scholastic' part of the poem.[53] It contains Langland's most sustained engagement with the conventional terms of 'clergie' in all senses: with a set of scholastic and clerical figures, with scholastic issues, and with the terms and modes of argument of scholastic discourse. On the basis of its scholastic mode of proceeding, then, rather than because of some notion of a necessity for formal completion, we would be justified in expecting that the dream will finish with an attempt to resolve the questions, responses, and objections that have emerged in its course. Ymaginatif assumes the

---

52 See the studies cited in n. 58.

53 See for example the seminal discussion by J. S. Wittig, *'Piers Plowman* B, Passus IX–XII: Elements in the Design of the Inward Journey', *Traditio* 28, 211–80; but almost every treatment of B's third dream remarks on its implication in academic argument. I will focus on the B text here, because its version of Ymaginatif's defense is longer and fuller, but will give cross references to C.

magisterial role at the end of the dream, in the manner of the determination with which a university master would resolve into a seamless whole the assertions and objections, arguments and counter-arguments, of a lengthy written or oral disputation in order to state a consistent final position – although this is not what Ymaginatif provides.

After rebuking Will for arguing with Reason instead of learning in silence and for writing poetry when he could be praying (XI 435–9, XII 16–19/not in C), Ymaginatif launches into a more general exposition about how people of various statuses can do 'as lewte techeþ' (XII 32/ not in C), postponing its application to Will until XII 92–8/XIV 43 – he should love clergie and kynde wit, and not 'lakke' logic or clerks – and the explanation for the long disgression into this topic until XII 155–8/ XIV 100–2:

> Why I haue told þee al þis, I took ful good hede
> How þow contrariedest clergie wiþ crabbede wordes,
> How þat lewed men li3tloker þan lettrede were saued,
> Than clerkes or kynde witted men of cristene peple.

The body of Ymaginatif's exposition, then, refers back to and takes up the issue raised at the point where the A text inconclusively ended at the equivalent of the end of B x: Will's assertion that a 'lewed' man's salvation is more assured than a clerk's.[54]

Will acknowledges the truth of both of Ymaginatif's initial rebukes. His defence, the closest B text analogue to the C v defence, is in terms of 'makyng' rather than 'clergie', but it similarly places Will amidst the clergy while at the same time attempting to excuse him from what he himself considers the proper activities of clerics. As for the rebukes within Ymaginatif's exposition, Will lets them pass, reserving his questions for the exposition's content. Indeed, the applications to Will Ymaginatif draws out are almost ostentatiously token: their import is disproportionate to the content taken as a whole, and the conceptual leaps Ymaginatif must make to arrive at them are jarring. Ymaginatif's attempt to address the issue of 'clergie' in general terms does not quite extend to an attempt to address a broader audience. But it runs into

---

[54] See B x 465–81; the same statement is made by Rechelesness in C XI 285–305.

some interesting difficulties even without that ambition, and even before Will's questioning of it.

On the one hand, Ymaginatif wants to offer a seamless defence of 'clergie' by asserting that its two referents, booklearning and clerical status, coincide; and that 'clergie' ought to be loved by all because it benefits everyone, through a harmoniously hierarchical system whereby the clergy diffuse the benefits of their learning to all (xii 99–154/xiv 44–98). On the other hand, Ymaginatif wants to counter Will's argument that being 'lewed' is better than being learned by asserting a contradictory point: that it is better for any given individual to have 'clergie'/booklearning than not (xii 155–91/xiv 99–130). The difficulty is that if Ymaginatif suggests that it is possible for *any* given individual to acquire 'clergie'/booklearning, then in doing so he distinguishes booklearning from clerical status and admits the possibility that the two could appear separately. And if he claims any given individual *should* learn, any reason he might give will have to acknowledge that some of the clergy are not adequately learned, or that the benefits of their clergy are not thoroughly diffused, or both. For if the clergy did in fact diffuse the benefits of their 'clergie' to all, then a learned person would not be better off than a 'lewed' one.

A further difficulty for both pieces of this argument is the doctrine Will invoked at the end of his 'lewed' condemnation: that God's grace operates to ensure salvation independent of 'clergie' in any sense. While advancing his hierarchical theory of 'clergie', Ymaginatif attempts to deal with this difficulty by suggesting that the clergy are the administrators of grace.[55] But even before he began the part of his exposition which defends 'clergie' he had placed grace beyond the grasp of either sort of 'clergie'.[56] Ymaginatif's suggestion that the shepherds were highly learned, and his assertion that Christ was born to a prosperous family, would surely seem incongruous to even the most 'lewed' among Langland's audience.[57] And the example of the

---

[55] See especially xii 105–12/xiv 50–7, where clerks are represented as essential to salvation, and xii 139–54/xiv 84–98, where clerks are key players in Ymaginatif's version of the Nativity.

[56] See xii 59–63/xiv 23–9.

[57] See xii 143–7/xiv 87–91 (modified in C; now clerks and keepers of beasts both exhibit 'clennesse', but are distinguished).

felon 'lolling' insecurely at the bottom of heaven with which Ymaginatif strives to reconcile clerical hierarchy and grace is, no matter how insecure the felon's position, an indictment of the system of administration which in the pro-clergial argument just completed left a group of felons 'lolling' on the gallows while another group were given 'benefit of clergy' merely on the basis of their ability to recite a psalm in Latin (XII 192–213/XIV 131–52).

Now, it could be argued that these internal incoherences are not a problem for Ymaginatif, and should not be one for us if we approach them correctly. Rather than demonstrating the gaps in the ideology of 'clergie' by virtue of his attempt to present that ideology as a seamless whole, Ymaginatif might be read as imaginatively bridging the deficiencies of logic to demonstrate truth. This sympathetic reading does fit with the prevailing mode of his exposition. He has set out to defend both 'kynde wit' and 'clergie', and though his argument focuses on defending 'clergie', the mode of that argument is that of 'kynde wit': it is laden with analogies to widely familiar events and examples, the sort of evidence 'kynde wit' can provide and apprehend. It has been suggested that these are just the sort of 'imagistic' arguments we might expect from the imagination, and that they transcend their contradictions, or bridge the gap between 'lewed' and 'clergie', by providing a more 'affective' sort of learning accessible to a wider audience, in rather the manner of the late medieval mystics. The strongest case for this interpretation is made by James Simpson; he suggests that the narrative and mode of argumentation of *Piers Plowman* move from *scientia*, or philosophical, ratiocinative knowledge, to *sapientia*, or theological, symbolic knowledge – a distinction between kinds of knowledge and specification of the rhetoric appropriate to presenting each of them drawn from   late medieval theological prologues of an Augustinian cast.[58]

---

[58] See *'Piers Plowman': An Introduction to the B Text, passim* for Simpson's theory about how the poem progresses, and 102–3, 136–9 for his comments on Ymaginatif's role in that progression. A more extended exposition of the medieval psychological theory involved appears in J. Simpson, 'From Reason to Affective Knowledge: Modes of Thought and Poetic Form in *Piers Plowman*', *Medium Aevum* 55 (1986), 1–23. Other attempts to argue that the poem transcends its contradictions include A. J. Fletcher's claim that it does so repeatedly throughout ('The Social Trinity of *Piers Plowman*', *Review of English Studies*, n.s. 44, no. 175 (1993), 343–61), and A. J. Minnis's argument

Certainly in the later passus Langland experiments with the reason-confounding possibilities of affective speech; he may well have been familiar with the theories about affective speech Simpson cites, or even others Simpson does not mention.[59] But it cannot be claimed that the poem moves smoothly from *scientia* to *sapientia,* or that Ymaginatif stands at the point of transition. Enigmatic forms of speech confound the dreamer and other introjected audiences from the Prologue onward, and (as we will see) the tensions of 'lewed clergie' continue to recur at intervals after passus XII/XIV up to the end of the poem. Even the experientially oriented portions of Ymaginatif's argument alone would seem to raise problems for a sympathetic reading. If 'clergie' can benefit everyone, then why can it not be defended before all by means of 'clergie' rather than 'kynde wit'? The inconsistency between the content and the method of Ymaginatif's defence seems to invite criticism rather than assent, and, instead of providing a medium between 'lewed' and 'clergie', to advertise the gap between them. But however sympathetically Ymaginatif's defence of 'clergie' may be read, Ymaginatif cannot in any uncomplicated fashion be construed as an authoritative spokesman for grace. His authority is compromised by the abrupt and startling shift in his mode of argumentation when Will questions him about salvation through 'clergie'.

When Will puts 'Alle thise clerkes' to Ymaginatif to suggest that any person who is not a Christian, and therefore lacks 'clergie' in both senses as well as any chance of benefiting from its remote effects, may be saved, Ymaginatif denies Will's point and asserts that 'clergie' is not needed for salvation. But Ymaginatif does not ground his argument on the unknowable operations of grace; nor does he proceed, as usual, by analogy. Rather, even as he denies the necessity of 'clergie' for salvation, he switches from his prevailing experiential or 'affective' mode to the most 'clergial' sort of argument; and by his denial he contradicts all the clerks Will has adduced, disregarding his own advice to Will not to 'countreplede clerkes':

---

for the success of Ymaginatif's exposition in 'Langland's Ymaginatif and Late-Medieval Theories of Imagination', *Comparative Criticism* 3 (1981), 71–103.
[59] See ch. 5, pp. 171–4 for Fitzralph's system of classification.

'Alle þise clerkes', quod I þo, 'þat [o]n crist leuen
Seyen in hir Sermons þat neiþer Sarsens ne Iewes
Ne no creature of cristes liknesse withouten cristendom worþ saued'.
　'*Contra!*' quod Ymaginatif þoo and comsed for to loure,
And seide, '*Saluabitur vix Iustus in die Iudicij*;
Ergo saluabitur,' quod he and seide na moore latyn.
(XII 277–82/XIV 199–204)

A narrowly logical argument in scholastic idiom, operating by means of contradiction and based on the grammatical point that '*vix*', 'scarcely', does not reverse the meaning of '*salvabitur*', 'will be saved', as '*non*', 'not' would, but merely restricts it, can scarcely be a suitable answer here in just the place where on the 'affective' account we would expect grace to celebrate its transcendent triumph.

It has, of course, been suggested that Ymaginatif's argument implies the mystical interpretation of the verse he cites, as for example it is given in this Wycliffite sermon:[60]

> . . . in þis word 'vnneþe schal þe iust man be sauyd' is menyd þis word 'Iesu', whoso coude vndurstonden it; for, in þis word 'vix' ben putte þre lettres, V, and I, and X; and V bytokeneþ fyue, I bytokneþ Iesu, and X bytokneþ Crist. And so þis resoun seiþ þat þe iust man schal be saued by þe fyue woundus of Iesu Crist oure lord.[61]

In the C version Will may perhaps have understood Ymaginatif in this mystical sense when he awakens in the next passus:

> . . . y merueyled in herte how Ymaginatyf saide
> That *iustus* before Iesu *in die iudicii*
> *Non saluabitur* bote if *vix* helpe.
> (XV 21–3)

The word 'vix' will help to save the just man on the Day of Judgement in the grammatical sense Ymaginatif employs – it restricts rather than reversing 'saluabitur' – but also in the sense that it is the mercy of Christ symbolized by the word 'vix' that will save him. Still, Will's interpretation obviously cannot be taken as a straightforward expan-

---

60　See Pearsall's note to C xv 22–3; he cites the earlier edition of the sermons, T. Arnold, ed., *Select English Works of John Wyclif*, 3 vols. (Oxford, 1869–71), i: 337.
61　Quoted from *Proprium Sanctorum* sermon 41, P. Gradon and A. Hudson, eds., *English Wycliffite Sermons*, 5 vols. (Oxford, 1983–96), ii, ed. P. Gradon (Oxford, 1988), 232/57–62.

sion of Ymaginatif's meaning. And even if, perhaps especially if, Ymaginatif's argument might imply this mystical sense, what is significant is the incongruity in context of the confrontational, analytic mode in which it is expressed.

What Ymaginatif says is rendered questionable not only by its internal incoherences, the tension between its mode and content, and by Ymaginatif's contradiction of his own advice, but – in the B version, at any rate – by uncomfortable resonances with statements by other speakers earlier in the third dream. Even if it is not always correct in *Piers Plowman* to assume that a concept or personification ought to be self-consistent, the scholastic character of the third dream entails considerable attention to (if not necessarily respect for) integrity of argument. Ymaginatif has associated his functions with those of memory, and elsewhere he does recall events earlier in the dream.[62] His suppressions of difference are therefore disquieting; it may even be right to view them as wilful misrepresentations to which our attention is meant to be drawn.

When Ymaginatif draws out from his more general exposition upon 'do as Lewte teacheth' the advice that Will should not argue with clerks, we should be uncomfortably reminded that Lewte taught Will something rather different in the inner dream of B passus XI. When Will asked whether he dare recount his dreamt experiences with corrupt friars, Lewte replied as follows:

> It is *licitum* for lewed men to [legge] þe soþe
> If hem likeþ and lest; ech a lawe it graunteþ,
> Excepte persons and preestes and prelates of holy chirche.
> It falleþ noȝt for þat folk no tales to telle
> Thouȝ þe tale [were] trewe, and it touche[d] synne . . .
> Ac be [þow] neueremoore þe firste [þe] defaute to blame;
> Thouȝ þow se yvel seye it noȝt first; be sory it nere amended.

---

62 J. Simpson, *'Piers Plowman': An Introduction to the B-Text* notes how Ymaginatif's exposition recalls the events of the inner dream within the B text's third dream (102–3, 136–7). In my view the links Simpson suggests between Ymaginatif's references backward and the rememorative psychological function that might arguably be attributed to him are perhaps over-specific: the philosophical affiliations of the kind of explanation Ymaginatif is giving account well enough for its tendency to return to and incorporate material from earlier in the discussion.

[T]hyng þat is pryue, publice þow it neuere;
Neiþer for loue [looue] it noȝt ne lakke it for enuye:
(xɪ 96–100; 103–6)

Because he is not a cleric, says Lewte, Will can 'publice' his dreams as
long as they do not present 'pryve', unblamed faults and provided that
his motives are disinterested – precisely the opposite of the advice
Ymaginatif attributes to Lewte's teaching.[63]

Ymaginatif may also misrepresent Will's encounter with Clergie;
there is a disjunction in his reference to 'clergie' that editorial interpretation has attempted to smooth over. Where Ymaginatif explains
that 'I took ful good hede / How þow contrariedest clergie wiþ crabbede wordes' (xɪɪ 155–6/xɪv 99–100), and then goes on briefly to
summarize Will's remarks at the end of B x: 'How þat lewed men
liȝtloker þan lettrede were saued,/ Than clerkes or kynde witted men of
cristene peple' (xɪɪ 157–8/xɪv 101–2), most editors attempt to specify
that Ymaginatif is referring to the concept 'clergie' in line 156, and thus
that Ymaginatif's only point of reference to events earlier in the third
dream is to B x 449.[64] But Ymaginatif's opening does not fit well with
the explanation that follows. 'Contrarien' is used in Middle English to
denote being, or acting, contrary to another thing or action;[65] it is just
conceivable that Will could be said to have 'contraried' the concept
'clergie' because he was *acting* contrary to it by directing 'crabbede
wordes' *at* it. But it seems much more likely that the phrasing 'contrariedest . . . wiþ crabbede wordes' is meant to describe a counterargument

---

63 In the C version this contradiction is removed: Ymaginatif does not ask Will to 'do as
   Lewte teacheþ', and most of the passage attributed to Lewte in B is assigned to Will
   instead (see C xɪɪ 23–38).
64 Schmidt uses a small letter here and a capital letter at B x 449 [Schmidt 440], as do
   Kane and Donaldson; Schmidt in addition refers the reader in his note to Will's
   condemnation of both kinds of 'clergie', 'i.e. at X 439–72a' (338, 157n.). The intended
   implication in both editions is that Ymaginatif is referring only to B X 449 [440].
   Skeat avoids the issue by using a capital letter in all versions both here and in the
   earlier passage, but glossing 'Clergie' in B x 449 [440] as 'Learning' (116, marginal
   gloss to 440) and providing no gloss to the later passage. Only Pearsall's C version
   capitalizes the word in the later passage at C xɪv 100, so as to imply that Ymaginatif is
   referring to the personification with whom Will spoke at C xɪ 138–62, and uses a
   small letter at C xɪ 276–84 where Rechelesnesse criticizes 'clergie'.
65 Elsewhere in *Piers Plowman* B see v 54; xv 569; xvɪɪ 335 and 344. See also examples
   listed in the *MED* s.v. 'contrarien', v. 4 a and b.

in just the sort of style that Ymaginatif employs to contradict all clerks, and that Will uses as well on several occasions elsewhere in the poem.[66] Ymaginatif seems to be suggesting that Will has argued against the figure Clergie with whom he spoke at B x 227–335 rather than, or at the very least in addition to, suggesting that Will acted against 'clergie' by means of words at B x 449.[67] In keeping with his project of papering over the contradictions in 'clergie', Ymaginatif appears to be lumping the concept 'clergie' together with the figure Clergie and suggesting that Will has 'contraried' them both. However, far from having 'contraried' Clergie, Will wholeheartedly agreed with him. For Clergie is one of the most outspoken critics of the clergy in the poem, and he argued that the 'lewed' play a key role in anticlerical complaint.[68]

Clergie's exposition in B x quickly veers from discussing the Trinity into a lengthy anticlerical complaint and prophecy. He warns that nobody should blame the guilty where he is blameworthy himself, but he directs his warning only to parsons and priests: 'This text was told yow to ben ywar er ye tauȝte / That ye were swiche as ye sey[d]e to salue wiþ oþere' (x 275–6), while tacitly permitting the blameworthy 'lewed' to censure priests, presumably because their faults may be blamed on the priests' poor governance. To release himself from the stricture on blaming by clerics that he has just imposed, he positions the blame he directs at parish priests in laymen's mouths rather than his own:

> Lewed men may likne yow þus, þat þe beem liþ in youre eiȝen,
> And þe festu is fallen for youre defaute
> In alle maner men þoruȝ mansede preestes.
> (x 282–4)

Having shifted the blame, so to speak, Clergie can produce a lengthy anticlerical statement that ends by prophesying that Dowel will

---

[66] For Ymaginatif's contradiction see above, pp. 44–5. Will uses the same 'Contra!' opening at B viii 20 and x 349, for example.

[67] Several manuscripts have 'contraryest' in place of 'contrariedest', perhaps in an attempt to make the reference more general. The reference is not consistent in C: even though Ymaginatif blames Will at xiv 99–100, it was Rechelesnesse who 'aresenede' Clergie earlier on (xiii 128), and he did so after the whole of his anticlerical remarks, not after the comment about salvation.

[68] In C Clergie merely delivers a short lesson on Dowel, Dobet, and Dobest, making no reference to failings in the contemporary church.

'dyngen hym [i.e. Caym, representing the four orders of friars] adoun and destruye his myȝte' (x 335).

Even if we allow that Ymaginatif ignores Will's encounter with Clergie and that his statement at B xii 156 refers only to Will's 'lewed role' at the end of B x, the relation to 'clergie' that Ymaginatif advocates is not the one Clergie himself recommends earlier in the dream. Much though it may be argued that Ymaginatif's inconsistencies are creative rather than destructive and that they point beyond the inadequacies of the system which has produced them, it remains that Ymaginatif contradicts himself, all the clerks adduced against him, and (in B at any rate) the personifications Clergie and Lewte. What Ymaginatif shows us is that clergie is not the province solely of clerics, nor is grace subject to clerical administration. His clerical apologism fails more strikingly than that of the priest who read Piers's pardon from Truth (vii 107–44) or the friars Will met before this third dream (viii 8–61) or the maister at the court of Conscience (xiii 25–214). Their smug complacency may, according to the conventional polemic strategy, be blamed upon their own personal failings.[69] But Ymaginatif's defence hinges on the ideal diffusion of 'clergie'; and although he may imaginatively bridge the fissures in the ideology he supports and advocates, his exposition presents those fissures gaping to the reader.

While his attempts at solution take a very different tack, Ymaginatif is attempting to deal with the same difficulty with 'lewed clergie' that Will and Piers have posed. Whereas they suggest it is possible for the 'lewed' to have 'clergie' through grace, Ymaginatif claims clerics are instrumental in the conferral of grace upon the 'lewed' by means of 'clergie'. Ymaginatif considers the social distribution of 'clergie' more fully than the briefly sketched extraclergial figures within the B version's third dream. He moves beyond Lewte's watertight separation between 'clergie' and 'lewed', which grants licence to speak truth only to the 'lewed' but does not explain where they will gain the knowledge that would enable them to speak. And he has a broader vision of the social role of 'clergie' than Clergie, whose interest was not in voicing concerns about their access to 'clergie' that the 'lewed' might want to express, but

---

[69] See Anne Hudson's discussion of older and newer polemic strategies in *The Premature Reformation*, 347–51.

instead in finding an extraclergial mouthpiece for his own critique of the institutional clergy. How, after all, are the 'lewed' to learn about the faults of the clergy if they themselves have no access whatever to 'clergie' and if, as both Lewte and Clergie recommend, the clergy keep quiet about their failings? But of course Ymaginatif is interested not in enabling 'lewed' critique, as Piers and Will are, nor even in the less straightforward way that Clergie and Lewte are, but in suppressing it. And Ymaginatif's hopeful solution, that the diffusion of 'clergie' might bring everyone to cultivate their own personal reform, is as hard to swallow as Piers's or Will's: the proposition that the clergy by diffusing 'clergie' will bring grace is if anything even more of an affront to ordinary common sense than the notion that grace could bring about Will's and Piers's 'clergie' in the absence of any institutional mediation.

SOCIAL 'CLERGIE': ANIMA

Ymaginatif does not explain what knowledge, if any, is communicated when clerics diffuse the benefits of their 'clergie'; and although even he is forced to acknowledge that there are abuses both by clerics and of learning, he gives no attention to how they might be dealt with. Any more practical consideration of how to distribute 'clergie' through society will have to consider the mechanics, and the consequences, of its dissemination. The speaker in *Piers Plowman* who devotes the most attention to the potential effects of new 'lewed' knowledge is Anima (Liberum Arbitrium in C), who Will encounters at the beginning of his fifth dream in B xv, or in the midst of his fourth dream in C xvi.[70] Anima's discussion voices the poem's most detailed and critical commentary on contemporary conditions, and its most thoughtful discussion of the social role of 'clergie'. In opposition to Ymaginatif, more thoroughly than Clergie, Anima speculates about the capacity of more

---

[70] Will meets Anima at xv 12/xvi 157. I will give cross references between the B and C versions throughout this discussion. In my view (as I will explain) the local changes to Anima's position on 'clergie' cannot, any more than Ymaginatif's, readily be attributed to any easily legible alteration in Langland's position: his presentation is neither more reticent, nor more cautious, nor more conservative.

widely distributed 'clergie' to produce a better-run England and even an ideally disposed Christian world – and not, or not solely, by the agency of clerics.

Anima's exposition, like Ymaginatif's, concerns itself with a wider public. But rather than merely dragging more general concerns back to their application to Will as Ymaginatif does, Anima makes use of the sort of homiletic pose that the writers of polemical sermons and tracts employ. He addresses himself beyond Will to a broadly inclusive audience: 'I shal tellen it for truþes sake; take hede whoso likeþ' (xv 91/not in C). He directs particular statements to a variety of specific groups (though displaying a marked bias toward those with money): 'Freres and fele oþere maistres þat to [þe] lewed [folk] prechen' (xv 70/ XVI 230), 'ye lettrede' (xv 103/XVI 255), 'ye lewed men' (xv 128/XVI 272), 'lordes and ladies' (xv 322/XVII 55), 'clerkes and knyʒtes and communers þat ben riche' (xv 332/not in C), 'wise men' (xv 548/XVII 210; 'lettred men'), 'ye clerkes' (xv 551/XVII 214), 'ye bisshopes' (xv 554/XVII 217). His style of exposition is both more self-consciously controlled and more modulated than Ymaginatif's: he grounds his statements of fact in common knowledge – 'þe peple woot þe soþe' (xv 79/XVI 237; as þe peple woet wel) – and his recommendations for change in the thoroughly clergial, textual domain of biblical and authoritative quotations: 'to witnesse I take / Boþe Mathew and Marc and *Memento domine* david' (xv 489–90/not in C).

Imbued though it is with 'clergie', Anima's homiletic pose also displays 'lewed' allegiances. As is usual among extraclergial writers, he distances himself from any clear clerical position, affirming his own 'lewed'ness to tell 'grete clerkes' 'If I lye on yow to my lewed wit, ledeþ me to brennyng' (xv 83/not in C). Of course there was as yet no direct imminent threat of burning when any version of *Piers Plowman* was written: no heretics were burned in England, nor was there even any law allowing this penalty, until 1401.[71] But nonetheless professed willingness to be burnt (presumably modelled on continental discourse) is common among English polemical writers before as well as

---

[71] On the prosecution of heretics in England before 1399 see H. G. Richardson, 'Heresy and the Lay Power Under Richard II', *English Historical Review*, vol. 51, no. 201 (1936), 1–28.

after 1401.[72] For Anima, as for other writers who deploy this strategy, voluntary self-subjection to punitive judgement provides a guarantee of veracity and implies some distance from the sway and influence of 'grete clerkes'. As a spokesman about the clergy to the 'lewed', authorized to speak by his 'lewed'ness yet deeply informed about the clergy and arguing by means of his 'clergie', Anima occupies precisely the position required of anyone who wants to 'legge the sothe' according to Lewte's recommendations.

But if Anima attributes one sort of 'lewed clergie' to himself, he imputes another to the clerics he criticizes. Their advice he labels 'lewed' in the pejorative sense typically applied to the laity: 'Allas, lordes and ladies, lewed counseil haue ye' (xv 322/xvii 55), meaning that it is ill-informed, bad, stupid, even though it is (in the status-linked sense) clerical in origin. Even worse, Anima accuses corrupt clergy of usurping 'lewed' status by imitating the way of life of the moneyed 'lewed', spending their tithes on clothes and building rather than the poor and showing off their 'heigh clergie' in endless discussions of the Trinity rather than teaching the essentials of faith. Because the clergy live 'lewed'ly they deprive the people of a proper example, with the result that charity is widely disregarded: corruption among lords, for example, is the fault of the clergy because they do not refuse ill-gotten tithes and because they set an example of lordly misspending which lords follow. Anima is careful to emphasize that the clergy, and 'clergie' in the sense of learning, have limited power: Certitude about charity is beyond the range of all clerks as well as all 'clergie', and it is possible for inadequately taught 'lewed' and heathens to be saved through grace without 'clergie'. But the clergy are the focus of Anima's programme of reform, as the redistribution of 'clergie' is its means.

Anima places his hope for reform in a wider dissemination of information about the clergy: by telling the 'lewed' about the gap between how the clergy should behave and how they do behave, he hopes to bring them to take action. However, Anima is less comfortable with the dissemination of potentially inflammatory 'clergie' about

---

[72] For a survey, and the suggestion that references to burning are consequently virtually useless for determining the date of texts, see Hudson, *Premature Reformation*, 15–16.

clerical misbehaviour than with that of the basic sort of 'clergie' that all those with pastoral responsibilities ought to teach. His variably meticulous translation from Latin to English is symptomatic of his ambivalence about undertaking the task of disseminating knowledge more widely himself, and of his concern about what effects it might produce. When he is explaining his names to Will (xv 23–39/xvi 182–200), or quoting Solomon to explain why one should not want too much learning (xv 54–9/xvi 215–20), he translates word for word. But when in the course of his sermon he quotes anticlerical passages, he threatens the effects of full disclosure while pretending to withhold it:

> Iohannes Crisostomus of clerkes [carpeþ] and preestes: . . .
> [quotation from Chrysostom]
> . . . If lewed [ledes] wiste what þis latyn meneþ,
> And who was myn Auctour, muche wonder me þinkeþ
> But if many preest [forbeere] hir baselardes and hir broches
> [And beere] bedes in hir hand and a book vnder hir arme.
> (xv 117; 119–22/xvi 271; not in C)

> [quotation from the gloss on Job]
> If lewed men knewe þis latyn þei wolde loke whom þei yeve,
> And auisen hem bifore a fyue dayes or sixe
> Er þei amortisede to monkes or [monyales] hir rente[s].
> (xv 319–21/xvii 53–4)

'Lewed men' would reform the clerics he is also addressing if they knew the meaning of these quotations, Anima says. He does not note that in point of fact he has already paraphrased and explained each of these quotations, and even named Chrysostom as the author of the first one, in the sections which precede them.[73] He masks his own role as the disseminator of the sort of knowledge that might cause trouble, just as at this point he lays a veil over the process by which 'lewed' men would bring priests to carry beads and books.

Even when Anima arrives at the more pointed suggestion that clerics should lose their lordship, he stops short of outlining how the loving knights and 'commune' will bring this about. Just as 'reson and rightful doom' judged the Templars,

---

73 See xv 92–102, 117/xvi 242–54, 271 for a close translation and identification of Chrysostom as the author of the first quotation; and for a looser paraphrase of the point of the second quotation, xv 269–317/xvii 7–50.

> Right so, ye clerkes, for youre coueitise er [come au3t] longe
> Shal þei demen *dos ecclesie,* and [depose yow for youre pride]:
> *Deposuit potentes de sede &c.*
> If knyghthod and kynde wit and þe commune [and] conscience
> Togideres loue leelly, leueþ it wel, ye bisshopes,
> The lordshipe of londes [lese ye shul for euere],
> And lyuen as *Leuitici* as oure lord [yow] techeþ:
> *Per primicias et decimas &c.*
> (xv 551–6/xvii 214–19)

The memory of the unpleasant fate of the Templars – mass trials and
executions as well as the confiscation of their property – should be
fresh enough even now to mark the distance between loyal mutual love
and what is threatened. But only in his peroration does Anima work
himself up to direct and specific exhortation:

> Takeþ hire landes, ye lordes, and leteþ hem lyue by dymes.
> If possession be poison and inparfite hem make
> [Charite] were to deschargen hem for holy chirches sake,
> And purgen hem of poison er moore peril falle.
> If preesthode were parfit þe peple sholde amende
> That contrarien cristes lawe and cristendom dispise.
> (xv 564–9/xvii 227–51; extended).

And even here the knowledge on which the exhortation depends is
carefully edged round with conditionals; Anima maintains to the end a
separation between the knowledge he is providing and the 'lewed'
activity that might result.

Anima's appeal is characteristic of a kind of polemic complaining
pose far less controversial, in a certain way, than Piers's and Will's. Like
the writer of the 'Petition' discussed in Chapter one, Anima addresses
himself most of all to the rich and powerful. He maintains the
conventional pastoral relation of 'clergie' to 'lewed': even though most
of the lords he is addressing must be literate, and many may know
Latin, Anima firmly classifies them as 'lewed'ly ignorant, in need of his
advice and dependent on his information. Despite his purported
advocacy of the 'lewed' in general, nowhere does Anima address the
uneducated ordinary lay people on whose behalf pastoral concerns are
(one might imagine) voiced.

54

'CLERGIE' AND WRITING: THE 'LEWED VICORY'

Only the latter part of B xix/C xxi goes further than Anima in considering the potentialities for reform through 'clergie' in order to envision their implications for the whole population.[74] But its social vision is an altogether darker one; and the extraclergial figure here, the 'lewed' vicar, is among the 'lewed' interruptors who disrupt Piers's aspirations toward reformed Christian community.

In the latter part of passus xix/xxi, Piers with the help of Grace has set up an ideally constituted Christian community endowed with grace and all the cardinal virtues. The concluding section of this dream may be viewed as an experimental consideration of the hope that 'clergie' properly distributed and administered through grace could bring about personal and institutional reform throughout the community. The dream as a whole is embedded in a mass, or symbolic creation of Christian unity, in which Will has fallen asleep, thus demonstrating one practical obstacle to the institutionally mediated spread of 'clergie': inattention.[75] The concluding section of the dream reveals other obstacles. At the point where the community has been established, Ymaginatif's ideal of harmonious hierarchy seems near to achievement. True, Pride and his host of vices earlier threatened to confuse the difference between virtue and vice,

> Conscience; and youre [caples two],
> Confession and Contricion, and youre carte þe bileeue
> Shal be coloured so queyntely and couered vnder [oure] Sophistrie
> That Conscience shal noȝt knowe who is cristene or heþene,
> Ne no manere marchaunt þat wiþ moneye deleþ
> Wheiþer he wynne wiþ right, wiþ wrong or wiþ vsure.
> (xix 345–50/xxi 346–51)

---

[74] Since the last two passus of C are unrevised and all differences between the edited texts are negligible, I will provide cross-references to Pearsall's edition but no separate discussion of any small variations.

[75] It was a convention of visionary literature that visions should arrive during mass; see K. Kerby-Fulton, *Reformist Apocalypticism and 'Piers Plowman'* (Cambridge, 1990), 118–20. Like other such visions, Will's dream might be regarded not as an abandonment of spiritual advancement, but a substitution of personal experience for institutionally mediated communal ritual.

And there are already a few cracks in the unified community; 'comune wommen' and a 'sisour and a somonour' are wilfully holding with the false (XIX 367–70/XXI 368–71). But everyone has been brought to contrition, and as the narrator hopefully puts it, 'Clennesse [of þe] comune and clerkes clene lyuynge / Made vnitee holy chirche in holynesse stonde' (XIX/XXI 379–80). The spread of 'clergie', and of grace mediated through 'clergie', seem at this moment about to produce a reformed community.

However, when Conscience tries to make the 'comune' pay its debts before entering Unity, an outcry erupts: '"How?" quod al þe comune; "þow conseillest vs to yelde / Al þat we owen any wight er we go to housel?"' (XIX/XXI 391–2). Considering that penance after confession is normally meant to be a prerequisite for communion, Conscience's does not seem too harsh a request: the 'comune's' incredulous, indignant reaction, and the brewer's affirmation of his intent to continue with business as usual, reveal the limits of any idealizing aspirations. When asked to put into practice something to which they normally pay lip service, to make their superficial knowledge of the 'clergie' that has been diffused to them into concrete, practical knowledge, the 'comune' refuse 'clergie' because it looks to them as though the costs of restitution outweigh the benefits.

But the brewer is the last figure in this passus whom Conscience can unequivocally condemn (XIX/XXI 403–8); and if the 'lewed' vicar's objection is accepted even that condemnation is overly harsh. For in the final section of this passus, as Pride promised, it is becoming extremely difficult to distinguish the perversions of virtue from their genuine practice.[76] The problem does not seem to be that the spokesmen here are *un*informed, lacking in 'clergie', but more that they twist their 'clergie' to purposes less virtuous yet disturbingly familiar. The knight is half-joking as he explains how the perversion of virtues licences him to take from his reeve all that his steward says is owing; but the king seems entirely serious when he explains that he is the source of all law and is entitled to act as he wishes – even though, as Baldwin explains, the kind of theocratic theory of rule the king is using

---

[76] Carruthers was the first to connect Pride's promise with its fulfilment near the end of the passus; see M. Carruthers, *The Search for St Truth: A Study of Meaning in 'Piers Plowman'* (Evanston, 1973), 157–8.

would not have been acceptable in England, still less in Ricardian England where control by other nobles of the king's excesses was a continuing source of conflict.[77] The way that the knight and king employ 'clergie' confirms Scripture's answer to Will's question (B x 336; not in C) whether 'dowel and dobet are dominus and knyȝthode': the principles and impetus of reform cannot, failing the clergy, be naively sought among the laity: they are no more a secure source of justice than anyone else. Clergie's prophecy about a just king (B x 322–35; not in C) cannot be interpreted as referring to any earthly ruler.

But the figure near the end of this passus, indeed anywhere in *Piers Plowman*, the quality of whose 'lewed'ness and 'clergie' modern scholars have had most difficulty in classifying, is the 'lewed' vicar who speaks directly after the brewer and before the knight and king. Like Will, like Anima, he is poised between the terms of 'lewed' and 'clergie'. But the polemic volatility of both the terms used to describe him, and their capacity to be applied in both laudatory and pejorative senses to persons at a range of levels in both the secular and ecclesiastical hierarchies, renders him difficult to classify – as, indeed, do the confusingly conflicted ideological commitments of the speech he makes.

Most straightforwardly, this 'lewed' vicar could be regarded as a parish vicar who is a clerk in minor orders, with a status and hierarchical position scarcely more secure than the one the dreamer claims in C v, 'lewed' in that he is a layman of quite limited education, and a 'vicar' in the common sense 'ordained cleric serving as parish priest in place of an absent rector'.[78] But his 'lewedness' might also, or instead, be read as an authenticating quality, as it is for Anima, whose claim to be 'lewed' both validates and excuses what he says; or a strategy of displacement, as it is for Clergie, who attributes his criticisms to the 'lewed'; or even a term of abuse meant to dismiss him from consideration.

Critics have been divided over the question of whether the vicar's

---

[77] On the knight and king in B xix/cxxi see A. P. Baldwin, *The Theme of Government in 'Piers Plowman'* (Woodbridge, Suffolk, 1981), 7–12. She mentions tensions in the contemporary governance of England only briefly; for a fuller discussion see ch. 3, pp. 74–5.

[78] See n. 81 for this sense of 'vicar'.

'lewed'ness is a positive, negative, or neutral quality.[79] But no one to my knowledge has focused attention on the multiple possible interpretations of not just 'lewed', but 'vicar' as well; nor has anyone that I know of examined the involvement of these terms in contemporary political debates.[80] 'Vicar' is used metaphorically to designate deputative functions in many sorts of contexts – as Ymaginatif uses it in C, 'For clergy is Cristes vycary to conforte and to cure' (xiv 70) – and in Latin writings produced in England it designates deputies lay as well as clerical serving at all levels of the secular and clerical hierarchies.[81] Polemical writers treating conflicts between spiritual and temporal jurisdiction contest in which ways 'vicar' can be applied to popes, emperors, or kings. Papal theorists attempt to claim that since the pope as God's vicar wields supreme temporal as well as spiritual power, therefore the emperor rules through the pope, as *his* vicar or minister: Hostiensis for example asserts that 'although the jurisdictions are separate as regards their exercise, nevertheless the emperor holds his imperial power from the Roman church and can be called its official or

---

[79] For a balanced assessment of the 'lewed' vicar's position, including bibliography on the views of previous critics, see J. Simpson, *Piers Plowman*, 229–30 and n. 9.

[80] For a general introduction to types of theoretical argument employed in political debate by late medieval English polemicists, see ch. 1, pp. 14–15.

[81] My thanks to D. R. Howlett and associates at the *Dictionary of Medieval Latin from British Sources* (hereafter *DMLBS*) for allowing me to consult their files s.vv., *vicaria, vicariatus, vicarie, vicarius*. To save space, I use *DMLBS* abbreviations where available. The pope is variously the *vicarius or vicariatus* of Christ; 'Proc. v. Alice Kyteler', in Camd. Soc. (1843), 18; *Ziz.* 249; Ockham, *An Princeps, Pol.* I 243–4; *Eul. Hist. Cont.* iii 337), or of Peter (*Ziz.* 259; Thos. of Elmham, *Cant.* 333; *Chr. Mon. S. Alb.* i 46); a bishop may also be called the *vicarius Christi* (T. Chobham, *Summa* 131); all sorts of ecclesiastical deputies are called *vicarii*, including parish vicars (*Ziz.* 345, 488), deputies for canons or deans who would take their place at Mass or in assemblies (*Reg. Bishop Halton* I 5; *Ch. Heref.* 74–5, 123–4, 210–15, 253; L. Somercotes 29; *Ac. Durh.* i 78), lay or choral vicars who seem to have been employed to sing mass (*Mun. Gild. Bond.* i 29), the *vicarius generalis* or bishop's deputy (*Sup. Clergy* 189; *Lit. Cant.* ii 500 and iii 352; Robert de Graystanes; *Mon. Francisc.* ii 81–2) and the *vicarius provincialis* or deputy for a Franciscan house (*Mon. Francisc.* ii 81; *ExchScot.* iv 462); the king is the *vicarius* or *vicariatus* of the emperor (Faust. B v 82v; *Chron. Monast.* (ed. Bond) ii 323; *Chr. Mon. S. Alb.* i 212), but also the *vicarius Summi Regis* (*Lib. Cust. Mun. Gild. Lond.* ii 630); and although he is more commonly called a *vicecomes*, a sheriff may also be a *vicarius* (*ExchScot.* iii 674, *Coram Rege* roll 64 m. 53 (in Selden Soc. 46, p. 35)); other secular deputies of unspecified office appear in Fortescue, *NLN* ii 15; Bacon, v *Secretum Secretorum* 150, 152.

vicar'.[82] Innocent IV's elaborate historical explanation for why it is the pope rather than the emperor who is God's vicar shows that the vicariate of ruling in place of God passed successively through Noah, patriarchs, judges, kings, priests and others who for a time were rulers of the Jewish people, Christ, Peter, then finally his successors the popes. Innocent concludes that therefore 'Although in many things the offices and governing powers of the world are distinct, nevertheless, whenever it is necessary, recourse is to be had to the pope.'[83] And late fourteenth century English polemicists give these jurisdictional arguments a more local application, contesting what powers and activities the clergy in England should have in terms of what temporal power Christ might be said to have.[84]

Langland's 'lewed' vicar gives voice to these controversies, in a way that in some ways seems to oppose the king's claim to supreme absolute temporal regal power conferred directly by God. But the content and tone of what he says are quite difficult to classify. He appeals to the ideal of a just pope who would rule Christendom, at the opposite theoretical pole to the theory of secular supremacy the king is about to assert; but he strongly criticizes the current pope (XIX/XXI 410–24). He is more pessimistic than most figures in this poem about any possibility of social reform; but he idealistically, or perhaps wistfully, reinstates the hope that Piers Plowman could rule as pope with the help of Grace (XIX/XXI 425–50). He invokes the common outcry of the 'lewed' with apparent approval in order to justify his claim that cardinals should stay in Rome or Avignon and Conscience at the king's court; but, bitterly it seems, he portrays the people as guileful exploiters of the forms of virtue (XIX/XXI 416–24, 451–8). It is his position between 'lewed' and 'clergie' that enables him, like Will, to point out the

---

82 This is Tierney's translation of this famous passage, found in his very useful collection of translated documents; see B. Tierney, *The Crisis of Church and State 1050–1300* (Toronto, 1988 [New Jersey, 1964]), 156.

83 See Tierney, *Crisis*, 154–5.

84 Although the 'lewed' vicar seems more interested in larger jurisdictional issues, his argument resonates with use of these arguments on more local issues by late medieval English writers. See for example ch. 1, pp. 14–15, ch. 3, pp. 79–81, and ch. 5, p. 142. For Wyclif's adaptation of Innocent's historical schema to explain why temporal rule by kings, without interference from the church, is the best system of governance, see ch. 5, pp. 147–8.

distance between theoretical ideals and practical reality without having to state his own position or expose his interests. But his inclusion here also fulfils a function similar to that of the king and knight who speak after him. Because his statements are disorienting, his readers may be led to weigh his extraclergial arguments critically and consider whether they deserve assent.

In the first and last lines of passus xix/xxi, as nowhere else in any of the waking interludes of the poem, Will recounts the writing of his dreams (xix/xxi 1 and 481).[85] Thus passus xix/xxi's vision of a society in which 'clergie' cannot finally have any effect upon just those recalcitrant elements one might want it to reform, but rather reinforces their arguments for continuing as they were, is framed as a *written* vision, itself capable of conveying 'clergie'. When Will falls asleep in mass in order to dream the vision he will write, forsaking a symbolic for an imaginary unity, the conflict between his waking duties and his clergial (or 'lewed'?) activity is the same as the one posed in Ymaginatif's initial accusation. At the very point where the dreamer gives us his vision of the worst misuse as well as the best use of 'clergie' by society as a whole, he also reminds us of his role as the mediator of 'clergie'. From Ymaginatif's and even Anima's blithe certainty of the saving powers of 'clergie' he has moved to a much less optimistic vision of how 'clergie' might be ignored or distorted; one which casts a different sort of light on his own work of recording and disseminating 'clergie' in the products of his 'makyng'. The references to writing at the beginning and ending of passus xix/xxi are the dreamer's closest approach to

---

[85] The narrator does mention writing on other occasions. In the midst of the A text pardon, internal to the dream, 'wille' becomes a scribe who benefits from the gratitude of merchants: 'þanne were marchauntis merye; many wepe for ioye,/ And ʒaf wille for his writyng wollene cloþis;/ For he copiede þus here clause þei couden hym grete mede' (viii 42–4). In the C text at the opening of C v, while awake, the narrator explains that 'lollares of Londone and lewede ermytes' disliked him because 'y made of tho men as resoun me tauhte' (v 4–5). However, only in B xix/C xxi does the narrator recount waking from a dream and writing about that dream. The narrator's ability to criticize his neighbours in C v may issue from what he has learned from the first dream, but the connection between dreaming and writing is not a direct one. It is true, as Middleton points out ('Acts of Vagrancy'), that even here Will does not specifically designate that the result of his writing is the book *Piers Plowman*. For my purposes, where it is writing rather than creating a book that is at issue, the distinction seems a narrow one; yet I agree that even here the relation between writer, narrator, book, and reading audience remains indirect.

considering the social function of his dream-writing activity. Still avoiding any direct reference to the audience for whom he is mediating 'clergie', he wraps his self-description as a mediator of 'clergie' around his darkest vision of its potential social effects. Without making the connection explicit, he juxtaposes his translation of the tools for argument into the vernacular with 'lewed' misuses of argument at every level of society – and even by an extraclergial like himself.

3

The 'publyschyng' of 'informacion': John Trevisa, Sir Thomas Berkeley, and their project of 'Englysch translacion'

John Trevisa is one of the best documented of late medieval extra-clergial writers.[1] We know just when Trevisa was at Oxford, and which colleges he belonged to; we even know which books disappeared with him and a group of colleagues when they were expelled from Queen's. We know roughly what years he was vicar of Berkeley. We know that the patron who financed the production of most of his work was Thomas Berkeley – and Hanna's work on Berkeley has helped to show why this relationship was a remarkably productive one[2] – and we have ample record in manuscript of the six translations and two short original works Trevisa is known to have produced.[3] So attractive is this fund of information about one particular education and relationship of patronage that there have been a number of attempts to assign to Trevisa other anonymous but now much better known late medieval English works whose sentiments and concerns resemble those expressed in works we can be confident in assigning to Trevisa. Thus, it has been suggested that Trevisa was the author of the revisions of *Piers Plowman*, and that he either translated the bible into English on his

---

[1] David Fowler's ongoing researches have helped to bring this documentation to modern attention. I am most grateful to Professor Fowler for allowing me to read in advance of publication chapter four of his book on Trevisa, *The Life and Times of John Trevisa, Medieval Scholar* (Seattle, 1995) and his collaborative edition (with Charles Briggs and Paul Remley) of the *De regimine principum*, *The Governance of Kings and Princes: John Trevisa's Middle English Translation of the 'De regimine principum' of Aegidius Romanus.*

[2] R. Hanna III, 'Sir Thomas Berkeley and his Patronage', *Speculum* 64 (1989), 878–916.

[3] See D. C. Fowler, *John Trevisa* (Aldershot, 1993), 45–7, and A. S. G. Edwards, 'John Trevisa', in A. S. G. Edwards, ed., *Middle English Prose: A Critical Guide to Major Authors and Genres* (New Brunswick, NJ, 1984), 133–46; 142–5, for convenient charts of the manuscripts of Trevisa's work.

own or participated in the Wycliffite translation.[4] Rather than an attempt to advance those claims, my reason for beginning with Trevisa is that his well documented position helps to show why the sentiments and concerns he shares with the author of *Piers Plowman* and later Wycliffite writers were of broad interest, and how they became so controversial.

The generally accepted corpus of Trevisa's works is as follows:

TRANSLATIONS
Gospel of Nicodemus
pseudo-Ockham, *Dialogus inter militem et clericem*
Richard Fitzralph, *Defensio curatorum*
Ranulph Higden, *Polychronicon* (completed 1387)
Giles of Rome, *De regimine principum*
Bartholomeus Anglicus, *De proprietatibus rerum* (completed 1398/9)

ORIGINAL WORKS
Dialogue and *Epistle*, prefaced to the *Polychronicon*

What this apparently ill-assorted group of texts has in common – apart from the *Gospel of Nicodemus*, which is probably Trevisa's first translation, and which I will disregard here[5] – is that each of them was well known in late medieval England, but had previously been available only in the original language, Latin, and in some cases in French translation. A large part of Trevisa's life work was therefore given over to producing English translations of works that were already well known and accessible to clerics, and were at the very least accessible to the nobility.

If clerics and nobles were already able to read these works in Latin or French, then why did Berkeley and Trevisa expend so much time,

---

[4] These are two of the more plausible suggestions. The idea that Trevisa translated the bible has a long history, conveniently summarized by A. J. Perry in *Dialogus inter Militem et Clericem, Richard fitzRalph's Sermon: 'Defensio Curatorum' and Methodius: 'þe Bygynnyng of þe World and þe Ende of Worldes' by John Trevisa, vicar of Berkeley* (London, 1925), (hereafter *Trevisa's Dialogus . . .*), cxv–cxxvi, and recently advanced by D. C. Fowler in, for example, 'John Trevisa and the English Bible', *Modern Philology* 58 (1960–1), 81–98. The first suggestion is Fowler's; see 'About the Author', in *Piers the Plowman: Literary Relations of the A and B Texts* (Seattle, 1961), 185–205.

[5] The work is edited in a thesis by H. C. Kim, and receives detailed, sustained attention in Fowler, *The Life and Times of John Trevisa*, 120–45.

effort, and money in producing English versions? Trevisa addresses this question in the *Dialogue* between a lord and a clerk that he prefaces to his translation of the *Polychronicon*: it forms the Clerk's first and most substantive objection to the Lord's proposal for an English translation.[6]

The Clerk first asks how an English translation of a Latin work could possibly make the work accessible to *more* men, as the Lord has claimed, since Latin is used all over Europe but English only in England: 'Þanne how scholde þe mo men vnderstonde þe cronyks þey a were translated out of Latyn þat ys so wyde yvsed and yknowe into Englysch þat ys noȝt yvsed and yknowe bote of Englyschmen alone?' (290/43–7). His characteristically clerical premise is that the only kind of literacy worth worrying about is literacy in Latin: all those within England who would want or 'need' to read the *Polychronicon* can use the Latin version. Although the Clerk's second question manages to acknowledge the possibility that there might be readers literate in English only and not in Latin, it does so only for the singular exceptional case of a member of the nobility, the Lord himself. And he disputes that example: 'ȝe cunneþ speke and rede and vnderstonde Latyn. Þanne hyt nedeþ noȝt to haue such an Englysch translacion' (290/53–5). What the Clerk's first questions amount to is a suggestion that there is no point to an English translation because there is no audience for it.

In contrast to the Clerk's stodgy, conventional objections, the Lord exhibits a detailed practical knowledge about the wider audience English translation might reach and the various constraints that prevent the ready spread of information to that audience. In the course of his sensitive explanation of the various impediments those who might want or need to read may face ('oþer maner bysynes . . . elde . . . defaute of wyt . . . defaute of katel oþer of frendes to vynde ham to scole . . .' (291/65–8)) and of hitches in the mediation process whereby the clerically educated should inform the uneducated ('þe lewed man wot noȝt what a scholde axe . . . noþer wot comunlych of whom a

---

[6] The *Dialogue* and *Epistle* appear in six of the fourteen extant manuscripts containing the full text of the *Polychronicon*, including three of the earliest manuscripts. They may be dated near the completion of the *Polychronicon* translation in 1387. For full details see R. Waldron, 'Trevisa's Original Prefaces on Translation: A Critical Edition', in Kennedy, Waldron, and Wittig, eds., *Medieval English Studies*, 285–99; 287–8.

scholde axe. Also noȝt al men þat vnderstondeþ Latyn habbeþ such bokes . . . [a]lso som konneþ noȝt and som wol noȝt and som mowe noȝt a whyle . . .' (291/84–90)) it becomes apparent that the poor, the stupid, the old, and those without leisure – the whole of the lay population, it seems – all belong to the potential audience he projects for an English translation.

What might the opinions of this Lord and Clerk have to do with those of Thomas Berkeley and John Trevisa? The rest of the textual apparatus to the *Polychronicon* encourages us to view the casting of Clerk and Lord in the *Dialogue* as expressive of the relationship between Trevisa and Berkeley, even if not necessarily limited to it. In a reversal of the usual relationship between cleric and layman, the Lord in the *Dialogue* instructs the Clerk, even perhaps inspires him after the manner of the Holy Spirit: by means of the Lord's arguments, the dialogue enacts the healing of the problem the Lord had bemoaned to begin with, that is, the estrangement of man from man and a dire need for learning, by bringing the Lord and Clerk into agreement with the result that the Clerk will translate the *Polychronicon*. In the dedicatory epistle from Trevisa to Berkeley that directly follows the dialogue – and that advertises its close relationship to the dialogue by echoing the alliteration of the prayer and repeating several of the Lord's phrases in Trevisa's voice – Trevisa emphasizes his subordination to Berkeley's will, placing it on a par with God's: 'Comforte Ich haue in medfol makyng and plesyng to God, and in wytynge þat Y wot þat hyt ys ȝoure wylle' (294/216–18). The colophon, too, places the impetus for the translation exclusively with Berkeley: Trevisa writes the age of his lord Thomas 'þat made me make þis translacioun' into the history he has just finished translating, alongside the year, day, and month 'of oure lord' and the regnal year, but includes himself only as the instrument of Berkeley's will.

But even if the *Dialogue* is accurate (or at the very least consistent with the picture Trevisa gives elsewhere) in showing that the translation project proposed here is very much Berkeley's idea, are the Lord's reasons Berkeley's reasons? The Lord's remarks about the lay audience he anticipates are effective in context: the Clerk finds them unanswerable, and retreats in disarray to an objection about the stylistic capacities of English. What is more, the Lord's remarks are unusual enough in both their sentiment and the detail of their conception to demand careful consideration. However, we cannot take them as a straightforwardly factual explanation of the impetus behind the translations Berkeley sponsored – not even if, like the *Epistle*, we transfer the views they express to Trevisa instead of Berkeley. Detailed, sustained attention to all the texts Trevisa translated for Berkeley – to the texts selected, the ways those texts are annotated and in some cases altered, the formats in which they are produced, and their early publication histories – suggests that informing the laity is far from being their primary concern. It is not worth belabouring that each work Trevisa and Berkeley collaborated in producing did not reach the audience the Lord describes and can scarcely have been chosen with the primary goal of educating that audience. Instead, it will be more worthwhile to allow that evidence to emerge obliquely, while investigating what the Lord's claim accomplishes. Why is the promotion of English translation figured as a promotion of publishing information to the broadest possible audience, and what might publishing information, or, better, an ethical commitment in principle to the publishing of information, achieve?

In the *Dialogue* and *Epistle* the potential effects of published information remain remarkably unelaborated; there are hints at social harmony and international understanding, an assertion that the material is 'profitable', but nothing more. Trevisa's translation of Bartholomeus Anglicus's *De proprietatibus rerum*, like the *Polychronicon* signed, dated, and ascribed to Berkeley's impetus 'that made me make this translacioun' in its colophon, is also hugely compendious but noncontroversial, and similarly delivers a wealth of information but does not recommend any specific application for it or indicate what its availability in the vernacular is meant to accomplish. Each of these two works does contain a number of annotations: the beginning of most is indicated by the word 'Trevisa' while the end remains unspecified. Those given in *De proprietatibus rerum* are purely explanatory in character,[7] but those in the *Polychronicon* venture beyond explaining, correcting and updating Higden to disparaging his attitude to Aris-

---

[7] See pp. 48, 83, 105, 108, 290, 312–13, 522–3, 792, and 823 of M. C. Seymour *et al.*, eds., *On the Properties of Things: John Trevisa's translation of Bartholomaeus Anglicus De Proprietatibus Rerum. A Critical Text*, 3 vols. (Oxford, 1975–88).

totle, his skepticism about Arthurian legend, and his pro-monastic leanings and even, in a note tellingly unsigned, recommending that secular lords should remove the superfluous possessions of monks:

> and now for þe moste partie monkes beeþ worste of alle, for þey beþ to riche, and þat makeþ hem to take more hede aboute seculer besynesse þan gostely devocioun; þerefore, as it is i-seide bifore in 4° libro in þe 26 capitulo, by Ierom, seþþe holy cherche encresede in possessiouns hit haþ decresed in vertues. Þerfore seculer lordes schulde take awey the superfluyte of here possessiouns, and ȝeve it to hem þat nedeþ, or elles whan þey knowen þat, þey beeþ cause and mayntenours of here evel dedes, seþþe þey helpeþ nouȝt to amende hit while it is in hir power, what evere covetous preostes seyn. For it were almesse to take awey þe superfluite of here possessiouns now, þan it was at þe firste fundacioun to ȝeve hem what hem nedede.[8]

To a standard anticlerical complaint – that monks are too rich and too involved in secular affairs – Trevisa appends a quite specific recommendation for reform: secular lords should give what the monks do not need to those who do need it. Trevisa urges lords to take on the pastoral role that the monks are not fulfilling: to give alms to 'hem þat nedeþ' rather than to the monks, and to take on themselves the monks' duty of distributing their superfluous possessions to the poor.

The kind of concern for the needs of the whole populace that Trevisa advocates here is very much in line with the Lord's sentiments in the *Dialogue*. Now it is not just intellectual capital that ought to be better distributed, as in the Lord's argument for translation, but money and land. Although Trevisa's argument in this note is concerned with needs more basic than the educational, it nonetheless turns upon the publishing of 'informacion', even while this 'informacion' is published only to lords. Once lords have been told about how monks are behaving, once that information has been linked for them with an interpretation of a patristic passage in an argument that counsels them about the action they should take; once, that is, lords have been

---

[8] R. Higden, *Polychronicon*, 9 vols., ed. C. Babington and J. R. Lumby (London, 1865–86), vi, ed. J. R. Lumby (London, 1876), 465/13–467/3. The first part of Trevisa's note recounts some 'lewed' deeds of Edgar. Fowler quotes this passage in *John Trevisa*, p. 5, and in modernized form in *The Bible in Early English Literature* (Seattle, 1976), 240.

provided with information previously available only to clerics, couched in a form that shows the influence of the sort of education clerics receive, then they are obliged to act: 'or elles whan þey knowen þat, þey beeþ cause and mayntenours of here evel dedes'. Some information, at least, entails or should entail direct practical consequences that will benefit the whole of the lay population, even when that information only reaches and is only meant for lords.

In addition to the practical, 'pastoral' knowledge about the capabilities of a wider potential audience that leads him to propose the *Polychronicon* translation, the Lord of Trevisa's *Dialogue* also relies for his credibility upon a broader base of what had traditionally been clerical 'informacion': he knows all about problems of communication between languages, and he reveals extensive familiarity with the history of translation as well as the academic controversies that have surrounded it (see esp. 291/100–292/109 and 292/128–46).[9] Already this well-informed Lord begins to show us why even information less inflammatory than that found in Trevisa's *Polychronicon* note, even quite neutral information of the sort found in the texts of the *Polychronicon* and *De proprietatibus rerum,* is of use to lords, and particularly to lords who might wish to argue with clerics: displaying intellectual capital by giving arguments from historical precedent or scientific analogy might be useful to anyone trying to win an argument, regardless of their social status.

One in particular of Trevisa's less securely dated and less neutrally informative translations illuminates why there is such a huge disjunction between the Lord's claims to want to be publishing information far and wide and the more restricted use to which any of Trevisa's translations, but especially this one, seems to have been put. Trevisa's translation of Giles of Rome's *De regimine principum* makes potentially accessible to all (though this potential was never realized; indeed any wider dissemination seems by contrast to the *Polychronicon*'s publi-

---

[9] For the controversies over translation see N. Watson, 'Censorship and Cultural Change in Late-Medieval England', 840–51, A. Hudson, 'The Debate on Bible Translation, Oxford 1401', *English Historical Review* 90 (1975), 1–18, and S. A. Hunt, *An Edition of Tracts in Favour of Scriptural Translation and of Some Texts connected with Lollard Vernacular Biblical Scholarship,* 2 vols. (unpubd. D. Phil. thesis, University of Oxford, 1996), i: 218–19, 234–7. Many thanks to Simon Hunt for allowing me to read his thesis in advance of its deposit in the Bodleian Library.

cation history to have been prevented rather than promoted) a kind of information that lords in general and perhaps Berkeley in particular would be anxious not to see just anyone successfully deploying in argument.

THE *DE REGIMINE PRINCIPUM*

Trevisa's translation of the *De regimine principum* is extant in only one manuscript, Oxford, Bodleian Library, Digby 233. It is intriguing that this exceptionally large and sumptuous manuscript contains so little overt reference to Thomas Berkeley, almost certainly its patron and first owner, or to its translator.[10] Instead, the lavish illustrations elaborately reconstruct the text's original circumstances of production for Philip the Fair by Giles of Rome.[11] In the first illustration on f. 1, the kneeling author offers the book to the enthroned king. The author's pose is typical of those found in contemporary 'presentation pictures', but the king's pose is a little more unusual. Conventionally the patron holds out one or both hands to take the book, grasping the book with at least one hand; sometimes the exchange has already been completed.[12] In this illustration, however, the king opens his robe toward the author, offering a place for the book near his heart, it seems, and laying that place open to the gaze of the kneeling figure. Of the two

---

10 Berkeley is mentioned in the colophon to the Vegetius translation (f. 227, printed in Perry, xcvi) and there are three internal annotations signed 'Trevysa' in the *De regimine principum* translation.

11 The two illustrations are conveniently reproduced in O. Pächt and J. J. G. Alexander, *Illuminated Manuscripts in the Bodleian Library, Oxford*, 3 vols. (Oxford, 1966–73), iii: plate LXXX 815a and 815b from ff. 1 and 62. Fowler points out that there is a missing leaf after f. 116 (removed before foliation) and suggests that on it was a third illustration which has been stolen (*The Life and Times of John Trevisa*, 191).

12 In Pächt and Alexander, *Illuminated Manuscripts in the Bodleian*, iii: plates XXXII 368b, LVI 562, LXIII 611, LXIV 635, LXXV 792b, LXXV 793b, LXXXIII 868a, XC 943a (to cite only examples of English manuscripts) illustrate the conventional configuration. See also J. J. G. Alexander, 'Painting and Manuscript Illumination for Royal Patrons in the Later Middle Ages', in V. J. Scattergood and J. W. Sherbourne, eds, *English Court Culture in the Later Middle Ages* (London, 1983), 141–62, plate 7. See L. Lawton, 'The Illustration of Late Medieval Secular Texts, with Special Reference to Lydgate's *Troy Book*', in D. Pearsall, ed., *Manuscripts and Readers in Fifteenth Century England* (Woodbridge, Suffolk, 1983), 41–69; 41–50 for some useful caveats about interpreting illustrations in manuscripts.

courtiers placed to the left, behind the author, the closer one, who holds a sword, looks back to the other as if to whisper to him, and the one behind him points at the author. The closest of the three courtiers on the right is, once again, looking backward, while the other two look toward the king, one of them pointing at him, but focus most of their attention on the figure looking back at them. The expressions as well as the physical attitudes of all five courtiers indicate a preoccupation with factional alliances among themselves rather than the central event, or indeed the proper central concern of the court with the governance of the king, while their foppish clothing – all are elaborately dressed, no one like another – reflects the misdirection of their energies.

In the second illustration, on f. 62, the author appears to be counselling the king. The king stands in the centre, holding his robe open as before. To the far left is a city or fortified building; a door is open in the near wall. Four men and four women, all simply dressed and watching the king, stand behind a single courtier holding a sword. In front of these nine the author kneels facing the king. He points urgently toward the buildings with his left hand, and points with his right hand toward the king's chest. The disposition of the five courtiers to the right contrasts with that of the men and women to the left; again they are more intent on their interrelationship than the king, although here their preoccupation suggests imminent confrontation. The closest courtier reaches out toward the king with both hands, his right hand touching the king's robe. He looks back toward the central figure among the five. This central figure is looking fixedly at the king. The two furthest back are, like the closest, staring at the central figure, while the one remaining man looks at them. As before the king ignores his court and focuses on the author.

The oddity of devoting so much expense, in this manuscript, to an anonymous reproduction of vanished circumstances is highlighted by the marked contrast with a more conventional book owned by Berkeley, Bodley 953, his copy of the glossed prose psalter in English by Richard Rolle.[13] The psalter, which was certainly a commissioned volume, incorporates Thomas's name and coat of arms in the border to

---

[13] For a full description of the psalter manuscript see Hanna, 'Sir Thomas Berkeley', 883–5, and the two descriptions he cites; for two reproductions, see Pächt and Alexander, *Illuminated Manuscripts in the Bodleian*, iii: plates LXX & LXXI 701a & b.

the first page, the illuminations, and two historiated initials. Privately commissioned pious volumes do often incorporate coats of arms in this manner; Berkeley may have been accepting an accustomed mode of production when he commissioned this volume, whereas for Digby 233 his own preferences may have had freer rein. But the contrast between this much more conventional sort of lay possession and Digby 233 is still marked – most especially if Briggs is correct that the same group of artisans produced both volumes.[14]

Digby 233 also stands out against the background of what we know about the publication history of the *De regimine principum* in England. Information about medieval ownership from booklists, wills, and medieval library catalogues shows that members of the higher ranks of the nobility who have left such records frequently owned either the *De regimine principum* or some other volume in the advice-to-princes tradition, and that libraries often had a copy. So, too, did tutors to the nobility: Simon Burley for instance, Richard II's tutor, owned a copy in

---

Hanna remarks on the iconography's heavy emphasis of Thomas's patronage, but does not draw any contrast with Digby 233.

[14] For Briggs's evidence see C. F. Briggs, 'The Manuscript as Witness: Editing Trevisa's *De regimine principum* Translation', *Medieval Perspectives* II (1996), 42–52; 47. There is no indication of when or where Trevisa produced the translation. In the manuscript in the same scribal hand is a translation of Vegetius's *De rerum militari* generally agreed now not to be the work of Trevisa, and finished (according to the colophon) in 1408. As Hanna notes ('Sir Thomas Berkeley', 897, n. 47), the initial plan for the manuscript's production seems never to have been completed: while the manuscript is very large, well written, extensively corrected, and beautifully decorated, the rubrication is not carried through to the end of the Vegetius text. The date of the second text may suggest that Trevisa's *De regimine principum* translation was his last work; we might even suppose that some of the many extensive erasures and corrections within and beside the text represent changes to Trevisa's text. However, there could of course be other reasons why publication of Trevisa's *De regimine principum* was restricted to a single manuscript and delayed until after his death even if it was not his last work. At the simplest, if Berkeley wanted a translation of *De proprietatibus rerum* it would make eminent sense for him to assign it to Trevisa, his most accomplished translator, and transfer Vegetius to a younger or less competent scholar, delaying the copying of Vegetius's designated companion text the *De regimine principum* until the Vegetius was complete. Fowler suggests that Trevisa produced the *De regimine principum* between the *Polychronicon* and the *De proprietatibus rerum*, from 1388 to 1392 (*John Trevisa*, 30). As we shall see, on the basis of its content it would have been appropriate for Trevisa to undertake it during this period. But throughout Trevisa's career – throughout, that is, the reign of Richard II, up until Berkeley's active participation in the deposition – the issue of the government of the prince, whether by himself or others, is crucially obtrusive.

French translation.[15] The handlist of manuscripts of English origin or provenance recently published by Charles Briggs surveys fifty-three manuscripts containing all or part of the *De regimine principum*.[16] Digby 233 is the sole English translation, and was at the time it was produced much larger than any other copy that has survived: against its dimensions of 460 x 325 mm, the more typical size is *c.* 300 x 175 mm. There are five copies of the French translation (two containing abbreviated versions of the text) all of which are illuminated, ten abbreviated Latin versions, and thirty-seven copies which contain or seemingly did contain all or part of the unabbreviated text. The *De regimine principum* is accompanied by other texts in twenty-nine manuscripts. Usually these accompanying texts belong to one of the two traditions of the text's reception in England as elsewhere, advice-to-princes or Aristotelian works and commentaries: Vegetius for example appears in six manuscripts, and Aristotelian works appear in ten.[17] Lay ownership can be proven for eight manuscripts: of these, a disproportionate number are abbreviated versions or French transla-tions; two contain Vegetius while none contain Aristotelian works; and all but one are illuminated, two lavishly.[18] Among the lay owned

[15] On fourteenth and fifteenth century ownership of the *De regimine principum* see R. F. Green, *Poets and Princepleasers: Literature and the English Court in the Late Middle Ages* (Toronto, 1980), 140–2. On Burley see p. 141.

[16] C. F. Briggs, 'Manuscripts of Giles of Rome's *De Regimine Principum* in England, 1300–1500: A Handlist', *Scriptorium* 47 (1993), 60–73.

[17] Any statement about the text or reception of Giles of Rome's *De regimine principum* must be qualified by the note that the critical edition of Giles of Rome's *De regimine principum* and a descriptive catalogue of all the manuscripts are still only in preparation for the series *Aegidii Romani Opera Omnia* (Rome). Briggs's findings about the company the *De regimine principum* tends to keep are however corroborated by the only volume of the descriptive catalogue yet to be published, F. Del Punta and C. Luna's catalogue of the manuscripts in Vatican libraries, or one fifth of the total number of manuscripts, *Aegidii Romani Opera Omnia*, vol. xii (Rome, 1993). See C. Luna's introduction, xxvi-xxx.

[18] The lay owned manuscripts are Cambridge, University Library Ee 2 17; Cambridge, Jesus College Q B 9; London, British Library, Royal 6 B V (not illuminated); Oxford, Bodleian Library, Bodley 234; London, British Library, Royal 15 E VI; London, Sion College, Arc. L. 40.2/L.26; Oxford, Bodleian Library, Digby 233; Oxford, Bodleian Library, Laud Misc 702; Cambridge, University Library, Ee 2 17; and British Library, Royal 15 E VI are French abbreviations, British Library, Royal 6 B V a Latin abbre-viation. Digby 233 of course is Trevisa's translation, Cambridge, University Library Ee 2 17 and Digby 233 contain Vegetius, and British Library, Royal 15 E VI as well as Digby 233 is lavishly illuminated. The other three manuscripts in French translation

copies are the only two comparable with Digby 233 in size. One, London, British Library, Royal 15 E VI, is larger, at 470 x 330: it was made in France *c.* 1445 at the order of John Talbot Earl of Shrewsbury for Margaret of Anjou, and its presentation picture features Henry VI and Margaret of Anjou. The other, London, Sion College, Arc. L. 40.2/ L.26, is 405 x 275; it was made in England in the 1430s at the order of Richard Duke of York for his son Richard III and is illuminated with his coat of arms. Seven Latin manuscripts for which lay ownership cannot be definitively proven include some illumination and decoration, and two of these include small pictures of Giles of Rome.[19] But no copy matches the thoroughness of the antiquarian impulse of Digby 233's illustrations: the only two copies that match it in sumptuousness and size are later, presentation copies for royalty, and are much decorated with the insignia of their intended recipients.

One obvious reason to reconstruct the original circumstances of production of a text is in order to detail an analogy to contemporary events; and it is clear, as Hanna points out, that the illustrations to Digby 233 lend themselves readily to fourteenth century analogy: factional alliances among late medieval English magnates and courtiers were notorious, and the clothing and physical mannerisms of courtiers were frequently satirised.[20] But it is significant, crucially significant in my view, that this manuscript does not spell out precisely which counselling relationship in its contemporary circumstances may be seen as analogous to the one it so elaborately recalls. It is not clear whether Berkeley might straightforwardly (and flatteringly enough) stand in as the recipient of the text, so that Trevisa would be the counselling figure advising Berkeley on governance; or whether Berkeley might mediate the counsel the text provides, and even perhaps present the manuscript itself, to someone else: to that prince-too-soon-

---

are Baltimore, Walters Art Gallery W 144, Durham University Library, Cosin v.i.9, and New York, Pierpont Morgan Library 122.

19 These two are Cambridge, Corpus Christi College 283 and Oxford, Bodleian Library, Bodley 234.

20 Hanna briefly describes the two illustrations in 'Sir Thomas Berkeley', 897–8. My description is based on my own observations, and my analysis differs from his. On satire directed at the attire and behaviour of late medieval courtiers see further ch. 4, pp. 121–4, and the references given there.

turned-king Richard II perhaps, or, as Doyle suggests, to the future Henry V.[21]

There is plenty of contemporary evidence to suggest that someone of Berkeley's social standing and position, and even Berkeley himself in particular, might during Richard's reign have wished to stand in as a mediator of counsel as well as its recipient. The three books of *De regimine principum* address in turn three levels at which proper governance must be instilled and maintained: they treat governance first of self, then of household, and then of realm. During the reign of Richard II, and particularly in the crucial early years after he ascended the throne at the age of eleven in 1377, the issue of how to counsel the young king into responsible governance on all three of these levels was one of the most prevalent concerns of public discourse. A variety of administrative documents record the appointment of a whole series of special councils and commissions.[22] In the first three years of Richard's reign a special continual council took on itself many governmental responsibilities: after 1380, this council was replaced by five principal officers of state. Committees were commissioned to recommend reforms focused on Richard's household in 1379, 1380, 1381, 1385, and 1386. Individuals or groups were appointed to attend upon Richard's person in 1381 and – in what might be viewed as merely the most forceful among many attempts to reform his administration – by the Lords Appellant in 1388. Many of these groups never met, and Richard or those around him obstructed the functioning of others. From 1389 onward, Richard consented to accept the advice of a council – but only

---

[21] Fowler notes advice that might have been directed to Richard II (*The Life and Times of John Trevisa*, 196–9); A. I. Doyle suggests the finished book was intended for Henry V in 'English Books In and Out of Court from Edward III to Henry VII', in Scattergood and Sherbourne, eds., *English Court Culture*, 163–81. The insecurity of either Richard II or Henry IV's rule would have made it politic to leave all possible analogies open. Since Trevisa very probably finished work on the *De regimine principum* before the generally accepted date of his death in 1402, circumstances of Richard's reign and deposition are likely to be most germane to his translation itself, even if not to the finished book.

[22] It is not the purpose of this chapter to provide an administrative survey of Richard's reign: see T. F. Tout, *Chapters in the Administrative History of Medieval England*, 6 vols. (Manchester, 1920–33), iii: 323–495 and iv: 1–68 for what is still the fullest, most comprehensive survey, and A. Tuck, *Richard II and the English Nobility* (London, 1973), for a more recent evaluation. The principal sources for the administrative tussles of Richard's reign are the *Rotuli Parliamentorum* and *Foedera*.

on the condition that he could select its members: thenceforward he arranged the membership of his councils and committees in such a way that they became very much the instruments of his personal rule, until 1399 when (according to the official account, the 'Record and Process', included in the record of Henry IV's first parliament) it was yet another committee that persuaded him to accept his deposition.

Relying on the same interlinked tripartite Aristotelian scheme of self, household, and national governance that forms the overall mode of organization of the *De regimine principum*, the writings that record these attempts at providing counsel are persistently hopeful about its efficacy: they blame problems with governance upon deficiencies or improprieties of counsel, and propose that reform can be effected if better advice is given by balanced, representative councils consisting of virtuous, upright counsellors. The fiction is always that a better conducted Richard and a properly ordered household can be produced through proper counsel, and that these two lesser (or at least smaller scale) kinds of governmental reform are crucial for any effort at re-forming the governance of the realm.[23] We need not dismiss altogether the familiar notions that Richard was hot tempered and that his household was expensive to maintain and influential in the governance of the realm in order to recognize this interesting correspondence between theory and a series of attempts at practice.

Hanna makes the interesting suggestion that Thomas Berkeley in particular might have been especially concerned with governmental reform precisely because he was not one of Richard's favourites, and as a result was excluded from a role in government commensurate with his rank and ambitions.[24] Hanna's hypothesis does not account for Berkeley's exclusion from the earlier councils and commissions of Richard's reign – here an explanation may be found in Berkeley's youth and his full engagement at that point in local government – but the evidence Hanna produces to suggest that late in his reign Richard interfered with Berkeley's local affairs and passed him over for prefer-

---

[23] Some especially good examples of optimistic tripartite rhetoric among would-be reformers are *Rotuli Parliamentorum* iii: 5–6 art. 18, 15–16 arts. 47–9, 73 arts. 12–14, 93 art. 28, 100–3 arts. 17–30, 115 art. 75, 216 art. 6, 246 art. 23, 249 art. 38.
[24] Hanna, 'Sir Thomas Berkeley'; on Berkeley's career, 879–92, and for this suggestion, 888–91.

ment is compelling. The contrast between Berkeley's continued exclusion from any wider influence while Richard remained on the throne and his prominence in public affairs early in Henry IV's reign helps to explain why Berkeley found alliance with Thomas Woodstock, duke of Gloucester, and membership of the committee of deposition attractive. Conversely, the fact that Woodstock's library contained Latin versions of two, possibly three, of the books Trevisa translated for Berkeley – and that Trevisa in each case translated from a Latin version rather than what Woodstock did not own, a French version – may suggest at the very least some literary association between the two men, hazy though this suggestion must remain, even if not a longstanding political likemindedness. That Berkeley associated with Woodstock at all, on any level, would help to explain Richard's disinclination to show any favour to Berkeley.[25]

Be that as it may, Trevisa's few signed annotations to his translation reveal that the proper role of counsel is at the forefront of his attention, and suggest that he viewed Berkeley as needing advice on how to counsel as well as on how to govern.[26] Two of these annotations are as purely informational as any of those in the *De proprietatibus rerum*: on 143v Trevisa explains the meaning of 'dyameter' and 'costa' (that is, side) with the aid of a diagram, while on 144v he explains the meaning of 'speculabilia' and contrasts it with 'agibilia'. But there is more to these two glosses than that. They appear in the midst of Giles's

---

[25] For the observation that Trevisa worked exclusively from Latin, see R. Waldron, 'John Trevisa and the Use of English', *Proceedings of the British Academy* 74 (1988), 171–202; 172. For the contents of Woodstock's library see (no initials) Dillon and W. H. S. Hope, eds., 'Inventory of Goods Belonging to Thomas Duke of Gloucester', *Archaeological Journal* 54 (1897), 275–308; 281, 300–3. The doubtful case is 'vagesse de Chivalrie'; Bartholomeus's and Aegidius's works are however clearly identified and specified as Latin versions. Like the corpus of translations Berkeley sponsored, Woodstock's library is unusually biased toward philosophic and informationally encyclopaedic works.

[26] The first two of these annotations were noted long ago by Perry, *Trevisa's Dialogus . . .*, xcix–c; the third was recently discovered by Fowler (*John Trevisa*, p. 31 n. 93, where, however, the passage is not quoted; it appears of course in the forthcoming edition and in *The Life and Times of John Trevisa*, 195). I am grateful to David Fowler for providing me with the further results of his meticulous researches, a full list of all divergences from the Latin text in Trevisa's translation, in advance of publication. A synopsis of these divergences and evaluation of which are significant is provided in Fowler, *The Life and Times of John Trevisa*, 195–9.

exposition on 'consaile', the second of four powers involved in ruling a city, and are themselves counsel for counsellors: they explain (even if Trevisa does get it slightly wrong) two topics on which it is neither advisable nor necessary for a 'consaile' to offer 'consaile'. If these are muted and advisory restrictions on the role of 'consaile', Trevisa's third signed annotation, recently discovered by Fowler, is much more pointed in its concern. Trevisa expands Giles's explanation of the four ways that tyranny is the worst sort of lordship that kings may exercise by interpolating the following definition of and comment upon oligarchy:

> Trevysa whanne fewe men ben lordes and ben not good *and* vertuous but riche *and* myȝty *and* louen not þe comune *pro*fit but desireþ here owne *pro*fite *and* ouersetteþ oþer men suche *pri*ncipate is i cleped eligarchia *and* here tirandise is i cleped þe worst eligarchia for it is most greuous to sogett*es*. (136v i 3–11)

Trevisa has a pretext in Giles's citation of a passage from Aristotle's *Politics* that mentions oligarchy, but his addition is nonetheless striking in its emphasis that a select group of lords, no less than a king, can be tyrannical. This piece of counsel is double edged, in rather the same way that the finished manuscript is: it might well serve, as Fowler observes, as a piece of admonitory counsel for Berkeley, but equally it is suitable for further mediation, if Berkeley should choose himself to act as counsellor or to present the manuscript to the reader that most needs it.[27]

If Berkeley might indeed plan to mediate further the 'consaile' of Digby 233, then the text offers him information on the same model as Trevisa's interpolation on monastic disendowment in the *Polychronicon*. It gives him 'clerical' information, copious in its citations of Aristotle, about the principles of good government. Of the absence of such government in England Berkeley does not need to be told. But once he has received the information the *De regimine principum* offers;

---

27 Fowler notes that Berkeley 'could have found Aegidius's distinction between a king and a tyrant an appropriate matter for reflection at a time when he was required to pass judgement on the king' (*John Trevisa*, 30) and Hanna (citing Fowler) suggests that the issues of good governance in *De Regimine Principum* 'provide a background appropriate to Berkeley's own political alienation from Richard II' ('Sir Thomas Berkeley', 892), but neither of them pursues the matter further.

once, as before, he has been taught this previously clerical knowledge, his knowledge requires him to act: to offer counsel, or even (in company with a few other lords) to 'overset' the king.

The manuscript evidence for this translation suggests that it was by far the least 'published' of Trevisa's translations, and if its import is anything like what I have suggested, then it is easy to see why.[28] The kind of 'informacion' that qualifies its recipients for counsel, or even for rule, will benefit those recipients most when it remains as privy as possible. The English translation of this text may plausibly claim to be aimed at the common profit, but the information it conveys is most decidedly not for wide publication, but for lords, and just a few lords, alone.

THE *DIALOGUS INTER MILITEM ET CLERICEM*

If the *De regimine principum* and Trevisa's unsigned note in the *Polychronicon* illustrate the direct and drastic consequences that may, and in some cases should, follow from information published solely to lords, then it is Trevisa's minor and generally less regarded polemic translations, of the pseudo-Ockham *Dialogus inter militem et clericem* and of Fitzralph's *Defensio curatorum*, that reveal just why it is that Trevisa's backhanded justification of 'Englysch translacion' in his *Dialogue* must postulate a Lord who blurs his status in two conflicting directions: by displaying a high level of ability in argument of a specifically 'clerical' sort, on the one hand, and on the other by allying his own interests and concerns with those of even the lowest of the laity.[29]

---

28 Hanna has suggested that the popularity of Hoccleve's poem *The Regement of Princes* blocked any further interest in a straightforward translation of Giles of Rome's treatise of the same title, ('Sir Thomas Berkeley', 913, n. 84) but this seems to me a less than full explanation: the appetite in the early fifteenth century for works claiming in one way or another to advise princes seems to have been less easily satiable than this hypothesis would suggest.

29 For the Lord's alliance with the lowest of the laity, see above, pp. 64–5. On the other hand, it is the Lord in Trevisa's *Dialogue* rather than the Clerk who makes extensive use of the terminology and techniques characteristic of academic argumentation: he introduces what looks as though it will be a confession of limited literacy with the technical term 'Y denye' (290/56); he skilfully uses a scholastic distinction on the senses of 'need' to explain in what sense it is true that all men

Like the *De regimine principum*, the *Dialogus* and *Defensio* bear no indications of date or external ascriptions to Trevisa; there is just one internal note signed 'Trevisa' between them, in the *Dialogus*. All six extant copies of these two texts are packaged together with the *Polychronicon* translation: the *Dialogus* is the first item in each of the six manuscripts where it appears, and is followed in each case by the *Defensio curatorum*, then prefatory material to the *Polychronicon*, then lastly the *Polychronicon* itself. These two texts are, in a sense, then, additional prefaces to the *Polychronicon*: they clarify and sharpen the impact of Trevisa's preface, and give added bite to the 'informacion' the *Polychronicon* publishes.

The *Dialogus* was written for Philip the Fair, as was the *De regimine principum*, and like the *De regimine principum* it addresses an issue whose political importance had recurred in the late fourteenth century: in this case secular jurisdiction, and in particular secular rights to taxation, over the clergy.[30] The Latin text of the *Dialogus* appears to have enjoyed fairly wide currency in England at least among educated clerics, but it is difficult to be sure how early it was known: six manuscript copies are extant in clerically owned fifteenth century collections of scholastic materials, but all of these postdate Trevisa's translation.[31]

Perhaps because this was the least familiar text among those he translated, Trevisa alters it most, to the point that his version reads as if

'need' to know the chronicles (291/65–8, 70–81); and he uses a syllogistic argument to show that because preaching in English is good and needful, so is translation into English (292/146–293/153).

[30] On the date, authorship, and reception of the Latin version of the *Dialogus* see N. N. Erickson, 'A Dispute Between a Priest and a Knight', *Proceedings of the American Philosophical Society* III (1967), 288–309; 288–90, as well as Erickson's Ph.D. thesis of the same title, Univ. of Washington, 1966. There are no firm indications as to the dating of Trevisa's version; Fowler, *John Trevisa*, 30 speculates that it may have been produced in the 1370s, while Edwards, 'John Trevisa', 135, suggests the 1380s.

[31] The six manuscripts are Cambridge, St John's College 115 and 160; Cambridge, Corpus Christi College 156; London, British Library, Cotton Nero D VIII; London, British Library, Reg. 6 E III, and Oxford, Bodleian Library, Rawlinson G 40. For the first five manuscripts listed see Erickson, 'A Dispute Between a Priest and a Knight', 290, and for some consideration of the last, recently discovered manuscript and comparisons between the Latin and Trevisa's version, see Fowler, *The Life and Times of John Trevisa*, 153–63. I have arrived at my own comparisons independently; while some of our examples overlap, our interpretations differ greatly.

it could well have originated in late fourteenth century England. He removes references which would distance his translation from its prospective audience, substituting '3oure cuntraye' for 'padue' (15/1), removing a reference to the duchy of Burgundy (15/7), and renaming 'Ropertus de flandria' 'Robart atte Style' (15/6), and reworks the way problems in relations between church and state are discussed in order to produce a closer fit to current concerns within England.[32] But the main drift of the argument does not need much changing, because the issues it raises have become, if anything, *more* topical, and *more* controversial, over the eighty years or so since the dialogue was first written.

For example, the knight's argument in the first half of the dialogue is devoted to showing that the clergy should have no temporal jurisdiction whatever, because if they did it would encroach on the king's regal prerogative, his 'regalie'. In the reign of Richard II, where the repeated attempts to provide Richard with better counsel discussed in relation to Digby 233 (see above pp. 74–5), are accompanied by repeated concerns that counsel should not impinge on his 'regalie', Wycliffites label any holding of temporal power among the clergy as a usurpation of the king's 'regalie' that deserves to be treated as a form of treason.[33] The second article of the 'Petition' supposedly written by Wyclif and presented to Parliament in 1382, for example, presents a radical assertion of regal and noble jurisdiction – and, incidentally, of the importance of publishing information.[34] Friars who have condemned the king and his council for removing the possessions of bad prelates

---

[32] For example, the knight's comments about various figures at the higher end of the ecclesiastical hierarchy are focused onto bishops, who were the ecclesiastical figures involved in governance (church and secular) that were generally of most immediate concern within England. Even the apparent lapse where a sentence begins with the king of France and finishes in the kingdom of England is probably topically astute rather than accidental: it avoids what could be an impolitic subordination of Richard II to the emperor (2/15–3/2).

[33] The definition of treason was officially broadened in Parliament in 1388 by the Appellants to include cases where counsel encroaches on the king's 'regalie'. However, radicals seem to have begun linking treason with encroachment on the king's prerogative in the early 1380s. For further discussion of the development of the law, and the discourse, of treason from the 1340s through into the fifteenth century, see ch. 5, pp. 142–52.

[34] 'A Petition to the King and Parliament', in T. Arnold, ed., *Select English Works of John Wyclif*, 3 vols. (Oxford, 1869–71), iii: 507–23. For discussion of the methodological

must be amended, it asserts, and their error 'publisshid' to 'men dwellinge in þe reume' (514/14). Kings in the past as well as now have removed the temporal goods of clerics 'by laweful cause, as perteynynge to here regalie, and of comun lawe, by counsail of pieres of þe rewme' (514/26–8); whoever claims that kings may not do so claims not only that the king has erred, 'but also his predecessours, and generally al his counseillores, as lords and prelatis, and alle men of þe Parlement counceilinge þerto' (514/29–31). In addition, anyone who makes this claim gives licence to all branches of the clergy to behave however outrageously they wish 'þouȝ þei maken on of hemself kyng' or 'conquere alle seculer lordship in þis eorþe' (515/29–31). The article's peroration, addressed to lords, makes the link to treason explicit:

> ȝee, lordis, seeþ and undirstondiþ, wiþ what ponisshinge þei deserve to be chastised, þat þus unwarly and wrongfully han dampnyd ȝou for heretikes, ffor as muche as ȝe don execucioun of riȝtwisnesses, by Goddis lawe and mannys, and namely of þe kyngis regalie. For þe chief lordshipe in þis lond of alle temporalties, boþe of seculer men and religious, perteyneþ to þe kyng of his general governynge. Ffor ellis he were not kyng of alle Englond, but of a litel part þerof. Þerfore þe men þat bysyen hem to take awey þys lordshipe fro þe kyng, as don freris and here fautours, in þis poynt ben sharper enemys and traitours þan Ffrensshe men and alle oþere naciouns. (515/33–516/8)

By this logic any holding of secular office by the clergy counts as an improper encroachment by the church upon secular government, in the end upon the king's regal prerogative or 'regalie', and can be viewed as a kind of treason.[35] The knight's tendency throughout the first section of the dialogue to oppose clerical powers to those of the king in order to deny their legitimacy, and his focus on questions of local power with potentially immediate local consequences instead of the rather academic and distant question of the pope's temporal power, ally him, in late fourteenth century England, with a far more radical tradition than they had eighty years before in France.

issues raised by the vexed question of the authorship and provenance of this tract, see ch. 1, pp. 6–9.

35 Cf. Dymmok's defence of secular office holding by the clergy against the *Twelve Conclusions* in ch. 4, pp. 116–20.

But if the radical argument that clerics should not exercise any temporal jurisdiction whatever is accepted, then there still remains the problem of defining what sort of power, if any, they *should* exercise. That is the issue in the one part of the dialogue where Trevisa's reworkings become less subtle, less invisible to the casual eye; where, to dismiss the clerk's argument that the pope has temporal jurisdiction because Christ did and the pope is Christ's vicar, the knight distinguishes two 'tymes' of Christ. Trevisa is unable to manipulate this distinction into a form he finds acceptable; and even apart from the lengthy note advertising his frustration which he interpolates into it, his rendering of the text reveals his struggles. For the convenience of the reader I quote Trevisa's translation of this argument and interpolated note in full:

> Myles. Ich haue herde of wise doctors þat we schal distingue twey diuerse tymes of Crist: oon of his manhed and anoþer of his power & mageste. Þe tyme of his manhed was from þat he toke flesch & blode anoon to his passioun. Þe tyme of his power & maieste was & is after þe resureccioun, whanne he seide: 'Al power is ȝeuen to me in heuene & in erþe.'
>
> (*Trevisa.* Here takiþ hede of þe knyȝtes menyng & of þe clerkes menyng also. For þe wordes beþ nouȝt fulle chambred. For al þe tyme of Cristes manhed, þat was tofore his passioun, was tyme of his myȝt, power, & maieste. For bifore his passioun he turned water into wyn; & heled blynde, & lame, & many maner seke men; & hadde þe see, & wynde, & weder, & fendes attondaunt to his heestes; & fedde fyue þousand of men wiþ fyue loues of breed & lefte twelue cupes of relef; & rered men from deþ to lif; & ȝaf his disciplis myȝt & power ouer alle þe deueles & fendes; and schewide of his blis to Petre, James, & Ioon; & ȝede vppon þe see in grete tempest of weder & of þe see. Also whanne he sent his disciplis to fecche hym þe asse to ride on into Jerusalem, he seide, 'ȝif eny man seiþ ouȝt to ȝow, seiþ þat þe lord haþ to do þerwiþ'; & in his ridyng he was worschiped as a Kyng, & somme spradde cloþes in his wey & somme bowes; & þanne was þe prophecie fulfilled, seiþ: 'Douȝtres of Syon, lo! þi kyng comeþ to þee, meke & mylde, sittyng vppon an asse'. Also in a tyme he drof biggers & sillers out of þe temple as lord & kyng. Also his lore was in myȝt & power, & he dide al þis & many oþer grete dedes bifore his passioun; þanne before his passioun was tyme of his power & of his myȝt & after his passioun was & is tyme of his manhed. For after his

passioun Seynt Steuene seyȝ hym in his manhed stonde in þe fader riȝt side. But how hit euer be of þe distinccioun þat is made bitwene þe clerk & þe knyȝt, of þe tyme of Cristes manhed & of þe tyme of his myȝt, power, and maieste, take hede how þei spekiþ eiþer to oþer. For þe knyȝt spekiþ in þis manere.)

Peter was ordeyned Cristes vicarie, for þe state of his manhed & nouȝt for þe state of his blisse & maieste. He was nouȝt made Cristes vicarie in doyng þat Crist doþ now in blisse; but for to folowe hym in his doying þat he dide here on erþe. Þanne he ȝaf his vicarie þat power þat he vsed here in erþe, deþliche . . . (6/1–7/14)

Trevisa's translation constructs a quite different sort of distinction; he alters the Latin's contrast between 'humilitas' and 'potestas' to one between 'manhed' and 'power and mageste'.[36] 'Manhed' now does no more than to pick out the period of Christ's human life, whereas 'power and mageste' specifies the kind of power Christ has, when he has it, as the regal sort exercised by kings. We might be tempted to explain Trevisa's alterations by supposing that he merely read 'humanitas' wherever we have 'humilitas'. But Trevisa also substitutes 'dethliche', that is 'mortal', for 'humilitas', elsewhere puts 'dethliche' in place of the amplifying explanation 'quia illa [activities] nobis necessaria sunt'; and adds two extra passages which stipulate that Christ did not exercise regal power during his time on earth.[37] It appears that Trevisa's aim is to restrict Christ's exercise of power to the second, heavenly 'tyme', and to represent that power as specifically and exclusively a regal power. But he cannot make this restriction complete: unless he were to modify the knight's distinction beyond recognition, he must retain one mention of a power which Christ did exercise on earth: 'þat power þat he vsed here in erþe, deþliche' (7/13–14; cf. 295 i 18–19). In Trevisa's version, the distinction does not answer to the knight's purpose of explaining what sorts of activities the clergy ought and ought not to engage in. Into the vacuum of the empty description of the earthly power Christ conferred on Peter might rush all sorts of undesirable activities.

Trevisa's complaint at the beginning of his interpolated note, that 'þe

---

[36] Forms of 'humilitas' become 'manhed' at 295 i 9 and 6/2, 295 i 10 and 6/3, 295 i 14 and 7/9–10; 'potestas' becomes 'power and mageste' at 6/3 and 6/5.

[37] See 295 ii 47 and 11/3, 295 i 18–19 and 7/14, 8/3–4, 8/9–10.

wordes beþ nouȝt fully chambred', that the terms of the distinction are not mutually exclusive or diametrically opposed, seems quite correct. But nor are they meant to be. The distinction in the Latin lies between Christ's renunciation of the greater part of his power during his human life and his assumption of full power after his passion. Christ does exercise some power while he is human, as the passage acknowledges, but this creates no difficulty for the original writer. Humility and power are not mutually exclusive states, and the limited power that someone who is being humble might exercise need not be different in kind from his full power.

It seems that Trevisa's troubles stem not just from the text of the dialogue, but from the difficulty of reconciling its distinction with more recent controversy over defining the proper powers and activities of the clergy in terms of Christ's temporal power. For example, in three questions on Christ's regalia that appear in the same manuscript as one of the Latin copies of the *Dialogus*, the friar Roger Conway makes just the combination Trevisa attempts here: he combines a distinction between Christ as man and as word of God, 'secundum quod homo et secundum quod verbum dei', with a discussion of whether Christ has any earthly kingship.[38] Conway denies any earthly kingship to Christ *secundum quod homo*, by either earthly law or title based on his innocence from sin. Instead, Christ is 'rex celestis et perpetualis', 'eternal heavenly king', and Conway denies that Christ's celestial kingship implies even for Christ *secundum quod homo*, let alone his vicar, any earthly dominion apart from over the church: his 'regnum secundum quod homo est ecclesia', 'realm as man is the church'. Conway's denial of temporal jurisdiction to Christ answers to his own purpose of justifying mendicant poverty; these questions were written in opposition to Fitzralph's *De pauperie salvatoris* for just that purpose.[39] But his argument does not, any more than Trevisa's, explain

---

[38] The Conway questions appear in Oxford, Bodleian Library, Rawlinson G 40 ff. 42–8. Here I summarize Conway's reply to the first question, 'Utrum christus hominum perfectissimus in statu huius vite habuit aliquod regnum temporale', ff. 42–43v; see esp. the conclusions on 43. In this and all subsequent quotations from manuscript, abbreviations are silently expanded and modern punctuation supplied. Manuscript spellings are retained; any emendations to manuscript readings are explained in the notes.

[39] On Roger Conway see K. Walsh, 'The *De Vita Evangelica* of Geoffrey of Hardeby

what kind of activities are implied by Christ's, or the pope's, dominion over the church.

The Wycliffite *Opus Arduum*, an anonymous commentary on the Apocalypse written in 1389–90, deals with the problem of aligning the pope's activities with Christ's by dissociating the issues of papal power and Christ's temporal dominion.[40] Perhaps because the denial of temporal dominion to Christ had become by this time strongly linked to a justification of mendicant poverty, the *Opus Arduum* incorporates into its commentary on Apoc. 19:16, 'et habet in vestimento et in femore suo scriptum "rex regum et dominus dominancium"', 'and he has written on his clothing and his thigh "king of kings and lord of lords"' a scholastic *quaestio* which affirms that the temporal realm of David does belong to Christ 'secundum humanitatem assumptam' both by title of innocence and by hereditary law. But the writer denies that this temporal dominion should be transferred to the pope. To the argument that

> Sequitur eciam, tunc cum papa sit vicarius Christi in terris, quod ipse titulo patroni sui Christi haberet dominium omnium terrenorum Dauid.[41]

> It would also follow, then, since the pope would be the vicar of Christ on earth, that the pope himself by the title of his patron Christ would have dominion over all the lands of David.

The writer replies,

> [P]lane sequitur oppositum, quia papa rationis neque titulum iuris hereditarii pro regno Israel temporali cum non sit de semine Dauid secundum carnem, neque titulum innocencie aut ius poli cum non sit iustus sed antichristus, pro dominio cuiusquam regni temporalis potest allegare. Ymmo hoc habet ex vicariatu Christi quod Christus contulit Petro, scilicet relinquere omnia terrena et Christum sequi in nuda paupertate. Et si sic faceret, tertium est quod iure poli sibi

(c.1385)' ii, *Anal. Aug.* 34 (1971), 5–83; 64–71; and on the text cited here, titled by Walsh *Tractatus de regalia Christi*, see 69–70. For extensive further discussion of the controversy over mendicant poverty and, in particular, Fitzralph's role in it, see ch. 5, pp. 162–77.

40 On the *Opus Arduum* see A. Hudson, 'A Neglected Wycliffite Text', *Journal of Ecclesiastical History* 29 (1978), 257–79, reprinted in *Lollards and their Books* (London, 1985), 43–65. For some revisions to this account see A. Hudson, *The Premature Reformation*, 264–7.

41 Brno, University Library Mk. 28 206r col. i.

deberentur omnia uicaria, siue ex decimis ecclesie, siue ex oblacionibus, siue ex dotatione regnum terrenorum; omnia superflua per manus dispensatorum in filiorum ecclesie et ministrorum suorum pauperibus et egenis fideliter largiendo; sed quia primum renuit, ad quod tenetur ex professione sui status apostolici, merito perderet secundum ut appostota infidelis.[42]

Clearly the opposite would follow, because the pope cannot reasonably claim dominion over any temporal realm either by title of hereditary law as regards the temporal realm of Israel, since he is not from the seed of David in flesh, or by title of innocence or law of the state, since he is not just, but the antichrist. Indeed, by the vicariate of Christ that Christ conferred on Peter, he has to forsake all temporal things and follow Christ in naked poverty. And if he does so, the consequence is that by law of the city all necessities will be due to him, whether from tithes of the church, or from offerings, or from the donation of terrestrial realms; and all that which is superfluous [to the amount due to him] is to be given faithfully to the poor and needy through the hands of those dispensing it among the sons of the church and their ministers; but because he has denied the first, to which he is held by the profession of his apostolic status, rightfully he should lose the second as an unfaithful apostate.

The pope is entitled to temporal dominion by neither hereditary right nor title of innocence. Instead, he has only the vicarship conferred by Christ, and unless he behaves like an apostle, imitating Christ in relinquishing all earthly things, he loses any entitlement to tithes, offerings, or gifts of land, and loses as well his pastoral role in distributing surplus goods to the poor. This argument denies the mendicants' grounds for their claims to voluntary poverty on the one hand, while insisting on the other that the pope should renounce any title to earthly riches.

Trevisa's note has a reductive, dismissive feel: using a common technique of reductive scholastic argument, he reverses the terms of the distinction already given in order to demonstrate that the reversed version is at least as unsatisfactory as the original – easy enough, since the reversed version's claim that Christ had power during his human life but not afterward directly contradicts the biblical quotation given just before the note (6/6). It is plain that Trevisa has not produced a

---

[42] Brno, University Library Mk. 28 206v col. i.

method satisfactory to himself of explaining the clergy's temporal dominion in terms of Christ's – though he does not, like the *Opus Arduum*, go so far as to deny that there should be any link. However, that is not to say that Trevisa thinks there is nothing to be learned from the Knight's argument.

In the remaining portion of the note, Trevisa makes what is probably the most revealing comment to be found anywhere, in any of his notes or prefaces, about the focus of his own interest in a particular work. Trevisa abandons exposition of his author's meaning in favour of instructing his reader directly, in his own voice, about how the dialogue ought to be read. 'But how hit euer be of þe distinccioun . . . take hede how þei spekiþ eiþer to oþer', he recommends (7/4–5, 7): he directs the reader's attention away from the content of the argument, and toward the kind of interchange taking place between the speakers.

The interchange between the speakers in this dialogue is likely to have influenced, or even inspired, Trevisa's own effort in the genre: as in Trevisa's dialogue, the contesting of the respective roles of 'lewed' and 'clergie' – there in education, here in government – carries with it a disturbance of the conventional pattern whereby learning, pastoral concern, ability in argument, and fine style are lodged with the clergy, while the 'lewed' are categorized as simple, inarticulate, and in need of guidance. Both dialogues stage a 'translacion', in the most literal sense of a bringing across from one side to the other, of conventional roles and the characteristics and typical languages of expression traditionally associated with those roles. But in the *Dialogus* matters are more complicated, less one-sided, than in Trevisa's *Dialogue*.

In contrast to the lengthy proem of Trevisa's dialogue, this dialogue begins with a rapid back and forth exchange which immediately marks for the reader, and allows the disputants themselves to comment upon, 'how þei spekiþ eiþer to oþer'. The knight objects straight away to the cryptic complaint of obscure reference with which the clerk begins:

> CLERICUS: Ich wondre Syr Noble Knyȝt þat in fewe dayes, tymes beþ chaungide, riȝt is y-buryed, lawes beþ ouertorned, & statutes beþ y-trode vnder feet.
>
> MILES: Ich am a lewed man & may nouȝt vnderstonde sotil & derk speche; þerfore þou most take more pleyn maner of spekyng.
> (1/1–6)

Trevisa has intensified the contrast in styles apparent even in the Latin version. He pares down the knight's objection, removing the knight's first characterization of the clerk's words (*Grandia verba sunt ista*, 'these are grand words'), his explanation of why he cannot understand them (*quamvis paucas litteras puer didicerim non tamen adeo in profundum veni*, 'although as a boy I learned letters, I did not go on to study profound matters') and the respectful conditional clause that gives a reason for his request (*venerande clerice, si mecum desideratis habere colloquium*, 'respected clerk, if you would like to have a discussion with me') (294 i 7, 8–9, 10–11). Elsewhere too Trevisa prunes the knight's flights of rhetoric, rare though those are, into pragmatic statement; for example, 'argumentum istud est cornutum cuius vanitas et infirmitas per argumentum similem repellenda est' (296 i 5–7) becomes 'Þis argument is riȝt nouȝt. For here ich argue in þe same maner . . .' (11/12–13). The effect is that the knight's self-characterization as a 'lewed man' serves as the only explanation, it seems the only explanation *needed*, for his style of expression, his opinion of the clerk's speech, and both the manner and content of his request. Especially in Trevisa's version, and as in Trevisa's own dialogue, style serves as a figure for status. But whereas for Trevisa's clerk 'lewed' style threatened improper debasement, here it exacts clarity and directness.

In the remainder of the opening exchange we discover that the correlation between the 'lewed' and 'clerical' styles Trevisa has so sharply distinguished and the ability in argumentation and level of erudition each disputant possesses is not the conventional one that we might, and the clerk certainly does, assume. Once the clerk has spoken more plainly and revealed the specific subject and grounds of his concerns, the knight attacks them using distinction, analogy, and reduction, in his and indeed the dialogue's first fully articulated argument. In reaction the clerk, in his turn, comments on the knight's mode of argument: 'ȝe spekiþ scharplich, slylich, & wilyliche y-nowȝ' (4/3–4). The clerk has been forced to readjust his condescension; the knight's 'lewedness' turns out not to imply any deficiency in understanding or ability – indeed in the course of the dialogue he will demonstrate his critical acumen, skill in argumentation, and knowledge of scripture – but rather a preference for clear, blunt argument.

There is more variety in the process of this dialogue than in Trevisa's:

both disputants have the opportunity to present arguments, pose questions, and make objections. Their argumentational styles differ somewhat: the knight dismisses the clerk's arguments through lengthy and ruthlessly meticulous *reductiones ad absurdum*, whereas the clerk produces short, easily demolished objections or else resorts to cryptic complaint.[43] The clerk's expositions are generally syllogistic whereas the knight's tend to proceed by analogy and (often scriptural) example.[44] But both demonstrate proficiency. Although the overall course of the dialogue favours him, however, the knight's exposition is not technically flawless. At approximately the halfway point the clerk catches him out in a contradiction – from the scholastic point of view, a fundamental error in the most basic principle of logic, and one which certainly invalidates any argument where it appears. In the course of an argument denying any temporal governance to the church, the knight introduces an Old Testament example which, even while its point is to show that kings have traditionally monitored the activities of priests, openly acknowledges that priests have temporal governance. Upon the clerk's observation of this contradiction this cryptic exchange follows:

CLERICUS: Me wondreþ þat ȝe seyn þat þe kyng vndertoke þe bischop in gouernaunce of temporalte.

MILES: Ȝe stireþ me & wakiþ me as hit were of my sleep, & makiþ me speke oþer wise þan y þouȝt.

CLERICUS: Lete þe hound wake & berke

MILES: For ȝe kunne nouȝt vse manhed suffraunce & pacience of princes, y trowe ȝe schal fele berkyng & bityng. (19/8–14)

The force of this exchange is not, even on the Knight's side, that of plain, self-evident logic; instead, its meaning is allusive, or 'coded'. Both the clerk and the knight are referring to Isaiah 56:10:

Speculatores eius caeci omnes, nescierunt universi, canes muti, non valentes latrare, videntes vana, dormientes, et amantes somnia.

---

[43] See, for example, the knight's reductive arguments at 2/15–4/2, 10/6–11/3, 11/12–12/2, 18/6–19/3. The clerk produces a short reductive argument (29/14–15), a counter-argument from scriptural evidence (30/10–31/5), an attempt to redirect the discussion (32/17–18), and an appeal to legal precedent (34/8–11) in addition to his retreats into complaint.

[44] For the clerk's syllogistic arguments see 5/8–16 and 11/7–11; for the knight's analogies see the bulk of his exposition: pp. 8–11, 12–16, 16–19, 20–3, 27–9, 31–7.

His watchmen are all blind, all ignorant, dumb dogs unable to bark,
seeing vain things, sleeping, and loving dreams.

Their reference would most likely be immediately recognizable to the
fourteenth century reader, because this verse was frequently employed
in criticism of the clergy, and far from needing to be updated for its
new audience, it had become rather more potent by the time Trevisa
was working on this translation.

Several roughly contemporary English texts employ this topos. In
the B version of *Piers Plowman*, for instance, Clergie exhorts clerics to
reform with the encouragement that then 'burel clerkes' would cease to
criticize them '[and] calle yow doumbe houndes: / *Canes non valentes
latrare*' (B x 293), whereas in the C version the commentary on Piers's
pardon includes an extended pastoral metaphor exhorting bishops to
wake and bark (C ix 260–70). The Wycliffite text Arnold prints as *De
apostasia cleri* (iii: 430–40) also employs an extended metaphor
criticizing the neglect by prelates of their proper pastoral activities of
barking and biting:

> siche prelats shulden be Cristis houndis, and berke bi hise lawe, and
> not bi lawe of wolves. Lord, what lettiþ þise houndis to berke, and
> lede Cristis sheep aftir his lawe? Certis it semeþ þat dowyng of þe
> Chirche, and too myche worshypyng of Antecristis lawe. For a
> lumpe of talowe strangliþ þe houndis, and lettiþ hem boþe to berke
> and to byte; and occupying of men in Antecristis lawes þat speken
> oonliche of worldliche goods drawiþ fro Goddis lawe and makiþ to
> love þe world. (Arnold iii: 440/1–9; repunctuated)

And there are a number of other examples.[45] In the *Dialogus*, however,
the usual situation found in all these texts is reversed. Normally the
mute or sleeping dogs are clerics who have failed in their pastoral
duties, and especially in preaching; typically clerics, or extraclerical
writers who occupy a position somewhere on the fringes of the clergy,
use the topos in urging them to reform. Here, however, the Clerk is
arousing the Knight – a layman, and what is more a layman whom he

---

[45] A. L. Kellogg lists a number of examples from Gregory onward including one other
Wycliffite example (from Arnold, *Select English Works*, iii: 133), but not the one I use,
in 'Langland and the "Canes Muti"', in R. Kirk and C. F. Main, eds., *Essays in
Literary History Presented to J. Milton French* (New York, 1955), 25–35.

is attempting to convince that clerics ought to be allowed their own sphere of temporal activity – with a call to reformative pastoral activity. It is not clear what effect the Clerk might hope for: if his remark is sarcastic, implying that it is ridiculous to impute pastoral negligence to a layman, then it backfires; and if he wants the Knight to wake and bark his agreement that the church should be allowed to maintain its temporal governance unmolested then he does not get his wish. The Knight takes the Clerk's pastoral invitation seriously, and threatens (in a way that anticipates the subsequent direction of his argument) not just an appropriation of clerical argument and the authority it confers, their 'berkyng', but, under cover of a broader 'translacion' of terms, 'bityng' as well.

Before his 'error' in logic and momentary 'lapse' into cryptic, prophetic language (rather like the sort characteristic elsewhere of the Clerk), the Knight presents anticlerical arguments that proceed on the assumption that the clergy can have no temporal jurisdiction whatsoever. Afterward, he presents arguments that accept the clergy's temporal governance (whether theoretically or merely pragmatically) yet argue that it ought to be subject to the supervision of the secular ruler. The shift in the argument allows him first to deny that the clergy should have any cake, so to speak, and then to proceed to tell them how they ought to eat it. Whereas before this point in the argument the Knight decries any exercise by clerics of temporal power as an encroachment on the king's jurisdiction – an effect Trevisa attempts to intensify by defining Christ's power as regal power – from here on he builds on the reversal of roles the Clerk has, oddly, requested.

The way the knight develops the meaning of 'sauacioun' over the course of the dialogue shows the logic of this 'translacion' of power. Before his 'error' the knight uses 'sauacioun' in the strictly religious sense to confine Peter's vicarship to spiritual matters: 'in þe first state Crist vsed no siche power, but put hit away from hym & vsed onlich þat longeþ to þe gouernaunce of oure sauacioun . . .' (9/12–14). Then, directly after he threatens the clerk with 'bityng', the 'sauacioun' (still in the religious sense) of the knight's own soul becomes his own business as much as the church's: 'Haue ich nouȝt to do to þenke on þe sauacioun of myn owne soule wiþ al þat y may?' (20/2–3). By this argument, laymen are justified in ensuring that clergy undertake their role in religious 'sauacioun' in the proper manner. The knight compares the clergy's duties with those of non-clerics, asserting that clergy who do not fulfil their duties should lose their money just as a knight would his wages or a vassal his fee (21/4–7).

On its next appearance, 'sauacioun' has shifted to a secular meaning: now it refers to the king's defence of the clergy from incursions both at home and abroad. The money the king asks he 'spendiþ . . . nouȝt in his owne vse, but in ȝoure owne sauacioun & in defence of holy chirche & of youre owne godes and catel' (24/9–10). And thus 'þe kynges . . . sauacioun is ȝoure sauacioun' (25/4–5). Trevisa intensifies the force of this argument by adding into his translation three threats in quick succession about the destruction of the church that would ensue in the absence of the king's protection: needy men and wasters would destroy all you have, all you have would be lost, neighbours and foreigners would destroy your possessions (25/3, 9–10, 14–15). Finally, now that the king's activity has been defined in the same terms as the clergy's, the knight argues that the 'sauacioun' the king provides is more fundamental, more indispensable, than that administered by the clergy. In order to show that converting church endowments to military use is not a perversion of the intentions of the donors but rather a fulfilment of them, he urges 'What is more holy þan þe sauacioun of Cristen men? What is licher to þe doom of God þan wiþstonde & put of enemyes, þeeues, mansleers, from Cristen men . . .' (30/4–7). To reinforce the knight's point, Trevisa removes value terms with specifically ecclesiastical connotations here, as he has done ever since the break in the argument: 'piis et sanctis vsibus' (299 i 40) becomes 'holy vse & mylde' (30/4) just as 'pietate' became 'myldenesse', 'religione' 'gode entent', 'religio' 'good entent', and 'religiose' 'gode vse & holy'. Trevisa's translation adds a final twist to this 'translacion' of roles by adding one more reference to 'sauacioun', 'for defens and sauacioun of þe kyngdom' (34/2) in place of the Latin's more neutral 'pro defensione regni vel communitatibus' (300 i 11): the clergy should give the king money for national defence even where they are by custom free from taxes not only in order to protect themselves, but for the 'sauacioun' of the people as a whole. Any delinquency in their duty of supporting the king financially becomes a failure in their primary obligation of administering 'sauacioun' to the people, a failure for which the king might well deem them unworthy of retaining their endowments (33/11–34/7).[46]

The 'translacion' the *Dialogus* enacts is a translacion to the secular side of not just the capacities associated with clerical education in Latin – ability in argument and the information necessary to make good arguments – but of the political activities and social obligations of clerics. This indirect consequence shows us just what is at stake in Trevisa's own *Dialogue* when the Lord, who combines with lordly command the ability to argue the Clerk into the ground, voices a pastoral concern better informed than his Clerk's. It is not necessary that the Lord's proposed redistribution of information to all the laity should extend in practice beyond the nobility and gentry. No more so than that when lords propose to usurp the pastoral obligation of clerics to give alms, so as to redistribute clerical possessions to all the needy, it is necessary that the poor should actually receive these goods; or that when lords and the king tax the clergy it is necessary they should spend the money on the 'sauacion' of the realm. Any 'English translacion', any 'translacion' to the laity, carries with it, for clerics, the threat of a kind of disendowment.

THE *DEFENSIO CURATORUM*

Trevisa modifies the *Defensio curatorum* far less than the *Dialogus inter militem et clericem*: he retains its setting at the papal curia; the speaker remains Richard Fitzralph, his diocese Armagh and the location of his differences with the friars London; and Trevisa does not alter the terms of the debate, modes of argument, or parties under discussion in anything like the systematic way he does in the *Dialogus*, nor include even one explanatory note. Wendy Scase's work on the importance of Fitzralph's ideas in later fourteenth century England has amply illustrated why it was feasible for Trevisa to deliver the text virtually unaltered to its new audience: Fitzralph was already of sufficient contemporary interest, as were the topics he had treated, that it would not have been necessary for Trevisa to fill in the gap between audience

---

[46] See 33/11–34/7 and 299 ii 52–300 i 17.

and work as he did in the *Dialogus*.[47] It takes little effort to perceive how translating Fitzralph fits in with Trevisa's anticlerical interests, and while the information Fitzralph provides in any of his polemical works would be of interest to Trevisa, the *Defensio curatorum* is the obvious candidate for translation in that it is Fitzralph's best known and most widely disseminated work. Once we have observed that it is almost too easy to explain why Trevisa would have translated the *Defensio curatorum*, however, there still remains more to be said about how Trevisa's 'translacion' of the *Defensio curatorum* fits into the larger project of intellectual disendowment that Trevisa's Berkeley-sponsored work accomplishes. What sort of difference does it make to have the potentially inflammatory 'informacion' in the *Defensio curatorum* available in English in manuscripts of the *Polychronicon*?

Even in Fitzralph's Latin version the *Defensio curatorum* disturbs conventional expectations of audience and argument. Fitzralph emphasizes the theme he reiterates several times in the course of his self-styled 'sermoun', 'Demeþ nouȝt by þe face but riȝtful doom ȝe deme', by presenting his arguments, or recounting how they were presented, to a nested series of audiences from which in turn he asks 'riȝtful doom'.[48]

Fitzralph's initial account of the process by which he has arrived before his present audience, the papal court in Avignon, introduces several audiences as a side effect of Fitzralph's, and the friars', avoidances of any direct interchange within the same set of generic constraints (39/1–19). On arrival in London from his diocese Armagh, Fitzralph encounters learned doctors debating among themselves theoretical issues having to do with Christ's mendicancy. He casts himself as an 'uplandish', extraclergial figure whose perspective upon the learned debate is validated by his distance from it: he has arrived from 'outside' the city, and, having taken the journey in order to satisfy needs within his diocese, represents concerns 'outside' the clergy. Further, he maintains that distance by refusing to enter the doctors' debate on its own terms; instead, he wrenches it from its conventional milieu and preaches in the vernacular to the 'lewed', 'to þe peple in her

---

[47] See W. Scase, *'Piers Plowman' and the New Anticlericalism*, 7–14, 16–32, and 47–83, and for further evidence, ch. 5 below, pp. 162–77.

[48] Fitzralph reiterates his theme at 39/1, 40/30–1, 51/28, 53/23, 70/24, 79/23, and 93/26–7.

owne tonge', the conclusions he has now to defend before the papal court. Fitzralph's 'translacion' broadens the scope of the learned debate, and sharpens it as well: his arguments are transformed from theoretical topics for discussion among scholars to more widely available assertions that ask of their 'lewed' audience a 'riʒtful doom' which implies pointedly practical consequences.[49]

The friars, like Fitzralph, do not simply reply in kind. Rather than translating their side of the argument into public sermons as well, rather even than maintaining the same scholarly debate as before, they appeal to the papal curia: they resort to a genre of argument in which it is normal to appeal for a kind of judgement that may carry direct punitive consequences, and to an audience that has traditionally been entrusted with delivering such judgements.

Appearing in the curia to deliver the *Defensio*, Fitzralph as before refuses the conventional role offered to him. He makes a show of his deference to the needs of his current audience: he promises to defend his conclusions using material from his public sermons, but presenting it in a different, 'somwhat harder' style, but continues to eschew academic discourse; though he could have produced an academic *quaestio*, 'argue[d] aʒenus me-silf & assoile[d] þe argumentes forto conferme þat ich haue seide' (93/22–3), on the present occasion he is tailoring his exposition to the present needs of his audience, and he has produced as much as they need or want: 'ich haue y-trauaylled ʒoure holynesse y-nowʒ & þe reuerence of my lordes þe Cardynals' (93/ 23–5). But even if his tone is respectful, the detailed directions about how the pope should evaluate them which Fitzralph submits with his arguments are rather presumptuous:

> And y pray ʒowre holynesse mekelich & deuoutlich, þat ʒe take hede to þe forseide conclusiouns & to þe resons þat ich haue made þerfore, and schal make at þis time; and also þat ʒe take hede to þe resouns þat freres makiþ for þe contrarie. & ʒif her resouns beþ strenger þan myn, y pray þat ich be punysched; & ʒif my resouns be strenger þan her resouns, be þei punysched for þat þei haueþ

---

49 Admittedly even interclerical discussions could be acrimonious and could on occasion lead to condemnations or to trials similar to Fitzralph's; but Fitzralph's interest is in contrasting his own activity with the typical mode of scholarly debate rather than in giving a history of academic antifraternalism.

sclaundred me, dispised, & diffamed priuylich & openlich. But touchyng þat, me is leuer suffre þan folowe þe lawe to her punyschyng. To holde alwey as y seide first: 'Demeþ nou3t by þe face but ri3tful dome 3e deme'. (40/21–31)

It may seem fair minded of Fitzralph to request 'ri3tful dome' even if it goes against him, but it is unlikely that the pope needs to be told how to preside over the papal court, and Fitzralph's attempt to refashion his case into a defamation suit against the friars is not likely to be sympathetically received.[50]

Even in the 'somwhat harder' style of the version presented to the papal court, the *Defensio curatorum* retains its prevailing concern with what it presents as an overriding public interest in the proper admin-stration of pastoral needs – an interest shared by, and open to the judgement of, even the lowest ranks of the laity to whom its arguments were originally presented. Fitzralph invokes the principle of attending to common needs above all to explain his ostentatious reordering of the conclusions that have been presented to him: 'for by lawe of God & of kynde, þe comyn nedes schal be sett tofore singuler nedes, ich wole bigynne atte mater of priuyleges þat touchiþ al þe clergie, & alle Cristen men' (41/1–3). Even if the original order was his rather than the friars', Fitzralph's reorganization affirms the importance of common needs and underlines the urgency of ensuring they are secured before any more specialized aims are pursued. But much more tendentiously, he repeatedly enlists the aid of the lay audiences he embeds within his presentation to the curia for the pursuit of those general aims.

A number of appeals in passing to 'lewed' experience bolster Fitzralph's claim that friars act against the common public interest, as here: '. . . but þe comyn opinioun of lewed men & of clerkes telliþ þat freres doþ so . . . [i.e. try to persuade men to be buried in their churches]' (46/23–4). However, Fitzralph's most interesting appeals to the 'lewed' are the ones that represent lay persons delivering 'ri3tful dome' 'not by þe face' against the friars. Fitzralph demonstrates, rather than recommending as he did in appealing to and instructing the judgement of the curia at the outset, the mode of judgement he is

---

[50] On defamation suits see R. H. Helmholz, *Select Cases on Defamation to 1600* (London, 1985), xiv–xlv.

advocating, reporting in the first person the internal argument that the parishioners he instances should conduct. But oddly, the fact that he is quoting the thoughts of one or more 'lewed' parishioners does not stop him from conducting that argument in a thoroughly scholastic mode.

Into the thoughts of a parishioner contemplating confession, Fitzralph substitutes a 'skilful' internal argument in place of the devotional introspection recommended by pastoral and penitential manuals as a prelude to confession:

> Þanne may þe parischon skilfulliche argue in his herte, why wolde þis begger sitte & here my schrifte & leue his beggyng & getyng of his liflode, but he hope to haue of me siche maner help, and nede driueþ to synne, by þe which synne þe nede myȝt be releued, as Proverbiorum 30 c. Salomon seiþ & prayeþ 'ȝeue me noþer beggerie noþer riches, but ȝeue me onliche what is nedeful to my liflode lest y be excited to denye & saye who is oure Lorde, & conpelled by nede for to stele & forswere þe name of my God'. Þanne hit folewiþ, þat for all maner synnes, he wole ioyne me almes dede for to releue his owne beggerie, & so y schal nouȝt be cleneliche byquyt of my synnes; þerfore whanne hise disciples axide of oure Lord: 'Why myȝt we nouȝt cast hym out?' & spake of a fende, oure Lord answerde & seide: 'Þese manere fendes beþ nouȝt cast out but wiþ bedes & fastyng'. Math 16 c. Of þis worde hit is y-take, þat as for euereche diuerse sekenesse of body dyuerse medicyns helpiþ; so for euereche gostlich seknese most be ordeyned his propre medicyn. And þis begger þat is bisy about his beggerye wole nouȝt with-out suspecioun ordeyne me siche medicyns for my synnes'. (47/10–29)

Rather than submitting himself without question to his confessor's judgement, this parishioner weighs the judging capabilities of two potential confessors against one another. Though the procedure of introspective self-questioning he undertakes is similar to the devotional process conventionally recommended by the manuals, its content is far different. This parishioner's reported internal argument is 'skilful' not only in the sense of being adeptly stated but in that it is full of scholastic 'skilles': it uses academic terminology ('hit folewiþ'), quotes from both the Old and New Testaments, glossing the second quotation with the aid of a medical analogy, and, like the Lord in Trevisa's dialogue, shows familiarity with contemporary arguments on 'need'.

Perhaps Fitzralph aims to foreclose the possibility that lay people will imitate his example by spelling out the internal argumentation involved in this process of judging 'not by þe face' and by presenting it as formidably technical. Nonetheless, Fitzralph has here opened up the possibility that any parishioner might evaluate the pastoral commitment of any confessor, and might be just as capable of doing so as the pope. The potential consequences of the second case I will examine are even more dangerous, and even more immediate. On this occasion the judgement of parishioners is introduced to illustrate why Augustine's claim that no lying ought ever to be permissible is correct. Fitzralph suggests a hypothetical case, based on the premise that the church allows preachers to lie, to show how parishioners listening to a sermon might evaluate it critically rather than simply accepting what they hear. Here too the critical method advocated is scholastic: the parishioners convince themselves that they need not believe what they hear because there is insufficient evidence to form a valid chain of reasoning:

> Þanne men þat hereþ hym preche my3t argue in her herte in þis maner: by his owne loore þis may lawfulliche lye & make lesyngis lawfulliche in many maner caas; y noot noþer may wite wheþer he haue sich a cause now oþer no; þanne y schal no3t trowe hym while he precheþ & techiþ. (57/8–13)

Since men may lawfully lie when preaching, but it cannot be determined and thus must remain in doubt whether this one is lying or not, therefore the audience here decides to withhold belief from the preacher's words. The difficulty is that the model of behaviour advocated here might equally well be extended to a situation in which the preacher is certainly not *permitted* to lie, but is thought to be doing so anyway.[51] Parishioners who have learned to be critical of what they hear can be critical whenever they see fit, and critical not just of friars, but of any preacher. Especially if he included this example in his public vernacular sermons in London, and even if it is new to his 'sermoun' before the curia, Fitzralph by these strategies of public appeal is leaving himself open to the 'dome' of the 'lewed peple' just as much as of the pope; he can only hope it will be 'ri3tful' and 'nou3t by þe face'.

---

[51] For the exemplary extension of this kind of 'lewed' withholding of belief in vernacular Wycliffite texts and especially in the *Testimony of William Thorpe*, see ch. 6, pp. 204–8.

Fitzralph's efforts at transferring across audiences, or 'translating' into one another clergial and 'lewed' languages, modes of argument, and audiences may be viewed as attempts to seize control of the debate: he asserts his superiority to the curia by condescending to their short attention span, and demonstrates his superiority to the 'lewed' by overwhelming them with difficulty. With one hand he gives the impression of being certain that he is in the right by expansively laying himself open to judgement not only by the papal curia, but even by the 'lewed', while with the other he attempts to prescribe in his favour the terms and conclusions of each judgement to which he is subject. But of course once Fitzralph has broken out of the conventional arena of scholastic debate, the technical tools of argumentation native to scholasticism cannot determine the results of all the judgements to which he is now subject. In redefining them, Fitzralph has unavoidably produced any number of new ways that he can be in the wrong.

When Trevisa translates Fitzralph's *Defensio curatorum* into English, its implications are widened yet further. Trevisa's further mediation of the text is transparent: he includes no notes and makes no systematic modifications, and he attaches no prologue or colophon to specify his role or that of his readership. Instead, he merely re-presents the text, and renders it at least potentially available to any person, clergy or lay, who can read English or (as the sermon form perhaps encourages) find a reader to do it for them. Trevisa's translation does not address Berkeley by name. It merely places him (as well as the extended future potential audience which his patronage may make possible) just exactly where the prefatory address and concluding remark put the pope in Fitzralph's 'sermoun'; and where the common people were placed at the London sermons from which Fitzralph claims to have drawn his present arguments; and also where Fitzralph puts the 'lewed' he instances during those arguments. All these audiences were asked to deliver the oft-reiterated 'ri3tful dome' of Fitzralph's theme. The innovation in Trevisa's version is simply that the newly extended audience are nowhere specifically addressed; nowhere are they assigned, as all Fitzralph's audiences were, to a carefully specified judgemental role.

While Trevisa's translation of the *Defensio curatorum* might seem to offer the utopian possibilities of universal 'informacion' that the Lord in Trevisa's *Dialogue* advocated, the extremely limited actual dissemination of the text should remind us also what possibilities the semblance of universal lay participation offered to lay lords. It might look as though Trevisa's translation offered lay readers of all sorts the opportunity to read like a pope, or a parishioner, and to arrive at their judgements by any of the means the text so thoroughly describes; and his translation certainly does fulfil that potential for unprecedented combinations of 'lewed' status and clergial learning that Fitzralph's text began to open up. Trevisa's English version does offer, however grudgingly, the possibility of clergially proficient 'lewed' introspection, and make available for the leisurely perusal of a vernacular readership matters which had previously been (on Fitzralph's account, at least) purely intraclerical issues. However, it only does so – initially at any rate, and according to the plan for publishing information on which Trevisa and Berkeley seem to have collaborated – for a very limited audience of lay nobility. What it offers that lay noble audience is the capacity Trevisa's *Dialogue* conferred upon the Lord: the ability to speak at once like a pope and a parishioner, advancing what are presented as the interests and concerns of the lowest of the laity while deploying clerical 'informacion' of the most sophisticated sort, all in order to inspire action.

PART II

Contesting vernacular publication

4

Answering the *Twelve Conclusions*: Dymmok's halfhearted gestures toward publication

As is often the case with heretical materials, we know of the *Twelve Conclusions* only through the efforts to record and refute them made by their orthodox opponents. Although our main concern here will be with their most dogged and thorough opponent, Roger Dymmok, we should first gather what we can from the form of the *Conclusions* he has preserved for us.

Like the 'Petition' examined in Chapter one, the *Conclusions* aim for the most important and influential audience in the land; the audience anyone wanting redress might want to achieve: 'þe lordis and þe comunys of þe parlement' (24/2). The *Conclusions* are broadly critical of church institutions, rituals, and rules, and in particular of 'prelacye' (the church hierarchy) and 'priuat religion' (orders of monks, canons, and friars). Their twelve points purport to aim at the 'reformaciun' of current institutions back toward the state of the primitive church, and the basis for their address to Parliament is that current ecclesiastical institutions do various kinds of harm to the people that it ought to be Parliament's responsibility to redress. However, like the 'Petition' in Chapter one, this petition does not use the official channels with which it associates itself. Although it apes the mode of address and presentation of a parliamentary petition, it is a hybrid product: it claims the virtues of poverty and championship of the people, but leaves the precise associations of its writers extremely murky.

The writers of the *Twelve Conclusions* set themselves apart from the institutional clergy. They strongly disapprove of clerical involvement in secular administration, calling the 'men of duble astate' who engage in it 'hermafodrita', and they censure the clergy's corrupt spiritual activities by linking them with dubious secular practices: bishops who ordain priests are giving out the livery of antichrist; sellers of letters of fraternity are selling the bliss of heaven 'be chartre of clause of warantise'; the pope by the logic of his claim to be able to grant pardons for sin is the treasurer furthest from charity. However, while the writers distance themselves from the sort of involvement with secular affairs they think typical of the corrupt clergy, contrasting themselves with the pope – if he is the worst sort of treasurer, they are the best; poor men and treasurers of Christ, holders of genuine spiritual rather than bogus salvific capital – they leave obscure whether they themselves are clerics or laymen. Patently they have had considerable access to clerical learning: they correctly use a distinction between 'latria' and 'dulia' worship and cite Wyclif's *Trialogus* in Latin. But they also make a bid for a role in public affairs that they would surely characterize as secular: as 'procuratouris' with an 'ambaciat', 'pursuing' a 'cause' before Parliament – even if they look beyond Parliament as well, petitioning God rather than (as a petition presented in Parliament typically would) the king or the commons,[1] and laying stress on their wish to see their ideas not only reach the lords and commons in Parliament, but be 'communid' 'in oure langage' to all true Christian men.[2]

In contrast to Walsingham, who allows the writers their extraclergial positioning, reporting that clerical 'Lollardi' worked in close collusion with a group of noble and knightly supporters who were certainly involved in the posting of the conclusions even if not in drawing them up, Roger Dymmok gives no credence to the *Twelve Conclusions*'

---

[1] On the procedure of presenting petitions in parliament see Roskell, *The History of Parliament*, i: 76–103.

[2] Admittedly 'true men' is one of the Lollards' 'coded' self-descriptions; it could be argued that the still wider audience the writers mean to reach will be made up of Lollards. (See A. Hudson, 'A Lollard Sect Vocabulary?', in M. Benskin and M. L. Samuels, eds., *So meny people longages and tonges: Philological Essays in Scots and Medieval English presented to Angus McIntosh* (Edinburgh, 1981), 15–30 for discussion of 'true men' and several other characteristic Lollard terms.) But even in the confined sense, the group 'alle trew cristene men' has the potential to include all who come in contact with the *Twelve Conclusions* and find they agree with them. The *Twelve Conclusions* are most conveniently available in A. Hudson, ed., *Selections from English Wycliffite Writings* (Cambridge, 1978), 24–9, 150–5.

efforts to associate themselves with lay as well as clerical authority.[3] He ascribes the writing and publication of the *Twelve Conclusions* solely to clerics, disparaging their address to the laity as evidence of ingratitude to the church that has educated them, and their use of English as revealing how little they gained from that education.[4] Any members of the laity who may be convinced count for Dymmok as audience, not participants. And the manner of the *Twelve Conclusions'* publication

---

[3] I cite Walsingham's *Chronica Maiora* from the edition printed as *Annales Ricardi Secundi et Henrici Quarti* in *Johannis de Trokelowe et Anon Chronica et Annales*, ed. H. T. Riley (London, 1866), 155–420, hereafter *Annales*. Walsingham claims the Lollards put together the list 'animati . . . favore quorundam procerum, et instigatione militum aulicorum', 'encouraged by the favour of certain nobles, and at the instigation of chamber knights'; and that chamber knights were responsible certainly for posting the poem appended to the *Conclusions* and bringing to them a tone of occluded menace, and perhaps for posting the *Conclusions* as well. As usual stressing Richard's defence of the church, Walsingham suggests the group were taking advantage of Richard's absence in Ireland to express their hostility to the church establishment, and that when at the request of worried bishops Richard returned he dealt severely with the chamber knights involved (*Annales*, 174–83; 174/9–10). In his *Historica Anglicana* Walsingham adds that the *Conclusions* were also affixed to the door of St Paul's (*Historica Anglicana*, 2 vols., ed. H. T. Riley (London, 1864), ii: 216). None of the other chroniclers mention the incident. The *Fasciculi Zizianorum* (*c.* 1439) claims in introducing them that the conclusions were 'in quodam libello porrectae pleno parliamento regis [or 'regni'] angliae', 'displayed in the form of a bill in the full parliament of the king [or 'realm'] of England' (*Fasciculi Zizianorum Magistri Johannis Wyclif Cum Tritico*, ed. W. W. Shirley (London, 1858), 360), while Netter (1426–30), (see for example T. Netter, *Thomae Waldensis Doctrinale Fidei Catholicae*, 3 vols., ed. F. B. Blanciotti, (Venice, 1757–9, repr. Farnborough, 1967), iii: 404a, 681 bc), a pamphlet on the Schism in Oxford, Bodleian Library, Digby 188, 66r–v (1395–8; see discussion by M. Harvey, *Solutions to the Schism: A Study of Some English Attitudes 1378 to 1409* (St Ottilien, 1983), 68–9 and 74–6), and the condemnation of five of the articles in a letter from Pope Boniface IX to the archbishops of Canterbury and York in September 1395 (*Calendar of Entries in the Papal Registers Relating to Great Britain and Ireland, Papal Letters*, vol. 4, ed. W. H. Bliss *et al.* (London, 1902), (hereafter *CPL*), 515–16) draw upon the conclusions without mentioning the manner of their publication. On reactions to the *Twelve Conclusions* see as well M. Aston, 'Lollardy and Sedition, 1381–1431', in *Lollards and Reformers*, 21–3, and 'Caim's Castles', 109–14; and A. Hudson, *The Premature Reformation*, esp. 92–3.

[4] On their ingratitude, see R. Dymmok, *Liber contra duodecim errores et hereses Lollardorum*, ed. H. S. Cronin (London, 1922), 13/31–8; on their lack of eloquence, see 25/10–11. (All subsequent citations from Dymmok's *Liber* will be by page and line number(s).) Boniface's letter also makes a point of the Lollards' ingratitude, while (in a way that would seem to weaken that accusation?) also suggesting that laymen as well as clerics are Lollards (*CPL*, 515).

counts for him as an unauthorized assumption of a kind of public role to which their writers are not entitled; he terms it their

> publicacione libelli famosi et eiusdem expansione apud Westmonasterium in ostio Aule Regalis, in pleno parliamento, in conspectu omnium prelatorum, procerum, nobilium et huius regni populi uniuersi. (15/23–7)

> publication of an infamous *libellus*, and display of that same *libellus* at Westminster, on the door of the Regal Chamber in full parliament, in the sight of all prelates, dukes, nobles, and the whole of the people of this realm.

Publicacio is the term used to describe public preaching, proclamation, and the promulgation of statutes, *libellus* is used to describe short legal documents such as deeds, writs, and bills as well as books, while *expansio* elsewhere describes, in a gesture reminiscent of the unrolling and display of the *Conclusions*, how the banners of kings are unfurled on the battlefield.[5] For Dymmok this unprecedented bid for the attention of the highest as well as potentially the broadest of publics is an untoward usurpation by clerics of status not so much (as in the *Twelve Conclusions* writers' complaints about the clergy) as laymen – for as we will see Dymmok will defend in the strongest terms the holding of secular office by ecclesiastics – but as what he calls 'public persons'.

Dymmok's category of 'public persons' includes influential figures in the secular and ecclesiastical hierarchies: kings, dukes, bishops, and scholastic doctors. Dymmok includes himself among this group, by virtue of his doctorate, but excludes the Lollards.[6] This representation

---

[5] See R. E. Latham, *Revised Medieval Latin Word-List From British and Irish Sources* (London, 1965), s.vv. 'libellus' and 'publicatio' for the senses mentioned here. See D. R. Howlett *et al.*, *Dictionary of Medieval Latin from British Sources* (Oxford, 1975–) s.vv. 'expansio', 'expandere' for king's banners. Knighton for example uses the verb 'expandere' to describe how Robert de Vere at Radcot bridge, seeing Henry of Derby approach, 'Statim pedem fixit, uexillum regis quod ibi paratum habuerat expandere iussit, et super lanceam erigere', 'At once he stood his ground, ordered the king's banner, which he had ready, to be unfurled and raised upon a lance' (G. H. Martin, ed. and trans., *Knighton's Chronicle, 1337–1396* (Oxford, 1995), 420–1).

[6] Dymmok specifies the membership of the group in most detail in this explanation of why public persons have an obligation to exemplary rather than eccentric conduct: 'quamuis forte persone priuate sine inconuenienti illud ieiunium possunt obseruare, tamen mihi uidetur quod persone publice hoc non facerent, sicud sunt reges, episcopi,

is, of course, skewed, and in at least two directions. For one thing, doctors rank with kings, dukes, and bishops only by an extraordinary kind of special pleading. Even Dymmok's inclusion of bishops and dukes is rather unusual: Aquinas, who is probably Dymmok's most immediate source on this as many other matters, calls only kings, princes, and other rulers 'public persons'.[7] For another thing, status as 'public persons' by Dymmok's definition is not what the Lollards are claiming. Instead, the secular roles they mention, those of ambassadors, procurators, or treasurers, are of just the kind occupied not by 'public persons', but by the clerics or gentry in their service who represent them in particular capacities – even if the 'public person' the Lollards claim to represent is Christ.[8] Dymmok is not prepared to accept the Lollard claim of direct service to Christ,[9] but neither is he comfortable with the notion that the Lollards have the support of some more tangible 'public person' or persons; he invokes national pride against the mere possibility: 'Per hunc enim modum faciendi ceteris nacionibus dare possent intelligere regem uel alias personas publicas et potentes regni ipsis fauorem . . . prebuisse . . . ', 'such behaviour might lead other nations to conclude that the king, or other public persons powerful in the realm, had shown favour to these' (27/6–10). Clerical service to 'public persons' is something Dymmok is concerned to defend, not decry – and I would suggest that despite his claim to be a

doctores, duces et tales, qui magnum regimen in populo sorciuntur, ne per hoc factum nouam inducant in ecclesiam consuetudinem', 'although perhaps private persons may fittingly observe that fast, nonetheless it seems to me that public persons, that is, kings, bishops, doctors, dukes, and such like, who are allotted an important role in government of the people, should not do so, lest by so doing they should bring in a new custom in the church' (122/32–7).

7   For Dymmok's citation of one of Aquinas's references to private (as opposed to public) persons as those persons not qualified by their status to wage war or (significantly) raise up a multitude of people in any way, see p. 262. All of Aquinas's references to public persons refer to rulers qualified to make laws and wage war: see the references listed in the *Index Thomisticus Sancti Thomae Aquinatis Operum Omnium indices et concordantiae*, ed. R. Busa *et al.* (Italy, 1975), vol. xviii.

8   The Lollards may be drawing on Wyclif's theory, expressed for example in *De potestate pape*, ed. J. Loserth (London, 1907), 7–21, that power does not exist absolutely *per se*, and is conferred directly by God rather than through human intermediaries.

9   Instead, he dismisses their claims as presumptuous (157–9), and defends the orthodox theory of ordination (53–70 *passim*; but especially 65–6, 146–7).

public person in his own right, this defence operates very much for his own benefit.

The status of Dymmok's family, who were Lincolnshire gentry of some importance, might well have disposed him toward the position he takes.[10] Sir John Dymmok, his father, was a retainer of John of Gaunt and member of Parliament in 1372, 1373, and 1377. He held in addition a position of considerable if largely ceremonial importance, acting as Champion of England at Richard II's coronation. After Sir John's death in 1381 the position of Champion would have been Roger Dymmok's by hereditary right if it were not for his ecclesiastical status; instead, in 1399 and again in 1413, it fell to his younger brother Sir Thomas Dymmok.[11] Roger Dymmok himself, however, although he did become a doctor of theology and thus by his own definition counts as a 'public person', seems never to have succeeded in gaining any important secular office. He was prior of the Boston Dominican house from 1379 onward and regent of the London house after 1396, but these offices involved him in purely ecclesiastical duties rather than in public affairs. He does not seem to have been offered any other opportunity to engage in affairs of state, and although he apparently preached a sermon before Richard II in 1391, there is no sign that he was ever in favour at court. Rather to the contrary: in the *Calendar of Close Rolls* there is an entry directed to the keepers of the passage at London, Dover, and Sandwich asking them to permit Dymmok passage; although previously, on account of information that he planned to pass to foreign parts in order to prosecute suits to the prejudice of the king and many of the people, he had been forbidden passage, now Dymmok has promised first, not to go abroad without special licence from the

---

[10] For records relating to Dymmok's life see H. S. Cronin's introduction to the *Liber*, xi–xv; and the entries for Roger Dymmok in A. B. Emden, *A Biographical Register of the University of Oxford to A.D. 1500*, 3 vols. (Oxford, 1957–9), ii, and L. Stephen and S. Lee, eds., *Dictionary of National Biography*, vi (Oxford, 1917). My thanks to Anne Hudson for discussing with me the new entry on Dymmok she is preparing for the revised *Dictionary of National Biography*.

[11] It seems most likely that Roger was the eldest of Sir John's sons; however, the very fact that Roger became an ecclesiastic may indicate that there were other obstacles, such as bastardy perhaps, to his inheritance. That there may have been other reasons why Roger did not inherit from Sir John does not of course stand in the way of my suggestion that Roger may have wanted the sort of public position others in his family held.

king, second, not to make any suit or attempt that might tend to contempt or prejudice of the king, or to hurt his people, or to impair the laws, customs, ordinances, or statutes of the realm, and third, not to send anyone else to make such a suit.[12] While the machinations behind this document are unclear, it is evident that Dymmok was not among the king's trusted servants.

In answering the *Twelve Conclusions*, then, Dymmok has no more ready access to sanctioned channels of broad public communication available to ecclesiastic and secular 'public persons' and those in their service in the late fourteenth century than his opponents did – an easy explanation for why his answer to them exploits none of those channels. His answer was not presented to parliament, whether as the sort of parliamentary sermon the chancellor might have addressed to the assembly or as a petition produced or advocated by members of parliament.[13] Still less did it become the more widely promulgated statute that might result from a parliamentary petition. It was not issued as a writ from Chancery to the bishops requiring them to ask the lower clergy to instruct the broadest possible public by means of sermons and of special prayers, masses, and processions.[14] Nor, even though it would have been perfectly legitimate for a licensed or invited preacher to address the public in this way and presumably Dymmok could have arranged such an occasion if he had wanted to, was his reply a public vernacular sermon given in London or Oxford and perhaps subsequently disseminated in written form.

Instead, Dymmok produces a voluminous treatise which discusses

---

12 *Calendar of Close Rolls*, membrane 23, no date or place given, but included among entries for autumn 1397; summarized in *Calendar of Close Rolls* (London, 1902–), vol. 29, 1396–99 (London, 1927), 150. Cronin discusses the affair: see Dymmok, xiii–xiv.

13 On parliamentary sermons see R. N. Swanson, *Church and Society in Late Medieval England* (Oxford, 1993), 93–4; on who could present various kinds of parliamentary petition and how they were dealt with see Roskell's discussion cited in n. 1.

14 This method of disseminating carefully doctored information, in particular about current foreign policy, appears to have been used frequently during the war with France. On its general mechanisms see W. R. Jones, 'The English Church and Royal Propaganda During the Hundred Years War', *Journal of British Studies* 19 (1979), 18–30, esp. 21 and 29. For a valuable survey of its use in the diocese of Lincoln see A. K. McHardy, 'Liturgy and Propaganda in the Diocese of Lincoln during the Hundred Years War', *Studies in Church History* 18 (1981), 215–27.

in detail and refutes in turn every point of each of the Lollard conclusions, and indeed argues over their heads, so to speak, with related issues raised by Wyclif and earlier polemicists.[15] The scholastic format and mode of proceeding of his text is just what we would expect from a man with Dymmok's training; these, after all, are the weapons he has been trained to wield. But Dymmok attempts to move beyond the extremely narrow audience of educated clerics we would expect for a treatise like his; he addresses himself to the king, and through and beyond him to the widest possible public:

> Scire etiam dignetur uestra precellentissima celsitudo, mei propositi non esse nimium subtilia et scolastica argumenta in presenti opusculo adducere, set talia que intelligi ualent ab omnibus, sicud omnibus supradicti ueritatis adversarii haurienda venenosa pocula doctrine infuderunt, ita ut et omnibus peruenire ualeat hoc antidotum catholice ueritatis, ut ex eo pateat uniuersis quam periculosum fuerit eorum documentum et quod nullum protulerunt pro sua assercione ualidum argumentum. (9/38–10/7)

> May it be worthy of the notice of your most excellent highness that my purpose in the present small work is not to adduce overly subtle and scholastic arguments, but arguments of a sort that may be understood by everyone – in the same way that the previously mentioned enemies of truth have poured out their venomous doses in such a way that everyone may drink them – so that this antidote of catholic truth may also reach everyone, with the result that it will be clear to absolutely everyone how dangerous their document is, and that they offer no valid argument for their assertion.

Dymmok claims to offer in his book a *universal* antidote; one that will make clear to *everyone* who might encounter the *Twelve Conclusions* the invalidity of the Lollard arguments and the danger of their document. One motive for referring to a universal audience here is perhaps to avoid telling the king that the work has been written simply enough for *him* to understand. But Dymmok does not have to appeal to the assent of *everyone* to his simplified argument in order to avoid insulting the

---

15 Margaret Aston has pointed out ('Caim's Castles', 113 n. 56) that Dymmok argues over the heads of the *Conclusions* in more than just the obvious example of the fourth conclusion, where the Lollards quote Wyclif's *Trialogus* and Dymmok in reply cites copiously from the history of the Eucharistic controversy. I will briefly examine another example below, pp. 116–20.

king. Rather, he is seeking not just the highest, but the widest ratification possible, in a bid for a public role designed directly to counter that assumed by the Lollards.

If part of what Dymmok intends in providing a self-styled public antidote to the *Twelve Conclusions* is to advertise his worthiness for office through a symbolic display – similar perhaps to that proffered by the Champion at a coronation? – of his would-be royalism, then it does not seem to have worked. Dymmok did become regent of the London convent after writing the *Twelve Conclusions*, but he seems to have incurred suspicion shortly thereafter. However, Dymmok's ostensible purpose of convincing a universal audience could not have been accomplished either, for the actual physical dissemination of his text was very limited. Along with the presentation copy presented to the king there are records of only four other manuscripts that include his text. None of them is pitched much lower than the one presented to the king; only one of them, indeed, a devotional volume of the sort typically owned by those in the upper reaches of the nobility, seems to have been owned by someone outside the narrow scholastic audience writing of this sort normally had.[16] Of the other three one was first owned by two bishops then given to the Cambridge University Library, a second, evidently a Dominican product, was owned by a master John Arnold, perhaps of Merton, in 1439, and the third, likely produced for consultation in scholastic argument and most probably owned by a monastery, is composed of anti-Wycliffite materials by Woodford and Dymmok.[17]

[16] The manuscript now Cambridge, Trinity Hall 17 is apparently the presentation copy that was given to the king: this is a very high quality volume, well written and ornamented throughout, with four illustrations; M. R. James dates it to the late fourteenth century. London, British Library, Cotton Otho c.xvi is the collection reflecting noble tastes; Dymmok's text, listed in the table along with seven saints' lives and two histories, has not survived. Catalogue descriptions of the manuscripts known to Cronin are conveniently reproduced in his introduction: see Dymmok, xvi-xxv. (On the Bodleian library manuscript not known to Cronin, see the next note.)

[17] Cambridge, University Library Ii.4.3, fifteenth century, belonged first to a bishop of Ely, then to Thomas Rotherham, Bishop of Rochester, Archbishop of York and Chancellor of England as well as of Cambridge, who gave it to the library in 1480. Oxford, Bodleian Library, Lat. th. e. 30, *c.* 1400, includes three Dominican letters of fraternity in its flyleaves and the note (f. 150v) that it belonged to master John Arnold – perhaps the same master John Arnold of Merton who owned the manuscript of

There is, nonetheless, one at least somewhat wider audience that Dymmok could realistically have hoped to reach even by means of the presentation copy alone, and one with whose concerns we might expect him by reason of his family connections to be especially familiar: that of lesser nobility and gentry in service at court. Although we need not believe that all books presented to Richard were read by the royal household (or indeed in some cases that he read them himself), it seems entirely possible that some courtiers literate in Latin could have read Dymmok's text, and others could have been told about it.[18] Much though Dymmok attempts to downplay as far as possible the notion that the Lollards had supporters and even collaborators at court, Walsingham's account tells a different story – as, indeed, do modern investigations of the 'Lollard knights'. And interest in the *Twelve Conclusions* need not even have been confined to knights and gentry who might be described as Lollards: the *Conclusions* contain much that would surely have appealed to anticlerical sentiments common among

meditations now Oxford, Jesus College 36 in 1440? Paris, Bibliothèque Nationale, fonds lat. 3381, early fifteenth century, includes as well as Dymmok's text a letter and a treatise against Wyclif's *Trialogus* by Woodford. While it cannot be conclusively identified with any of the five known copies, we do in addition have one further record of ownership: John Carpenter, common clerk to the city of London and noted bibliophile, mentions a copy in his 1442 will; it may have been one of the books his executors Reginald Pecock and his relative Master John Carpenter later bishop of Worcester selected for inclusion in the Guildhall Library. As a book collector with bishops among his close relatives and friends John Carpenter may not be an entirely typical representative of the literate gentry of his day. Still, his ownership and the possible further dissemination through his bequest of a copy of Dymmok's treatise fulfil somewhat after the fact the potential for reaching a wider readership that Dymmok seems to have made little effort to achieve. (On Carpenter see M. Aston, 'Bishops and Heresy: The Defence of the Faith', in *Faith and Fire*, 73–93; 90–1.)

[18] N. Orme has investigated how courts, and monasteries, universities, and the households of bishops and nobles as well, were centres for the education of at least a few members of the nobility and the gentry ('The Education of the Courtier', in Scattergood and Sherbourne, eds., *English Court Culture*, 63–85). Even members of the household who did not have sufficient skill in reading Latin would presumably have access to tutors, confessors, and other educated clerics in the household who would be entirely competent to read a book like Dymmok's and retail it to whomever they saw fit. Fellow Dominicans in the royal household might have been especially eager to pass on the content of Dymmok's text; Richard's confessor in 1395, John Burghill, was for example a Dominican. (On clerks in the royal household see C. Given-Wilson, *The Royal Household and the King's Affinity: Service, Politics and Finance in England 1360–1413* (London, 1986), 175–83.)

this class and at court.[19] Interest at court in the proposals put forth in the *Twelve Conclusions* might dispose nobles and gentry to consider Dymmok's reply, even if only as a prelude to dismissing its arguments: if Dymmok knew about such interest, it might dispose him all the more toward attempting to appeal to nobles and gentry at court – at least insofar as such an appeal would not obstruct his address to the king.

What evidence is there that Dymmok makes any attempt to pitch his text to this audience at court or indeed any wider audience? On most occasions where Dymmok differentiates the membership of his audience rather than addressing an amorphous 'omnibus', he shows a bias toward its upper end. Typically an *ad status* address invokes the public good and advises representative groups at all levels of society about how they should behave in order to maintain it, whether by discussing members of the three estates in turn or by anatomizing society according to the extended metaphor of a body, building, boat, or what have you.[20] But when Dymmok explains how each person should behave in accordance with his status, when he tells 'unusquisque . . . in gradu suo' how to combat the heretics, for example, it is those

19 A number of studies since K. B. McFarlane's rehabilitation of the evidence (*Lancastrian Kings and Lollard Knights* (Oxford, 1972)) have investigated Lollardy, support for Lollards, and/or sympathy with Lollard views among the nobility and gentry. See, for example, M. Wilks, 'Royal Priesthood: The Origins of Lollardy', in *The Church in a Changing Society: CIHEC Conference in Uppsala, 1977* (Uppsala, 1978), 63–70; J. A. Tuck, 'Carthusian Monks and Lollard Knights: Religious Attitude at the Court of Richard II', *Studies in the Age of Chaucer, Proceedings* 1 (1984), 149–61 (though Tuck focuses on more general trends in lay noble devotion); P. McNiven, *Heresy and Politics in the Reign of Henry IV: The Burning of John Badby* (Woodbridge, Suffolk, 1987); and Hudson, *Premature Reformation*, 110–19. See also n. 24 below.

20 On estates literature in general, the most illuminating survey is J. Mann, *Chaucer and Medieval Estates Satire* (Cambridge, 1973); appendix A lists which estates are included in a number of texts which aim at a comprehensive address to all of society, and will give the reader an idea of the more usual breadth of address. While Mann concentrates mainly on literary texts rather than sermons, A. J. Fletcher's 'The Social Trinity of Piers Plowman' places the use of *ad status* address in *Piers Plowman* in the context of uses of these conventions in contemporary sermons (*Review of English Studies*, n.s. 44 no. 175 (1993), 343–61). For other examples of this sort of address not included in Mann or mentioned by Fletcher, see *Lollard Sermons*, ed. G. Cigman (London, 1989) expansion to sermon 11, 137/202–139/300, and *Sermon of Dead Men* 222/524–224/618. On vernacular sermons *ad status* see also Spencer, *English Preaching in the Late Middle Ages*, 65–8.

he classifies as pastors who concern him, not their sheep: doctors, kings, and princes, not the 'simplices', the 'Christianum populum', that they protect:

> contra quos [aduersarios] ecclesie diligencia pastorum inuigilet, ne gregem dispersum morsibus uenenosis interimant. Sancti doctores eosdem suis predicacionibus ac disputacionibus compescant, ne simplices seducant per apparenciam ueritatis. Reges uero et principes accincti armis contra ipsos insurgant, ne uiolent[a][21] adunacione peruersorum nouiter insurgencium Christianum populum opprimant . . . . . . unusquisque prompto animo eidem in gradu suo respondeat illud Ysaie VI: 'Ecce ego, mitte me,' ut debita cooperacione omnium fidelium sancta mater ecclesia ab istorum malignancium defendatur . . . (314/32–315/7)

> against which [adversaries] let the diligence of shepherds of the church keep watch, lest they should destroy the scattered flock with their venomous bites. Let holy doctors suppress them with their preaching and disputation, lest they should seduce the simple with the appearance of truth. Let kings and princes girded with arms rise up against them, lest the raging throng of their perverse insurgencies should oppress the Christian people. Let each in his degree with a ready mind reply to Him as in Isaiah 6: 'Here I am, send me', so that with the due cooperation of all the faithful, holy mother church may be defended from their malignance.

The way Dymmok demarcates pastors from the 'simplices', the undifferentiated remainder of the 'Christianum populum' whom those pastors protect from seduction, is unusual. Normally the church's metaphorical shepherds are those clerics at whatever level who are engaged in those duties typically regarded as pastoral: preaching, teaching, administering sacraments, and so on. Here, however, Dymmok picks out as his pastors a mixed group of important laymen and clerics from among that group he has defined as 'public persons': scholastic doctors who engage in disputations as much as preaching, and kings and princes whose martial role can be viewed as pastoral only by a sort of blinkered extension. Much though Dymmok calls on the 'debita cooperacione omnium fidelium', the undifferentiated *simplices* these pastors protect can hardly be said to contribute, except perhaps in

---

[21] Emending Cronin's misprint 'uiolent'.

demonstrating the dangers of Lollard publication: they are fragile in their virtue, ready to be led astray at the slightest intellectual temptation.[22]

But are only scholastic doctors, kings, and princes, (as this passage seems to imply) excluded from the ranks of the simple and capable of the required 'cooperacio'? If the lesser nobility and gentry are granted pastoral capacities anywhere, it seems likely that it will be where Dymmok (adapting the method anticlerical writers so often employ) attempts to show this audience that his interests coincide with theirs. While other examples might be considered, nowhere does Dymmok's approach stand out better as a counter to anticlerical appeals to knights and nobles on the basis of common interest than in his response to conclusion six, where he defends the capacity of clerics to hold secular office.

The anticlerical complaint that the clergy ought not to have temporal jurisdiction had featured for some time in ongoing conflicts over the respective powers of ecclesiastical and secular government.[23] In the more traditional version of this argument, secular authorities are typically exhorted to reform some section of the clergy by forcing them to attend to their proper spiritual jurisdiction and their pastoral duties. At the same time, as we saw in Chapter three, the exercise of secular power is itself often represented as a pastoral activity, and secular power may even be encouraged to take over activities associated with the clergy's pastoral ministry but inadequately performed by them.[24]

---

22 Dymmok does allow the *simplices* virtue: 'contingit simplices, nullam uel paruam potestatem habentes, maiores esse et meliores quoad Deum illis, qui regali uel episcopali fulserant dignitate', 'on some occasions the simple, having no power or little, are greater and better in God that those who shine out with regal or episcopal dignities' (61/14–17). See also 44/13–24, 45/14–18, and 80/20–2. But he also remarks frequently on its fragility: see 13/2–15, 14/16–19, 15/4–8, 251/8–13, and 274/35–275/29, as well as the *ad status* address just quoted in the text.

23 For an introduction to the main points of contention and some examples see ch. 1, pp. 14–15 and n. 28, ch. 2, pp. 56–60, and the reference to ch. 3 that follows.

24 In the pseudo-Ockham *Dialogus inter militem et clericem*, the speaker *Miles* suggests that the king's role as defender of the realm is a pastoral one, whereas clerics who neglect to support him through taxation are delinquent in their pastoral obligations. An annotation in Trevisa's *Polychronicon* translation asks that lords should remove the superfluous possessions of monks and take over the neglected monastic duty of administering alms to the poor. See ch. 3, pp. 91–3, 66–7. On late fourteenth and

Conclusion six puts forth an elaboration of this argument characteristic of Wyclif and his followers:

> Þe sexte conclusiun þat mayntenith michil pride is þat a kyng and a
> bisschop al in o persone, a prelat and a iustise in temperel cause, a
> curat and an officer in wordly seruise, makin euery reme out of god
> reule. Þis conclusiun is opinly schewid, for temperelte and spirituelte
> ben to partys of holi chirche, and þerfore he þat hath takin him to þe
> ton schulde nout medlin him with þe toþir, *quia nemo potest duobus
> dominis seruire*. Us thinkith þat hermofodrita or ambidexter were a
> god name to sich manere of men of duble astate. Þe correlari is þat
> we, procuratouris of God in þis cause, pursue to þis parlement þat
> alle manere of curatis boþe heye and lowe ben fulli excusid of
> temperel office, and occupie hem with here cure and nout ellis.
> (26/62–72)

Not only should ecclesiastical government be denied any secular role,
but individual members of the clergy ought not to hold positions in
the secular hierarchy. Secular authorities ought to secure pastoral
benefits for the people by forcing not just the church administration to
attend to its proper pastoral duties, but also each one of the church's
clerical members.[25] Dymmok's inference that an argument based on
Hugh of St Victor's *De sacramentis*, book 2, part II, 3 lies behind the
Lollard conclusion and its corollary is characteristic of the way he
argues over the heads of the *Twelve Conclusions*; here he is very likely
thinking of Wyclif, who frequently cites *De sacramentis*, book 2, part II
when arguing for strict limits on the powers and activities of clerics.[26]

---

fifteenth century interest in disendowment more generally see Aston's survey in
'Caim's Castles'.

[25] Hudson, *Premature Reformation*, 346, mentions this argument as the last of three
arguments on the temporal power of the church characteristic of the Lollards, and
gives several examples of its use in Lollard texts. Wyclif's most extensive and specific
comments on the holding of particular secular offices by clerics are in *De blasphemia*,
ed. M. H. Dziewicki (London, 1893). See especially his comment on the Chancellor:
'Quid, rogo, pertinet ad archiepiscopum occupare cancellarium regis, que est
secularissimum regni officium?', 'How, I ask, can it be appropriate for the archbishop
to occupy the post of Chancellor of the king, which is the most secular office in the
realm?' (194/16); and his list of numerous secular offices that the lower clergy ought
not to occupy (261/3–264/5). For Wyclif's theoretical justification of this position see
below at n. 27.

[26] The nine chapters of Hugh of St Victor's 'De Unitate Ecclesiae', book 2, part II of his
De sacramentis Christianae fidei, appear in J. P. Migne, ed., *Patrologia Latina* 176
(Paris, 1854), cols. 173–618; 415–22.

In *De Ecclesia*, for example, Wyclif uses *De sacramentis*, 2, II, 3 to assert that clergy should have no secular jurisdiction, that they are not entitled to own but only to use what they hold, and that they must employ lay officials not only to fight for them (as even Dymmok concedes), but even to pursue justice on their behalf.[27]

Both the sixth conclusion and the argument from Wyclif upon which Dymmok seems to be drawing demonstrate a detailed awareness of the extent to which 'secular' and 'spiritual' powers and personnel interpenetrate one another in fourteenth century England – in company with the impossibly idealistic notion that it might be possible to disentangle them at every level, removing 'curates' from secular offices ranging from the king's council to the judiciary to clerkships on the one hand, and handing over secular tasks involved in church administration to laymen on the other. But whereas the more traditional version of the argument is straightforward in its offer to secular power of an increased sphere of influence that the pope, or the particular order being criticized, would wish to deny, both the Wycliffite version and Dymmok's attempt to counter it are obliged to develop a more nuanced approach. Both want to cast themselves as royalists supportive of the claims of secular power, but both on the other hand also want to criticize some of the practices of secular rule.

Elsewhere, as we have already seen, Dymmok attributes pastoral roles to kings and princes as well as scholastic doctors: he is no less willing than anticlerical polemicists to suggest that figures at the very top of the secular hierarchy, at least, may share spiritual power of a sort with clerics. In his reply to conclusion six, however, Dymmok counters its restriction of clerical roles on pastoral grounds with a new alter-

---

[27] Dymmok's concession that clergy should hire others to fight for them appears on pp. 148–9. Wyclif uses Hugh's *De sacramentis*, 2, II, 3 in *De Ecclesia*, ed. J. Loserth (London, 1886), 316/11–318/26, 378/29–380/5. See also 'Determinacio ad argumenta Wilhelmi Vyrinham' in *Opera Minora*, ed. J. Loserth (London, 1913), 415–30; 422, where Wyclif cites Hugh in arguing that secular lords cannot grant to clergy regal prerogative, secular lordship, or capital dominion; and *De potestate pape*, ed. J. Loserth (London, 1907), 7–21; 8/4–5, where to launch a complex discussion of the nature and sources of secular and spiritual power Wyclif counterposes Hugh's demarcation of the two powers with the observation that 'clerici nostri videntur habere potestatem secularem concessam eis a regibus', 'our clerics would seem to have secular power granted to them by kings'.

native theoretical justification, also based on pastoral grounds, for clerical involvement in secular affairs.

Dymmok suggests that on many occasions curates can best help the souls under their care not by residing in their parishes, but by serving their lord in some temporal capacity, for they will then be able to direct the lord about how best to administer his goods for the good of his subjects:

> nonne talis meritorie ageret licitum ministerium tali domino inpendere ad sui correctionem, et omnium subditorum ipsius domini alleuiacionem et solacium, et malorum exemplorum extinctionem? Immo certe . . . de licencia sui prelati domino certo ministraret sua temporalia bona ministrando, cuius industria dominus suus de multis malis se corrigeret . . . (153/25–9, 20–2)

> May it not be meritorious for some curate licitly to devote his ministry to a lord, for that lord's correction, and the relief and solace of his subjects, and the removal of bad examples? Indeed, certainly . . . with license from his prelate, the curate may assuredly minister to the lord by administering his temporal goods; and by his labour, his lord may correct himself from many evils . . .

This moral and indeed fiscal advisory power will enable curates to curb all manner of abuses: 'puta de extorsionibus falsis, decimacionibus, adulteriis et huiusmodi, quorum exemplum pestiferum patriam infecerat uniuersam', 'as for example false extortions, tithes, adulteries, and suchlike, the pestiferous example of which infects the whole country' (153/22–5). By transferring the accepted method by which clerics offer spiritual guidance into the secular sphere, Dymmok offers a new sort of justification for clerical activities that most at best try to ignore; one that bolsters the moral authority of clerics over the lords they serve and dignifies the kind of service they offer. Far from there being a need for nobility and gentry to ensure that the clergy carry out their pastoral role, the work clerics are doing in the secular sphere is already a kind of pastoral work that ensures that lords fulfil their secular role.

But Dymmok does not simply want to suggest, in counterposition to the Lollards, that clerics should take over or at the very least supervise secular governance: that would be no way to persuade a secular audience.

Instead, he goes on to propose an ethical ideal for both gentry and clerics. While he unsurprisingly makes no attempt to rehabilitate the term 'hermafodrita', Dymmok redefines its companion epithet 'ambidexter' into an ideal to be aspired to by any holder of 'pastoral office', gentry or cleric:

Debet igitur mens hominis non esse mollis, ad modum cere mutabilis ad cuiuslibet sigilli inpressionem, set dura, quasi adamas inflexibilis et totam fortunam mundi in sui conuertere qualitatem, et sic uere fortis esset eo quod aduersa sicud et prospera equanimiter portaret, nec ex illis deiectus, nec ex aliis elatus, et talis solus maxime dignus esset pastorali officio insigniri eo quod uerisimile est talem nec auaricia nimia uel ambicione laxatum prosequi mundialem fauorem, nec ex alio latere propter metum mortis uelle gregem deserere, uel recedere a iusticie rigore, de quibus dicit Christus (Iohannis x) 'Pastor bonus animam suam ponit pro ouibus suis, set mercenarius fugit, si uiderit uenientem lupum, quia mercenarius est et non pertinet ad eum de ouibus.' (156/20–34; punctuation modified)

Therefore a man's mind should not be soft and changeable as is wax at the imprint of any seal, but hard, inflexible as adamant, able to convert any worldly fortune to its own quality, and in this way truly strong, so that it may bear both adversity and prosperity with equanimity, neither dejected by one nor elated by the other. Only a man of this sort is most worthy to be marked out for pastoral office, because it is unlikely that such a one, made slack by excessive avarice or ambition, will seek worldly favour, or on the other hand that he will wish to desert his flock for fear of death, or depart from the full rigour of justice. Christ speaks of such men in John 10: 'The good shepherd lays down his life for his sheep, but the hireling flees if he sees a wolf coming, because he is a hireling, and the sheep do not belong to him.'

The ideal Dymmok holds up here is typical – up until its fifth line, at least – of the sort of Boethian advice offered in courtly literature in the exemplary fall-of-princes mode. As always, the advice about fortitude in the face of changing fortunes this sort of writing offers is meant at least as much for those in service to royalty and subject to its whims as it is meant for the king or prince subject to changes of fortune. But not content merely to desanctify the ambidextrous ideal he has set up so as to extend it to laymen as well as clerics, Dymmok goes on, quoting the passage from John 10 most frequently used in describing the ideal of pastoral service by clerics, to dignify all those who embody the ambidextrous ideal as being worthy of an office designated as pastoral: 'talis solus maxime dignus esset pastorali officio insigniri'. By the end of his arguments for why clerics should hold secular office, Dymmok has dignified as pastoral and endowed with moral authority not only the secular activities of clerics, but even those of knights and gentry.

Where Dymmok assumes the pastoral role for clerics who hold secular office that he defends in conclusion six and attempts to cast himself as a pastoral advisor to the king, it is rather more difficult for him to stake out common ground with the gentry. Both in his reply to the corollary to conclusion ten and in his reply to conclusion twelve (260–71, 292–304), Dymmok slips from a more generally focused discussion, applicable to nobility and gentry as well as the king, to a defence of regal magnificence by reference to the example of Solomon. Kings who tax heavily and spend lavishly on external display, as Solomon did, impress neighbouring kings into maintaining peaceful relations, and intimidate their subjects into obedient compliance. The special appeal of these arguments for Richard II, never much of a fighter but a lover of magnificent display, is obvious: equally obvious is that not only Dymmok's shift to discussing the king alone, but especially the kinds of regal behaviour he approves in these passages, might badly damage any wider appeal.

Still, although it has been argued that Dymmok's defence of magnificence wholeheartedly endorses Richard's policies, or as Eberle puts it, is a 'sympathetic presentation of Richard's own point of view', it must be noted that along with upholding the king's entitlement to heavy taxation and the ostentatious display of wealth, Dymmok also holds himself up as an advisor to the king by including, in however muted and cautious a fashion, recommendations about the limits that even kings ought to observe.[28] Might the qualifications to Dymmok's approbation also salvage his wider appeal?

[28] P. J. Eberle, 'The Politics of Courtly Style at the Court of Richard II', in G. S. Burgess *et al.*, eds., *The Spirit of the Court* (Dover, NH, 1985), 168–78; 173.

Directly after the defence of regal magnificence in conclusion twelve which follows his more general argument that need is commensurate with status rather than absolute, Dymmok devotes a chapter to five abuses of clothing. Included among them is his only other reference to *mollicia*, the vice that his ethical ideal of pastorship in his reply to conclusion six had pointedly excluded. Even if Dymmok attributes this list of five abuses to Aquinas and interleaves them with repeated reassurances that it is always proper to make use of the clothing commensurate with one's status, the terms in which these abuses are described have acquired a new polemic volatility in late medieval England. The reassurances Dymmok interposes before and after Aquinas's description of two defects of proper attention to clothing cannot neutralize Aquinas's examples:

> Cum quibus omnibus stat quantumcunque solempnis apparatus uestium conueniens statui hominis debitis circumstanciis usitatus absque peccato. *Alio modo ex parte defectus potest esse duplex deordinacio secundum affectum; uno modo ex necligencia hominis, qui non adhibet studium uel diligenciam ad hoc, quod exteriori cultu utatur, sicud oportet. Unde dicit Philosphus (VII Etichorum) quod ad molliciem pertinet, quod aliquis trahat uestimentum per terram, ut non laboret eleuando ipsum; alio modo, secundum quod defectum ipsum uestium ordinat ad gloriam. Unde Augustinus (in libro De Sermone Domini in Monte) dicit: 'Non solum in rerum corporearum nitore atque pompa, set eciam in ipsis sordibus luctuosis esse posse iactanciam, et eo periculosiorem, quo sub nomine seruitutis Dei decidit;' et Philosophus dicit (X Etichorum), quod superabundancia inordinatus defectus ad iactanciam pertinet. Et* sicud homines se possunt licite secundum sui status congruenciam ornare sumptuose et artificiose, ita artifices talium ornamentorum licite possunt suas artes exercere, et tales artifices non sunt destruendi set permittendi et fouendi, ut necessarii coadiutores hominum in conuersacione eorum politica et ciuili.[29] (296/24–297/9)

With all of this it remains consistent that a show of clothing, if fitting to the status of a man and used in the appropriate circumstances, however solemn it may be, can be used without sin. 'In another way,

---

[29] My italics: Cronin, who uses italics to demarcate Dymmok's quotations from authorities from Dymmok's own commentary and exposition, does not notice the resumption of quotation from Aquinas here.

on the side of lack or defect, there can be a disorder of affect in two ways. In one way from the negligence of a man who does not give proper attention or diligence to his attire. And thus the Philosopher says (*Nicomachean Ethics*, book 7) that it pertains to softness, that someone drags his clothing on the ground to avoid the labour of lifting it. In another way, as that defect of clothing is ordered toward vainglory. And thus Augustine (in his book about the Sermon of our Lord on the Mount) says "Not only in the elegance and pomp of bodily things, but also in those that are sordid and muddy, there can be boastfulness, and the second is more dangerous in that it goes by the name of service to God", and the Philosopher says (*Nicomachean Ethics*, book 10) the overabundance of a lack is a kind of boastfulness.' And just as men can licitly ornament themselves sumptuously and with artifice, in a manner fitting to their status, so the artificers of such ornaments may licitly exercise their artistry; and such artificers are not to be abolished, but permitted and even cherished, as necessary to men's political and civil life.

From the mid 1380s onward in England the most frequent referents for the second abuse of boastful insufficiency are the Lollards: Dymmok himself elsewhere comments on the Lollards' 'apparenciam humilitatis . . . in uestimentorum deiectione', 'appearance of humility . . . in the lowliness of their clothing (307/12–14).[30] But *mollicia*, and its association with the dragging of clothing, were in late medieval England acquiring a new set of associations in court satire. These associations are perhaps rather less compatible with Dymmok's supposedly wholehearted approval of unlimited regal magnificence – and even with his attempts at wider appeal.

Aquinas himself in his commentary on the passage from the *Ethics* that he cites in describing the first abuse commented that dragging one's clothing creates as much work as it saves: 'Et licet imitetur laborantem in hoc quod vestimenta trahit, et per hoc videtur non esse miser, habet tamen similitudinem cum misero inquantum fugiens laborem sustinet laborem', 'And although he acts like a laborer in that he drags his clothing, and in this he seems not to be wretched, he

---

[30] See the discussion of the surrounding passage on pp. 131–2. See Hudson, *Premature Reformation*, 145–7, for various other discussions of clothing by Lollards and their opponents, and W. Scase, *'Piers Plowman' and the New Anticlericalism*, 168 n. 18 for the wider tradition in antifraternal satire and criticism of beguines.

nonetheless resembles the wretch in that while fleeing labour he undergoes it.'[31] Late medieval English court satiric examples similarly focus on the misdirection of effort that dragging one's clothing betokens, even if they generally associate this misdirection with excessive rather than defective concern. *Richard the Redeles*, for example, describes courtiers' preoccupation with the design of their clothing in these terms:[32]

> And, but if the slevis slide on the erthe,
> Thei woll be wroth as the wynde and warie hem that it made;
> And [but] yif it were elbowis adoun to the helis
> Or passinge the knee it was not acounted.
> (III, 153–6)

And Hoccleve in his *Regement of Princes* suggests that the dragging sleeves require so much effort that courtiers who sport them cannot defend their lord as they ought.[33] The implication is the same later in *Richard the Redeles*, when 'the sleeves' say 'Let sle him', '*have* him slain', but then rather than carrying out the action they have urged, merely mock Wisdom's clothing – though this may be a fate worse than death in their view.[34] If, as seems likely, the association of *mollicia* with dragging clothing (as here in Dymmok's reply to conclusion twelve) and unworthy service to one's lord (as in Dymmok's reply to conclusion six) already in the 1390s evokes the sort of early fifteenth century court satire in which these associations are combined, then Dymmok's quotation of Aquinas imports a rather more critical attitude to Richard's household: it is significant too that Dymmok omits from his description of Solomon's household in the previous chapter any mention of the detailed description in III Kings 10:5 of the possessions and clothing of Solomon's household as well as Solomon himself. While

---

[31] Thomas Aquinas, *S. Tho super Ethica Sancti doctoris Thome de aquino in decem libros ethicorum Aristotelis profundissima commentatio cum triplici textus translatione antiqua videlicet Leonardi aretini nec non J. argyropili* (Venice, 1563), f. 124v iF–iiG; iiF; abbreviations silently expanded. In the standard modern reference, the passage under discussion is *Nicomachean Ethics* 1150b, book 7, chapter 7.

[32] Quoted from the edition of the text in H. Barr, ed., *The Piers Plowman Tradition* (London, 1993), 101–33; 121–2.

[33] See T. Hoccleve, *Regement of Princes*, ed. F. J. Furnivall (London, 1897), lines 463–9, and also 421–7, 533–6.

[34] See *Richard the Redeles*, III, 234–8, p. 125.

Dymmok's muted criticism might, like later satire against courtiers, appeal to a wider gentry audience, it is not clear whether those within the king's household, or aspiring to enter it, would be equally appreciative.

If this example of Dymmok's criticisms of the king and court's expenditure is circumspect even to the point of nonexistence, then within Dymmok's defence of taxation in part ten there is a much more overt example, however strongly undercut by Dymmok's subsequent blaming of women, and however couched in quotation from authorities. In the midst of his defence of taxation and expenditure by the king especially for defence of the country, but equally as appropriately for the display of his majesty, Dymmok mentions the possibility of abuse:

> Set cum secundum Philosophum (in *Politicis*) regem oporteat copiam habere diuiciarum et possessionum ad sui et suorum defensionem, cauere summo opere debent reges et domini temporales, ne bona sua indiscrete consumant in expensis excessiuis aut suas possessiones notabiliter diminuant eas aliis indebite conferendo et sic semetipsos impotentes efficiant maliciis aduersariorum resistere aut honorem regium in necessariis sumptibus conseruare, ne populum sibi subiectum in sui defectum in taxis et aliis exactionibus onerosis compellantur, plusquam necesse fuerit, onerare. In cuius rei euidenciam (Deut. xvii) mandauit Dominus regibus uniuersis, ut haberent tam in expensis et sumptuosis negociis, quam in exactionibus in populo faciendis, moderamen debitum et mensuram, dicens: 'Cum rex fuerit constitutus, non multiplicabit sibi equos, ne reducat populum in Egiptum', id est, pristinam Egipciacam seruitutem, 'equitatus numero subleuatus; non habebit uxores plurimas, que illicitant animam eius, neque argenti et auri immensa pondera', scilicet a populo suo talia exigendo. Cui precepto rex Salomon contraueniendo secundum Magistrum in Historiis diuinam incurrit offensam et sui regni demeruit diuisionem et scissuram perpetuis temporibus duraturam. (264/3–27)

> But since according to the Philosopher (in the *Politics*) the king should have an ample store of riches and possessions in order to defend himself and his realm, kings and temporal lords should take great care, lest they should indiscreetly consume their goods through excessive expenditure, or significantly diminish their possessions through unduly bestowing them on others, and in this way render

themselves incapable of resisting the malice of their enemies or maintaining their regal honour with regard to necessary expenditures; and lest they should be compelled to make up the lack by burdening the people subject to them with taxes and other onerous exactions more than is necessary. As evidence of this, the Lord (Deut. 17) ordered all kings to maintain, both in expenditures and in exactions from the people, the proper moderation and measure, saying, 'when he is made king, he shall not increase the number of his horses, nor lead back the people into Egypt' – that is, their former Egyptian servitude – 'he shall not increase the number of his knights, nor have many wives, who would lead him into licentiousness, nor an immense weight of gold and silver'. – requiring these things from his people, that is. According to the Master of Histories [Peter Comestor], king Solomon by contravening these precepts incurred divine anger and brought upon his realm everlasting divisions and factions.

The statement Dymmok attributes to the 'Magistrum in Historiis' here makes explicit a danger in Dymmok's defence of Richard as a type of Solomon, latent in his replies to conclusions ten and twelve. Even if after coming to the throne in his youth Solomon ruled for a time with exemplary wisdom, so that the comparison might flatter Richard II, Solomon later became what Richard is in 1395 coming to resemble all too closely, a tyrant. The implication of the cautious and authority-hedged limitations suggested here is that Solomon's tyranny was linked to his taxation and expenditure. When we consider how frequent complaints about excessive taxation and irresponsible expenditure were throughout Richard's reign, Dymmok's argument seems perilously strong. Even Dymmok's protests two chapters later that Solomon degenerated into tyranny not because he exacted huge taxes, but because he took foreign wives, may not do much to soften his implied criticism: while Dymmok might not yet have known it, Richard was soon to cement a controversial treaty with France by means of a marriage with Isabella of France. Dymmok may have done a better job of reconciling his advisorial pose with his efforts to appeal to an audience of nobility and gentry here, but he has also put himself at a greater risk that his advice will offend the king.

If we accept what circumstantial and internal evidence suggest, that addressing a court audience is at least part of Dymmok's concern, then could his book have shown even this more restricted audience what he promises in his address to the king to show everyone? If the lowest common denominator Dymmok aims for is not an average villager but a regionally influential member of the gentry resident at court, then how does the content of his book measure up to the project of convincing his public that the Lollard document is dangerous and contains no valid arguments?

In massively expanding each Lollard conclusion into a set of three to ten opposing conclusions, Dymmok makes plenty of room for showing the dangers of the Lollard document as well as the invalidity of its arguments. Along with presenting the manner of its publication as a usurpation upon the proper domain of public persons, Dymmok builds up a frightening picture of the implications that might logically, or else through 'vulgar understanding', be adduced from Lollard beliefs. He sums them up here:

> isti se fingunt Christi thesaurarios et nuncios et tamen contrarium dicunt et faciunt euangelice ueritati . . . (311/26–8)
> Docent namque mulieres **nulli petenti** ex caritate **negare** corpora sua, que doctrina, si licita credatur, aufert uerecundiam de fornicacione. Asserunt insuper **titulo** caritatis, quemlibet omnia temporalia possidere, quod si uerum sit, ad intellectum uulgarem populi quilibet posset bona cuiuscunque sibi assumere, et tunc nullus de furto uerecundaretur, cum nullus homo nisi propria accipere posset. Dicunt insuper nullum peccato mortali innodatum aliquid **iusto titulo possidere**, ex qua doctrina nichil aliud restat, nisi ut quilibet contra alium peccatum mortale obiciat, et eius bona auferat per uiolenciam, si eo sit forcior, et sic rapina ducetur in consuetudinem et putabitur satis licite exerceri, et sic suis peruersis doctrinis licenciam tribuunt, uiciis uirtutibus conculcatis. (311/36–312/13; my emphases)

> These pretend to be treasurers and messengers of Christ, but speak and do the opposite of gospel truth . . .
> For they teach women for the sake of charity to deny their bodies to no petitioner; which teaching, were it believed licit, would remove the shame from fornication. They assert, moreover, that each person possesses all temporal goods by title of charity. If this were true, then according to the vulgar understanding of the people anyone could take for himself the goods of anyone, and no one would be ashamed of theft, since no man could take what was not his own. They say, furthermore, that no one snared in mortal sin can possess anything

by just title. From this teaching it would come about that anyone might accuse another of mortal sin and take his goods by violence, if he were stronger than him; and thus seizure would become customary and be thought licit. Thus their perverse teachings give licence that vices should tread virtues underfoot.

Through an echo of their initial self-description as 'tresoreris of Cryst', through quasi-legal terminology, Dymmok hints once again at the presumption of the Lollards' manner of publication. But in addition, here he moves furthest from the meticulous if fastidious quotation of what the Lollards have actually written that characterizes his refutations.[35] In tarring the Lollards with the brush of the *reductiones* he has drawn out from their views, he produces three conclusions guaranteed to horrify anyone threatened by the 'vulgar understanding', the *intellectum vulgarem*, he mentions.

While any property owner will see the force of Dymmok's assessment of the dangers of the *Twelve Conclusions*, however, how many of his audience will be able to assess his arguments and judge whether they are better than those the Lollards supply? In his initial promise, as we saw, Dymmok places the burden of sufficient explanation squarely upon his own shoulders: he commits himself to using 'talia [argumenta] que intelligi ualent ab *omnibus* . . . ut ex eo pateat *uniuersis* quam periculosum fuerit eorum documentum et quod nullum protulerunt pro sua assercione ualidum argumentum'. He attributes to *everyone* the capacity to give an informed assent to his side of the case, and what is more, he represents that capacity here as an academic one: it is specifically the superiority of his arguments that his universal audience is expected to recognize. We have already noted that in

---

[35] There is no basis in the *Twelve Conclusions* for any of Dymmok's three conclusions here. The first is a misrepresentation of the claim found in conclusion eleven, that religious women should not be permitted to take vows of continence; but the reader will note that the eleventh conclusion nowhere approves fornication in place of vows of continence; indeed, it recommends marriage for widows. The second converts to a general claim and attributes to the writers of the *Conclusions* a frequent scholastic contention arising in controversies over poverty, that there was no individual proprietary possession in the state of innocence: in fact the writers have made no such claim. The third pretends the writers of the *Conclusions* have stated a garbled version of Fitzralph's or Wyclif's arguments on dominion, whereas the closest they have come is to criticize the church in England and the priesthood in conclusions one and two.

practice Dymmok denies the *simplices* the capacity to make an informed judgement. But the boundaries of this group are not clear. Will only kings, princes, and doctors be allowed to weigh Dymmok's arguments? Or at the other extreme, will only those for whom the *intellectum vulgarem* of Dymmok's *reductiones* is attractive be excluded?

Since none of his other works are extant it is impossible to determine whether Dymmok has, as he claims, written in a more straightforward style than usual. But he does seem to have made some effort to pitch his text to a nonacademic audience. He anticipates the need to explain more fully than usual argumentational techniques and concepts from grammar, logic, biblical interpretation, and natural science.[36] He makes use of the conventions of academic genres such as the determination, lecture, and disputation, proceeding by demonstrative argument and embedding arguments staged in dialogue form[37] and discussions in *quaestio* form[38] in his prose, but he is more clear about his procedure than scholastic treatises often are: he spells out what he is doing step by step rather than using the scholarly abbreviations and 'therefore etc's frequently found in university lecture notes or records of disputations.[39] Though on many occasions he loads his prose down with the machinery of argumentation, typically such machinery is

---

[36] One example of each for the reader to consult, though there are many more of each sort: 54/7–9, 30/15–16, 48/8–10, 147/5–11, 98/32–99/3.

[37] See the reply to the Lollard's question posed to a posited pilgrim (195/18–30); and for a lengthier exchange, Dymmok's demonstration of how Behemoth attempts to tempt people (273/28–274/30).

[38] Chapter four of the seventh part is in *quaestio* form, built around a passage from Aquinas which reconciles two views (167–9).

[39] For example, Maidstone's *Determinacio*, dated by Edden to between 1384 and 1392 and probably before 1390, and produced solely for a clerical audience in opposition to Ashwardby's sermons given before mixed audiences, contains this rather obscure passage: 'Et ideo ad argumentum. Cum arguitur: doctor ille dicit sic, ergo sic est; dicitur negando contrariam', 'And so to the argument. When it is argued "that doctor says so, therefore it is so", it is said by denying the contrary'; or to amplify, 'And so, let us move on to consider our adversary's argument. Where he argues "that doctor says so, therefore it is so", we can show that the argument is false by denying that its contrary [that doctor says not, therefore it is not so] is true' (V. Edden, 'The Debate Between Maidstone and Ashwardby', *Carmelus* 34 (1987), 113–34; 121/1–2; see pp. 114–15 on the dating). Maidstone's argument is not ill-formed, but it does in places employ a cryptic academic shorthand characteristic of university-produced prose.

nonfunctional, intended for display, and his meaning readily apparent despite it.[40]

Still, the methods Dymmok uses to make his text accessible reveal other motives than comprehensibility. Other motives are particularly conspicuous where he uses that hallowed technique of lay instruction, the analogy. In replying to conclusion five, for example, when explaining how material things gain supernatural power without being altered in any way apparent to the senses, Dymmok makes an analogy to how a mayor, or similarly a temporal or spiritual lord, acquires a new power of governing without sensing any change in himself:

> sicud maior ciuitatis nullam sensibilem mutacionem in se sentit nec habet, quam prius non habuit, et tamen potestatem habet nouiter sibi commissam uirtute officii a rege totam ciuitatem gubernandi et nociua illi ciuitati compescendi. Similiter, cum homo de nouo adquirit dominium uel dignitatem siue temporalem, ut regiam dignitatem, siue spiritualem, ut papatum uel episcopatum, nulla in eo fit mutacio sensibilis, et tamen uirtutem magnam spiritualem recipit, quam prius non habuit, ex diuina ordinacione ad talem populum gubernandum, et populus a Deo inclinacionem accipit, ut eidem obediat et ipsum timeat ceteraque faciat ad eius imperium, que suo regimini conueniunt. (128/18–30)

> just as when he takes office the mayor of a city neither feels nor undergoes any sensible change, but nonetheless has a power for governing the whole city and preventing harm to it newly committed to him in virtue of his office by the king. Similarly, when a man newly acquires lordship or honour or temporal possessions, as for example regal dignity, or spiritual dignity (such as the papacy or an episcopate), no sensible change is made in him, but nonetheless he receives by divine ordination a great spiritual power that he did not have before for governing that people, and the people are inclined by God to obey him and fear him and do whatever else befits his reign.

What is startling about Dymmok's analogy is that it advances his theory of governance so boldly and, as it were, offhandedly. Contrary to the writers of the *Twelve Conclusions*' implicit theory that all power is held directly from God, Dymmok here claims that all offices below those of king and pope or bishop are held through those authorities

---

[40] See, for example, the passage quoted in the middle of p. 131, or 274/35–275/29.

rather than directly. Furthermore, unlike the more usual sort of royalist argument, here Dymmok attributes divinely ordained and popularly accepted regal power not only to the king, but to the pope and his bishops as well.[41]

Some of Dymmok's analogies, too, show quite clearly the sort of audience for whom he hopes to elucidate his point. When he compares the case of a corrupt order which, he argues, ought not to be disendowed but instead reformed, with a case where the laws of inheritance would dictate that a traitor's lands should be kept for his son, the special appeal to landowners is blatant, especially in the late 1390s when Richard's attempts to take to himself the inheritance of traitors' lands were highly controversial (176/17–25).[42] Similarly, where Dymmok likens the behaviour of pilgrims with the outward signs of secular love, it seems obvious that he hopes to appeal to the sort of audience that is familiar with courtly love poetry (193/18–32).

Still, even if these analogies carry heavy ideological freight, not all Dymmok's analogies are as helpful; some seem deliberately intimidating. In countering conclusion two, for example, where the Lollards began to use scholastic terminology in earnest, Dymmok deploys prolonged disgressions on logic and natural science in which, as in the examples just examined, the material has little or nothing to do with the matter at hand beyond the analogy it offers.[43] Unlike the previous examples, however, here Dymmok chooses not familiar examples that illuminate the concept to be explained, but unfamiliar and probably daunting material. In this case he seems more concerned with showing

---

[41] Paul Strohm explores the ideological implications of another of Dymmok's explanations of imperceptible change: see P. Strohm, 'Chaucer's Lollard Joke', 40–1.

[42] On the development of penalties of forfeiture for treason see J. G. Bellamy, *The Law of Treason in England in the Later Middle Ages* (Cambridge, 1970), *passim*. C. D. Ross suggests that Richard's attempts in 1397 to impose the strictest possible penalties of forfeiture on traitors, even disinheriting their heirs, were one important cause of his deposition (in 'Forfeiture for Treason in the Reign of Richard II', *English Historical Review* 71 (1956), 560–75).

[43] See especially 54/11–32, 57/34–58/4, 58/11–30; Dymmok uses analogies to the hierarchy of powers in the human soul and to the 'propagation of species' which was thought to be involved in vision (for a lucid introduction to which see K. H. Tachau, *Vision and Certitude in the Age of Ockham: Optics, Epistemology, and the Foundations of Semantics, 1250–1345* (Leiden, 1988)) in order to justify his assertion that priests accept from Christ a higher power than that of the angels.

that he knows more than the Lollards than making sure his readers understand why his argument is better.

But this temporary lapse into obscurantism is not as telling an index to the authenticity of Dymmok's desire to submit his arguments for public judgement as are the final few pages of his text, where he returns to his initial promise and devotes his full attention to explaining how his audience should be able to distinguish the Lollards' semblance of holiness from the authentic sanctity of legitimate preachers and teachers. As Dymmok has been emphasizing from the beginning, not everyone has the information and abilities they would need to tell a good argument from a bad one; here it finally becomes clear just who it is that he views as irremediably incapable of informed judgement. Dymmok exhorts all the faithful not to believe the Lollards, giving the specious impression that he has reached a logical conclusion by introducing his recommendation with a logical formula:

> Igitur a multo forciori, nullus fidelis debet eis prebere **assensum**, cum **constat** eos directissime **contraria** sentire euangelice **ueritati** et nullum **signum** ostendunt in sue **assercionis euidenciam**, nec in uita aut in moribus sanctorum **congruunt** disciplinis. (307/7–12; my emphases)

> Therefore, all the more ought no faithful man to offer them assent, since it has been established that their meaning is most directly contrary to gospel truth, and that they show no evidence for their assertion, nor do their teachings correspond to the life and mores of the saints.

The impression that the skill required will be clergial and the decision based on academic criteria is intensified by the density of terminology of argument packed into this directive: one might think Dymmok was telling his readers how to test whether a proposition is well formed. But as the more specific condemnation that immediately follows reveals, the process of discrimination is not so clear cut:

> Nichil amplius habent, nisi quandam apparenciam humilitatis in gestu, in capitis demissione, in uestimentorum deiectione et ieiunii simulacione, simplicitatem pretendunt in uerbis, caritate Dei et proximi se feruere affirmant, cuius feruore excitati se continere non posse pretendunt a doctrina pestifera prius dicta, dicentes se non timere quantumcunque mundi aduersa aut mortem subire, si oporteat, pro defensione sui erroris. (307/12–19)

They have nothing more than a kind of appearance of humility in their demeanour, their lowly clothing, and their simulated fasting. They pretend simplicity in their words, they affirm fervently that they live in charity as regards God and their neighbours. Excited by that charity, they pretend they cannot contain themselves from the pestiferous teaching mentioned before; they say that they do not fear to undergo however much worldly adversity or even death, if it should be necessary, in defense of their error.

The problem is that every aspect of the *appearance* Dymmok describes is associated with the outward aspect of Christian virtue as much as with hypocrisy. If the Lollards are hypocrites as accomplished as he claims, if every aspect of their *appearance* is good, then Dymmok can offer no experiential proof that this appearance is a false front, and no method by which his readers can tell the difference.

Dymmok tries to suggest that the difficulty of telling whether someone follows Christ is the same as that of telling an ape from a man:

> Simia quidem omnia membra hominis habet et per omnia hominem imitatur – Numquid propterea dicendus est homo? Sic eciam heresis omnia misteria ecclesie habet et imitatur, set non sunt ecclesie . . . (308/4–7)

> An ape has all the members of a man, and imitates a man in all things. Should it on that account be called a man? So too heretics have and imitate all the mysteries of the church. But they do not belong to the church.

Then Dymmok swings to the opposite extreme, to warn that careful attention is required:

> Non dixit 'aspicite' set 'attendite;' 'aspicere' enim est simpliciter uidere, 'attendere' autem est caute considerare, ubi enim certa est et indubitabilis, aspicitur, ubi incerta et dubitabilis, attenditur. Quia igitur in illis aliud pro alio uidetur, aliud desuper positum, aliud intus inclusum, ideo dixit 'attendite,' ut scias, quia non corporali aspectu attendendum est set uigilancia spirituali. Attendendum igitur est per opera bona. (308/8–15)

> He did not say 'look' but 'attend'; for 'look' means simply to see, but 'attend' means to consider carefully. Where something is certain and not subject to doubt, one looks at it; where it is uncertain and doubtful, one attends to it. Because therefore in these matters one

thing seems like something else, one obvious and the other concealed, therefore he said 'attend', so that you would know; because one does not attend by means of corporeal looking, but by spiritual vigilance. One should attend, therefore, through good works.

Even at this point the mental effort required for discerning good from apparent good seems within any conscientious person's capacity, and if the project of maintaining spiritual vigilance were a bit hazy, the explanation that one 'attends' by doing good works gives a concrete recommendation. But in what follows it turns out that the judgement upon the reader's powers of discernment and his probity is to be made in reverse order, and retrospectively:

> Ipsa res facit errare, que facit alterius errorem non cognoscere; qui autem non cognoscit mendacium alterius, non cognoscit eius ueritatem. Sicud, quamdiu facimus opera bona, ipsum lumen iusticie ante oculos nostros adaperit ueritatem, sic et peccata peccancium sensus tenebrescere faciunt, ut non uidentes mendacium cadant in illud. (308/15–21)

> This same thing makes him err, which causes him not to recogize another's error. In the same way that as long as we do good works, the light of justice before our eyes adapts itself to truth, so also the sins of sinners make that sense become dark, so that not seeing the lie, they fall into it.

Not only must Dymmok's readers do good in order to discern apparent from authentic good. If they disagree with Dymmok, then that shows not that he might be wrong, but that they have erred; and, further, that they were not doing good after all. For they could only have made their mistake because they were sinners already: 'non possunt errores preualere in homines, nisi precesserint peccata, prius enim peccatis plurimis excecatur homo, et sic diaboli seductione cadit in errorem', 'errors cannot prevail in men unless sins have gone before them, for first many sins blind a man, and thus by diabolic seduction he falls into error' (308/24–7).

Dymmok shifts the boundary between pastors and *simplices* as it suits his need to exact assent: even if gentry and clerics alike are dignified as pastors in his reply to conclusion six, only the highest public persons qualify as pastors when he addresses 'unusquisque in gradu suo', and in the end only those who agree with him count as undeceived. It is clear that he has little interest in exposing himself to any broader public judgement. That his text promises to do so in its preface and conclusion despite the way this gesture toward wider audience cuts against the grain of his own disapproval of illicit publicity, shows how useful the gesture can be – however empty it may be – in establishing any writer's status as a 'public person'.

5

The *Upland Series* and the invention of invective, 1350–1410

The *Upland Series* is an extended series of textual interventions upon a set of antifraternal questions, posed and counterposed over the course of the time period on which this book focuses and advertising that period's shifting and sharpening concerns. The rather surprising neglect of these texts can partly be blamed on the editor of *Jack Upland, Friar Daw's Reply, and Upland's Rejoinder*, P. L. Heyworth.[1] Heyworth dismissively presents the *Upland Series* as three not-very-competently executed literary texts from which corruption and interpolation must be cleared away and upon which some semblance of style and grammar must be imposed; he was unaware of the full extent of the series, and unwilling to grant participating status even to all the components he knew of. Further, Heyworth rather controversially assigned the texts he did consider to an oddly late range of dates: he places *Friar Daw's Reply* in late 1419–early 1420, *Jack Upland* not long before, and *Upland's Rejoinder* around 1450. Although everything in this chapter will support it, I reserve for an appendix my detailed

---

[1] *Jack Upland, Friar Daw's Reply, and Upland's Rejoinder*, ed. P. L. Heyworth (Oxford, 1968). The same three texts have subsequently been published again in J. M. Dean, ed., *Six Ecclesiastical Satires* (Kalamazoo, MI, 1991), 115–226; Dean largely relies on Heyworth's edition, though he restores many of Heyworth's less convincing emendations and line reorderings. Although Dean's edition is useful as an inexpensive, readily available student text, it cannot be used without reference to Heyworth: its introductions and notes to the texts sometimes present Heyworth's conclusions in summary form, as the general consensus on the poems, whereas students ought instead to be encouraged to question Heyworth's presentation; and Dean omits altogether the passages from *Upland's Rejoinder* that Heyworth places in his notes. (On Heyworth's omissions see below, n. 3). The *Upland Series* deserves a new critical edition in which all the texts in the series might be included in full, thoroughly reconsidered, and provided with a full introduction and much more extensive notes.

rebuttal of Heyworth's datings and presentation of my alternative suggestion that all four of the texts *Jack Upland*, William Woodford's *Responsiones*, *Friar Daw's Reply*, and *Upland's Rejoinder* may be dated between 1382 and 1410, and that very probably Woodford's *Responsiones* were written in 1395, *Friar Daw* after 1388, and *Upland's Rejoinder* soon after 1402. I begin here by expanding the series to include the parts of the textual record Heyworth did not know, and also the parts he relegates, as 'the work of an interpolator', to his notes.

Jack Upland (*JU*) poses a long series of questions probing every aspect of fraternal behaviour, and pointing out every embarrassing difference between fraternal profession and fraternal practice: he takes up, for example, the oddity of fraternal regulations about the wearing of the habit, the discrepancies between the friars' requests for alms and their possessions and between what charity would seem to require and what methods of raising money the friars use, and finally the slanderous accusations friars make against those who profess the truth about the Eucharist, when in fact it is friars whose Eucharistic beliefs are heretical. The five extant copies of *Jack Upland* reveal that the questions were available in a number of versions from the late fourteenth century to the 1530s: there are two late medieval manuscript copies, one in Latin (*JU*1a) and one in English (*JU*2a); and three early sixteenth century copies in English, two copies of a version printed in 1536 (*JU*1b), and one in an early sixteenth century Lollard manuscript (*JU*2b).[2]

---

[2] *JU*1a, a Latin version of the questions preserved in a response to them by William Woodford (on whom see the next paragraph of text and n. 4), appears in Oxford, Bodleian Library, Bodley 703, ff. 41–57. We need not assume that both Latin and English versions of *JU*1 were extant before Woodford wrote: Woodford might have translated an English text. *JU*1a was apparently unknown to Heyworth; along with Woodford's response it was edited by Eric Doyle as part of his dissertation in 1964, and published as E. Doyle, O.F.M., 'William Woodford, O.F.M. (c. 1330–c. 1400): His Life and Works, Together with a Study and Edition of his "Responsiones Contra Wiclevum et Lollardos"', *Franciscan Studies* 43 (1983), 17–187 (hereafter *Responsiones*). The *Responsiones* and Doyle's edition are mentioned in J. I. Catto's much-cited thesis *William Woodford O. F. M. (c. 1330–c. 1397)*, (unpublished D. Phil. thesis, University of Oxford, 1969), 31–2, 305, 311. *JU*1b, an English version printed in 1536, is close to the version in Woodford in both content and order of material, with the exceptions that the final question on the Eucharist is missing in *JU*1b and that *JU*1a lacks any introductory or concluding material for the questions. Heyworth consulted *JU*1b but for the most part discounted it as a later adaptation; he describes and dates the two copies in San Marino, Huntingdon Library (STC 5098) and in Cambridge, Gonville

Short responses are appended to the manuscript copies of *JU*2a and *JU*2b.[3]

A full scale systematic reply to the questions of *JU*1a was given in Latin scholastic prose by William Woodford, a Franciscan friar based first at Oxford then after 1390 in London, and who was one of Wyclif's most prominent and prolific early opponents.[4] Marginal comments in the single manuscript of Woodford's *Responsiones* show readers' points of interest.[5] A writer who calls himself Friar Daw (though the colophon for his reply labels him John Walsingham) replies rather more selectively than Woodford to what seems to have been a version of *JU*2, using English alliterative verse into which a number of Latin quotations are incorporated.[6] Into the margins of the single manuscript copy of

and Caius College Library (used by W. W. Skeat for his edition in *Chaucerian and Other Pieces* (Oxford, 1897), 191–203) in 'The Earliest Black-Letter Editions of *Jack Upland*', *Huntingdon Library Quarterly* 30 (1967) 307–14. The *JU*2 copies have different introductory and concluding material than *JU*1 (though some material is shared) and differ slightly in wording and emphasis throughout: *JU*1 tends to focus on Franciscan friars, typically as representatives of friars in general, while *JU*2 takes a broader view, on occasion targeting the church hierarchy as a whole. *JU*2a (English) appears in London, British Library, Harley 6641, and was Heyworth's base text for *Jack Upland*. *JU*2b (English) was copied in the early sixteenth century together with the Lollard sermon *Omnis plantacio* and a version of the Lollard *Epistola Sathanae ad cleros,* and is now Cambridge University Library Ff.6.2, ff. 71–80. *JU*2b poses the same questions as *JU*2a apart from some minor differences in wording, and was collated by Heyworth for his edition. Anne Hudson has compared *JU*1b with *JU*1a as well as Heyworth's edition of JU2ab, concluding that the sixteenth century version is 'substantively a reliable transcript of a lost medieval exemplar' (in ' "No Newe Thyng": The Printing of Medieval Texts in the Early Reformation Period', in *Middle English Studies presented to Norman Davis,* ed. D. Gray and E. G. Stanley (Oxford, 1983), 153–74; reprinted in Hudson, *Lollards and Their Books,* 227–48; 238–40; quotation from 240).

3 Heyworth includes the response to *JU*2a in his textual variants (72, line 411n.), and the response to *JU*2b in his notes (137, line 411n.). Both are quoted below, pp. 153–4.

4 Woodford's *Responsiones* are the only work he wrote against not Wyclif himself, but an opponent he describes as a disciple of Wyclif (see, for example, below, p. 163). A single copy of the *Responsiones* is preserved in a manuscript of Woodford's works formerly held in the library of the Franciscan convent in London, now Oxford, Bodleian Library, Bodley 703, ff. 41–57. In addition to the edition by Doyle and reference by Catto cited in n. 2, see for a brief introduction to Woodford's life and writings Hudson, *The Premature Reformation,* 46–9, and for further information other articles by Doyle cited below, nn. 45, 47.

5 These marginalia are included *passim* in Doyle's edition of the *Responsiones.*

6 *Friar Daw's Reply* (hereafter *FDR*) quotes extensively from the text it answers: several passages quoted are absent in *JU*1b, fewer in *JU*1a, and none in *JU*2ab. The single copy

Friar Daw's Reply (*FDR*) before it was sewn into its present binding was written *Upland's Rejoinder* (*UR*), a reply to some of Daw's answer written in two hands, *UR*1 and *UR*2: this rejoinder like Daw's reply is written in alliterative verse, and it quotes Latin authorities even more copiously than Daw.[7]

Because the composition of the *Upland Series* extends over a span of several years including the turn of the century, the work addresses the transition to Lancastrian rule in a way no other work discussed in this book can. But there are other good reasons than this to look first at the series' brief excursion, in the debate over one of Jack's questions, into the profession of Lancastrian allegiance: the way the *Upland Series* treats this issue illustrates well both how it differs from kinds of Lancastrian writing that have received a good deal of attention recently, and also how it is unique among the extraclergial works this book examines in its attitude to its potential audience and in the character of its commitment to the vernacular.

Henry IV's first parliament of October 1399 legitimates his kingship and founds the Lancastrian succession on Henry's promises to provide just, well-counselled rule in place of Richard's tyranny. Needless to say, these promises went unfulfilled. But they did not sink without a trace. Instead, they left a paper trail, in the years just following, in the writings of aspiring Lancastrian royalists. Self-legitimating, self-authorizing foundational moments grounded in the assertion of Lancastrian kingship proliferate in the wake of October 1399. Would-be-Lancastrian writers held Henry's espoused principles up to him: in so doing they of course flatteringly upheld Henry's position as king, but also their own as his loyal supporters. Like Henry's first parliament, the writings of Henry's would-be-Lancastrian subjects are revisionary, but at the same time careful not to look too closely at what has been left behind. Quietly rewriting an earlier version of a prologue or

---

appears in Oxford, Bodleian Library, Digby 41, ff. 2–17, Heyworth's basis for *Friar Daw's Reply.*

7 Anne Hudson has pointed out to me that *UR*1/2 could not have been positioned as it is if written into *FDR* in its present binding. Heyworth provides a convincing argument that *UR* is written in two different hands (40–1), but his editorial decision to place *UR*2 in his notes is rather more questionable, as I will show (see pp. 167–8).

superseding earlier poetry written for Richard with new work addressed to Henry, what-have-now-become Lancastrian writers relegitimate their own position by confirming Henry's new model of rule.

Some examples of this sort of aspiring Lancastrian writing have received a fair amount of attention recently.[8] One obvious, simple reason why the *Upland Series* has so far been overlooked is the dating Heyworth has assigned to it. But the other, more significant reason for the neglect of the *Upland Series* is that it is a different *kind* of Lancastrian writing than, for example, Gower's *Confessio Amantis*, or Hoccleve's *Regement of Princes*, or *Richard the Redeles*. The *Upland Series* is not courtly and self-consciously literary, and advertises no ties with the advice-to-princes tradition. Instead, momentarily at any rate, at the point where Upland, Daw, and the Rejoinder fix on the issue of regal jurisdiction and treason, it participates in another tradition of self-serving address to the king: that of highly educated polemic argumentation in support of the king's policies – but also, typically, in support of one's own position as a political advisor.[9] That most texts in this tradition are written in Latin is not the only reason for their relative neglect: it stems also from the fact that despite their ostensible address

---

[8] D. Lawton's 'Dullness and the Fifteenth Century', *English Literary History* 54 (1987), 761–99 suggested reasons to investigate early fifteenth century writings directed to the king; other studies on Ricardian and/or Lancastrian writers include L. Scanlon, 'The King's Two Voices: Narrative and Power in Hoccleve's *Regement of Princes*', in L. Patterson, ed., *Literary Practice and Social Change in Britain, 1380–1530* (Berkeley, 1990), 216–47; D. Pearsall, 'Hoccleve's *Regement of Princes*: The Poetics of Royal Self-Representation', *Speculum* 69 (1994), 386–410; H. Barr, 'Legal Fictions', ch. 5 in *Signes and Sothe: Language in the 'Piers Plowman' Tradition* (Woodbridge, Suffolk, 1994), 133–66, J. M. Bowers, '*Pearl* in its Royal Setting: Ricardian Poetry Revisited', *Studies in the Age of Chaucer* 17 (1995), 111–55; F. Grady, 'The Lancastrian Gower and the Limits of Exemplarity', *Speculum* 70 (1995), 552–75. On difficulties in coping with the memory of Richard see especially P. Strohm, 'The Trouble with Richard: The Reburial of Richard II and Lancastrian Symbolic Strategy', *Speculum* 71 (1996), 87–111; and M. J. Bennett, 'The Court of Richard II and the Promotion of Literature', in Hanawalt, ed., *Chaucer's England*, 3–20.

[9] For an introduction to the careers and writings of late medieval royal propagandists or 'publicists' see 'Notes on the Publicists and Anonymous Works', Appendix III in M. Wilks, *The Problem of Sovereignty in the Later Middle Ages: The Papal Monarchy with Augustinus Triumphus and the Publicists* (Cambridge, 1963), 548–59 (some parts of these notes are now outdated, but they are a valuable overview); J. Miethke, 'Zur Einführung', in J. Miethke and A. Bühler, eds., *Das Publikum politischer Theorie im 14. Jahrhundert* (Munich, 1992), 1–23; and J. Coleman, 'The Science of Politics'.

to the king (or at the very least on behalf of his policies), these polemic writings make very little effort to render themselves accessible to any audience other than educated clerics. Their method of procedure is adversarial rather than straightforwardly didactic – so that frequently it is difficult for the uninitiated to pick out which arguments the writer finally accepts – and their idiom is compressed and specialized, frequently alluding to topics and arguments familiar only to those with a particular kind of university training. Even though it is written in English, the *Upland Series* shares these characteristics; if anything, the allusiveness of its arguments is intensified in translation.

Where the *Upland Series* differs crucially from other sorts of Lancastrian writing that have received attention recently is in the attitude of its participants toward what they oppose. From the point where Jack begins to challenge the legitimacy of the friars' foundation onward, the *Upland Series* stages a contest over the legitimacy of modes of writing and learning and living: Latin vs vernacular, institutionally sanctioned vs unprecedented, regular vs secular. Each participant's reply aims not only through its overall formal choices (English or Latin, prose or verse), but through redefining in its favour the terms of debate over each question, to bolster its own position at the expense of its predecessor's. In the successive answers to Jack's question about how it can possibly be justified for priests to imprison people, this sequential contest for legitimacy comes to hinge on the difference between Ricardian and Lancastrian royalism. Rather than suppressing the transition from a Ricardian to a Lancastrian model of rule – so that Ricardian loyalty is either quietly forgotten, as in Gower's revisions to the *Confessio Amantis*, or else very cautiously evoked as a bad example, as in *Richard the Redeles*, the *Upland Series* puts it to use. Whereas court writers discard Ricardian ideals of kingship in favour of Lancastrian ones without remarking on the fact, here the difference between them is drawn into the contest.

Daw opposes his own royalism to what he labels as Jack's treason here:

> Þou seist also ferþermore þat prestis shul not enprisoun
> For it nys not foundid in al Goddis lawe,
> But vndirnym bi charite & so wynnen her broþir,
> And ȝif he wil not be so wonnen haue him as heþene;

& þus bi þin opynyon no man shulde be enprisound.
But, Iakke, in þi frensy þou fonnest more & more –
Þou wenyst to make to me a diche, þou fallist þi silf þerinne.
For if þou pursue þi purpos þou assentist þi silf in tresoun,
Menusynge þe kyngis maieste, priuyng him of his power.
For if we taken þe gospel aftir þe menynge,
Neþir emperour ne kyng may honge ne drawe,
Heued ne enprisoun ne haunte no domes,
But al in fair manere shulen ben vndirnomen;
And who wil not amenden him ȝeue him þe brydil,
And boþe robbers & reuers, mansleeris & treytours,
And al maner mawfesours, shulden ben vnpounishid.
Iak, þe pope haþ a prisoun & ȝit he is a prest,
Þe bishop of Cantirbury & of Londoun also,
And many oþer bishopis bi leeue of her kyng.
Art þou hardy to seien it is not Goddis lawe?
But y blame þee not gretli þouȝ þou bere hem heuy,
For goldsmythis of þi crafte ofte haue þei hem haunted
And ȝit þei shulen ofter, bi þe helpe of heuen.
(*FDR* 554–76)

And this is Upland's reply:

Daw, I do þee wel to wite, frentike am I not,
Bot it semiþ þi sotil witte marriþ many man.
Bot how stondiþ þis to gedir: ȝe sle men in ȝour prison,
Ȝe haue ȝour conspiracies when ȝou gode likiþ,
Ȝe damne þe trwe, ȝe hyen þe false, deme Dawe wher þis be gode.
And þe kyng by his juges trwe execute his lawe
As he did now late whan he hangid ȝou traytoures,
Wilt þou Dawe, allegates, compere ȝou to þe kyng
Or to oþer lordes þat han her grounde in God?
Lefe, fole, þi losengerie & studie Cristis lyf.
(*UR* 266–75)

Daw construes as treason Jack's attempt to restrict priests' power by
arguing that priests are subordinate to kings within one and the same
hierarchy. Bishops, including even perhaps the pope, exercise whatever
power they may have subject to their king's permission. Kings, rather
than the bible, are the final authority on 'Goddis lawe': bishops are
permitted to imprison 'bi leeue of her kyng'. Any attempt to question
any coercive juridical power mediated through the king, no matter who

the king might have sanctioned to exercise it, is treason on the grounds that it restricts the royal power, 'diminishes' the king's 'majesty'.

Daw's staunch royalism should come as no surprise. To those who have studied the long-running medieval controversy over conflicting claims for papal and royal or imperial power it may seem odd that any writer, and especially any cleric, should so readily subordinate the church's jurisdiction to the king's power. However, clerical polemic discourse within England in the late fourteenth and early fifteenth centuries is virtually unanimous in professing royalism under some description or another. Writers like Daw and Upland – who does not contest that the king and other lords 'han her grounde in God' (*UR* 274) – are far more concerned with local ecclesiastical issues than with any potential competing claims of the pope's. They typically look to the king, not the pope, to resolve those issues; and they construe their own positions, however contortedly, as supportive of the king. What is more remarkable about Daw's argument is the substance of his accusation of treason. 'Menusynge þe kyngis maieste, priuyng him of his power', the limitation or appropriation of the king's regal pre-rogative, or to call it by its technical legal name the charge of 'accroach-ment', is a specifically Ricardian charge of treason, and one that Henry's first parliament in 1399 eliminated from the possible grounds for an accusation of treason.

Prominent among the concerns of Henry's first parliament are a set of reforms to the definition as well as the prosecution of treason. Directly after it records the grant of the subsidy requested by the crown – in the position that is generally reserved for a parliament's most pressing business – the offical record of the October 1399 parliament in the *Rotuli Parliamentorum* records that Henry at the request of Parliament and after extensive consultation with those present annulled Richard's parliament of September 1397, and reinstated the parliament of February 1388, itself annulled in September 1397, in which a group of magnates known as the Appellants had suppressed Richard's favour-ites.[10] Next, again according to the official record, Henry is said to

---

[10] *Rotuli Parliamentorum* iii: 425 arts. 66, 67. Adjustments to these sweeping pronounce-ments are recorded later, in 428 art. 83, 432 art. 94, 442 art. 145, 445 art. 157, and the separate section where the cases of the lords who had presented appeals in the September 1397 parliament is considered, 449–53.

have affirmed, to the great rejoicing of lords and commons, the most significant result of these reversals:

> come en dit Parlement tenuz l'an XXIe [i.e. September 1397] y feurent ordeignez par Estatut pleusours peines de Traison, si qe y ne avoit ascun homme qe savoit coment il se deust avoir de faire, parler, ou dire, pur doubt de tielx peines; [Henry] dist, Qe sa volunte est tout outrement, qe en nul temps advenir ascun Traison soit adjuggez autrement q'il ne feust ordeignez par Estatut en temps de son noble aiel le Roy Edward Tierce, qe Dieu assoile. (*Rotuli Parliamentorum* iii: 426 art. 70)

> since in the said parliament held in the 21st year there were established by statue many penalties for treason, such that no man knew how he ought to act, talk, or speak for fear of such penalties, he said that his will was entirely otherwise, [and] that in no time to come should any treason be judged otherwise than was established by statute in the time of his noble grandfather the king Edward III, whom may God pardon.

Previous to this point the parliament record has carefully subordinated Henry's personal will to God's will and the counsel of true judges; in contrast to the conventional brief formula for the king's assent to a petition, 'le Roi le voet', 'the king wills it', Henry's agreement to annul the September 1397 parliament and reinstate that of 1388 has been hedged round with consultation processes that take almost as much space to record as the petitions themselves. Now the king states for the first time in the parliament, indeed in his reign, what he himself wills: he pronounces that on the issue of treason, his will is 'tout outrement' than Richard's; but entirely in conformity with the provisions of the 1352 Statute of Treasons.[11]

Of course not all of Henry's extensive rulings on future procedure and annulments of previous convictions for treason elsewhere in the 1399 parliament match up precisely with the provisions of the 1352 Statute, itself promulgated in response to a specific set of circumstances some fifty years earlier.[12] But recalling the Statute of Treasons of 1352

---

[11] The 1352 statute is printed in *Statutes of the Realm*, 10 vols. (London, 1810–28), i: 319–20. Of course this statute's account of Edward's pronouncement is no less a carefully rigged representation of regal authority.

[12] Henry annuls particular judgements of treason from Richard's reign (430 art. 90 and 434 art. 104 (on Haxey), 434–6 arts. 109–11 (on the Arundel family), 436 art. 112 (on

allows Henry to align his coming rule with that of his much respected grandfather Edward III rather than his cousin, and to present his modifications as reversions to previously accepted precedent rather than as innovations. Even more importantly, Henry's recourse to the limiting and clarifying provisions of 1352 allows him to eliminate from the scope of treason all the offences against the king's 'regalie', all the varieties of 'diminution' of the king's 'majesty', that had been added to it during Richard's reign.

Space does not permit a full survey of the Ricardian modifications to treason; but we should briefly examine what might be seen as their culmination in the parliaments of 1397. The best instance of the kind of Ricardian atmosphere Henry criticizes, where 'y ne avoit ascun homme qe savoit coment il se deust avoir de faire, parler, ou dire, pur doubt de tielx peines', is provided by the case of Thomas Haxey from the January 1397 parliament – this case too was annulled in Henry's 1399 parliament (430 art. 90). Haxey had arranged for the presentation of a parliamentary petition that criticized, among other things, the conduct and personnel of Richard's household. Richard pronounced that the petition was 'econtre sa Regalie et Estat, et sa Roiale Liberte', 'against his regality and estate, and his royal liberty', and had Haxey convicted of treason for presenting it. Haxey's pardon, into which the record of his trial is incorporated, gives the grounds for his conviction:

> si aliquis, cuiuscunque status seu condicionis fuerit, moverit vel excitaverit Communes Parliamenti, aut aliquam aliam personam, ad faciendum remedium sive reformacionem alicuius rei que tangit nostram personam, sive nostrum Regimen, aut Regalitatem nostram, teneretur et teneatur pro proditore. (*Rotuli Parliamentorum* iii: 408)

> if anyone, of whatever status or condition he may be, should move or excite the Commons of Parliament, or any other person, to make a

---

Warwick)), and makes a number of rulings on how treason is to be treated in future: he secures the inheritance of widows and children of traitors (440 arts. 130–2), establishes that a parliament may not pronounce (as the 1388 and 1397 parliaments did, though only 1388 is mentioned here) that any future attempt to repeal it will count as treason (442 art. 143), and bans parliamentary appeals of treason in favour of trial in the courts (442 art. 144). This last reform is reinforced obliquely by 446 art. 162 and 433 art. 97; these return all personal actions to the courts and affirm that lords and judges will be expected to give honest and just counsel and will not be subjected to any form of coercion.

remedy or reform of anything that touches our person, or our rule, or our regality, they should be held as a traitor.

If anyone of any status should incite the commons, or indeed anyone else, to advocate reforms affecting the king's person, conduct of his household, or rule, they will be considered a traitor. By this definition any attempt to exert influence over the king by any person through any third party whatever is potentially treasonous on the grounds of accroachment. The September 1397 parliament could scarcely go further, but it could be still more systematic.[13] By statute it repealed the February 1388 parliament of the Appellants 'come chose fait traitoirousement et econtre sa [Richard's] regalie sa corone et sa dignite',[14] reinstated the answers given by a panel of judges in Nottingham in 1387 in reply to Richard's questions about the commission appointed to review his finances in 1386 – these answers had suggested that several actions potentially restrictive of the king's power ought to be punished as treason[15] – included a new list of four offences against the king that were henceforth to be considered treason,[16] and classed as a traitor as well, by way of insurance, anyone who might in future attempt to create a commission like that of 1386,[17] and any attempt to repeal the present statute of September 1397.[18]

Once we have reminded ourselves of just how expansive the scope of treason on the ground of 'diminishing the king's majesty' had become by September 1397, it is abundantly clear just why one of Henry's first concerns on coming to the throne was to annul that parliament. It was essential to the justification of Henry's usurpation that the 1397 statutes should be thoroughly extirpated, for if they were allowed to stand they

---

13 For the parliament see *Rotuli Parliamentorum* iii: 347–73; the statutes appear only in *Statutes* ii: 98–110, and not in the parliament roll.

14 *Statutes* ii: 98 art. 2; the quotation appears at 98/28–30.

15 *Statutes* ii: 101–5, art. 12.

16 'chescun qi compasse et purpose la Mort le Roy, ou de luy deposer, ou de susrendre son Homage liege, ou celuy qi leve le poeple et chivache econtre le Roy a faire de guerre deinz son Roialme . . .', 'anyone who plans and intends the death of the king, or to depose him, or to abandon his allegiance, or he who raises the people and rides against the king, making war in his realm . . .' *Rotuli Parliamentorum* iii: 351 art. 18. See also *Statutes* ii: 98–9, art. 3. The first and fourth of these were familiar charges found in the 1352 statute, but the second and third relate directly to charges against the Appellants (Bellamy, *The Law of Treason in England*, 114–15).

17 *Statutes* ii: 98 art. 2. 18 *Statutes* ii: 99 art. 4.

would directly challenge the legitimacy of Henry's rule, and label him and all his supporters as traitors. From the perspective of the first decade of the fifteenth century, soon after Henry's reformative first parliament, any attempt deliberately to recall and employ the grounds for treason that Henry had removed in 1399 must have looked especially and even menacingly Ricardian. If Daw's argument were written before 1399,[19] then circumstances have subsequently imposed a very striking change on the public meaning of its professed allegiance. The ditch Daw thinks Jack has fallen into (see *FDR* 560) has been filled in and redug elsewhere.

Upland's rejoinder is just as royalist as Daw's reply, and just as determined to label his opponent a traitor. But writing from the perspective of the first decade of the fifteenth century, Upland avoids simply reversing Daw's accusation. Arguments that claim the friars 'diminish the king's majesty' are very common in Wycliffite tracts dating from the 1380s and 90s.[20] But this is not what Upland claims.

[19] See the Appendix for consideration of this issue.
[20] Some Wycliffite tracts datable before 1399 that use arguments on accroachment: 'The Grete Sentence of Curs', in Arnold, ed., *Select English Works of John Wyclif*, iii: 267–337, may probably be dated to the early 1380s since it refers to the Despenser crusade of 1383 in a way that implies that it is still going on (329/10–29) as well as to the 'newe dampnacion' of the Earthquake Council of 1382 (313/22). This tract repeatedly accuses clerics of treason in addition to heresy and blasphemy: it invokes the terms of the 1352 statute, as at 276/6–12 and 303/8–10 where clerics are accused of raising banners against the king, or at 314/18–25, where the possibility that clerics might murder the king, queen or lords or 'defoule' the queen is raised, but its most frequent suggestion is that clerics behave treasonously by encroaching on the king's 'regalie' (298/2–299/3, 300/9–12, 300/26–301/9, 306/27–307/5, 307/14–21, 314/34–315/16), whereas the 'poor priests' whom the clergy persecute labour to uphold the king's 'regalie' (272/28–34, 287/33–6). Other early Wycliffite works that label derogation of the king's 'regalie' as treason include 'Fifty Heresies and Errors of Friars' (Arnold, 366–401; 391/8–27, datable to *c.* 1383–93: contains a reference to the Despenser crusade of 1383 (such references appear in precisely datable Wycliffite works up until 1393, see Hudson, *The Premature Reformation*, 14, 368)); 'A Petition to the King and Parliament' (Arnold, 507–23; 514/11–516/8, datable before February 1399: addresses Richard II and the Duke of Lancaster in a way that would have been impossibly controversial after John of Gaunt's death in February, let alone Richard's deposition.); and 'Of Clerks Possessioners' and 'Of Poor Preaching Priests' (in Matthew, ed., *The English Works of Wyclif Hitherto Unprinted*, 114–40; 130/17–30 and 275–81; 279/27–32, 280/13–17, both very probably datable before 1399: they appear in Cambridge, Corpus Christi College 296, a late fourteenth to early fifteenth century manuscript that was itself copied from an earlier manuscript distributed piecemeal for copying (Hanna has persuasively argued this in 'Two Lollard Codices', and see ch. 1,

Instead, Upland characterizes the kind of rule the friars exercise as unjust and tyrannical, 'ʒe sle men in ʒour prison, / ʒe have ʒour conspiracies when ʒou gode likiþ, / ʒe damne þe trwe, ʒe hyen þe false'. He contrasts the friars' rule with an ideal of just, well-counselled kingship 'þe kyng by his juges trwe execute his lawe'. And he links that second, more desirable type of administration to an allusion to the trial and execution for treason of several friars in 1402, 'As he did now late whan he hangid ʒou traytoures'.

The basis for the juridical contrast Upland sets up here is partly bibilical: his contrast between the rule provided by kings and that of ecclesiastical rulers who slay men, conspire, damn the true and raise the false draws on the Wycliffite account of biblical history according to which in the Old Testament men were first ruled by judges from the time of Moses until Samuel, then by kings, and then (after kings succumbed to idolatry) by priests, whose misrule eventually culminated in their conspiracy to kill Christ. Wycliffites typically emphasize that this progression represents a decline from pure adherence to God's law, and draw a parallel to New Testament and subsequent history. Under Christ and his apostles Christians were ruled as by judges. When kingdoms began to convert wholesale to Christianity then Christians were ruled as by Old Testament kings. Where this system of rule by kings works well, under a good king who governs in accordance with God's law, it is the best kind of rule that can be achieved in a Christian state in this world. But where regal rule is corrupted and adulterated by the institutional church's meddling in secular affairs,

---

pp. 6–7). Datable Wycliffite tracts from after 1399 that eschew or modify arguments on accroachment: William Taylor's sermon (preached 21 November 1406; see Hudson, ed., *Two Wycliffite Texts*, xiii) focuses on how priests injure the people rather than the king. The sermon *Omnis plantacio* (c. 1409–March 1413) discusses how the king's 'regalie' may be affected by clerical activities, but with reference only to biblical and early Christian kings, or to God's 'maieste' (London, British Library, Egerton 2820, ff. 34, 44rv). The *Tractatus de Oblacione Iugis Sacrificii* (March 1413–February 1414) makes reference to 'regalie' only in wholly positive, affirmative terms; interestingly, its explanation of how God confers 'regalie' employs the terms of Henry's coronation oath (London, British Library, Cotton Titus D.v, f. 30v; see also f. 78). My thanks to Anne Hudson for the loan of transcriptions of *Omnis Plantacio* and the *Tractatus*. On the datings and manuscripts of these works see Hudson, *The Premature Reformation*, 10, 12, 184–5, 286–8.

Christians are ruled as the Jews were by priests, scribes, and Pharisees.[21]

The close biblical scripting of Upland's juridical contrast in itself has force for his argument. Daw had criticized overly close reliance on literal historical biblical interpretation, reducing to absurdity what would happen 'if we taken þe gospel aftir þe menynge': Upland is defiantly showing the direct political application of an argument that conforms closely to Old Testament history. But the direct political application Upland makes is at least equally important: Upland's topical allusion imports a new kind of accusation of treason to replace the former Ricardian polemic against accroachment. The problem with the friars executed in June 1402, as with Daw, was not so much a simple *failure* of loyalty as a *misplaced* loyalty: reputedly the friars' conspiracies and efforts to 'damn the true and raise the false' were devoted to the service of their continuing *Ricardian* royalism.

There is considerable evidence of official disquiet in 1402 over suspicions about the activities of Ricardian friars.[22] The fullest account we have of the friars' trials appears in the *Continuatio Eulogii*, which

---

21 The parallel is referred to in 'The Clergy May Not Hold Property' (*The English Works of Wyclif*, ed. Matthew, 362–404; 370). In the extended version of this tract, the sermon *Omnis Plantacio*, the writer discusses the Old Testament model and its New Testament parallel at length. Wyclif in *De civili dominio* develops the parallel in an extended discussion of what form of rule is best for England: unsurprisingly, the best form of governance achievable turns out to be kingship (J. Wyclif, *De civili dominio*, 4 vols., vol. 1 ed. R. L. Poole (London, 1885), vols. 2, 3, and 4 ed. J. Loserth (London, 1900, 1903, 1904), i: 194–9). Although he does not cite it here, Wyclif's argument may be designed to refute Innocent IV's very similar historical argument (quoted in ch. 2, p. 59) for why supreme terrestrial power rests with the pope. However, any origin for this argument in papal and antipapal polemic is suppressed in all the Wycliffite treatments I have encountered.

22 The lay defendant John Sperhauke in his trial for treason in 1402 claims a friar was the ultimate source of his conviction that Richard was alive in Scotland: see G. O. Sayles, ed., *Select Cases in the Court of King's Bench* (London, 1971), vii: 123–4. A writ of 5 June 1402 asks every sheriff to have it proclaimed that the rumours promulgated by enemies of the king and realm to the effect that Richard is alive in Scotland and preparing to invade are to be distrusted, and those involved in spreading them to be arrested and imprisoned (*Foedera . . .* , 3rd ed. vol. 4, ed. T. Rymer, (London, 1740; reprinted Farnborough, Hants., 1967), 29; see also the translation in *Calendar of Close Rolls*, vol. 30, 1399–1402 (London, 1927), 570). Records of the arrest and imprisonment of fifteen friars, two monks, and three priests in May and June of 1402 are preserved in the Close Rolls and Patent Rolls. Although all the trial records are not preserved, four trials for treason involving friars are extant in the *Coram Rege* roll.

gives a Franciscan chronicler's detailed description of the events surrounding the executions, reporting in dialogue form the encounters
between friars loyal to Richard and their challengers.[23] The reporting
of the disputes as dialogues is of course a stylistic device for presenting
opposed views: but they are valuable precisely as a digest of those
opposed views presented from a fraternal perspective. The dialogue
inserted before the account of the June 1402 trial, a dispute between
Henry IV and a friar supposedly staged before the lords and the archbishop of Canterbury, presents an opposition between Henry's and the

These trial records have most recently been edited by R. L. Storey, in 'Clergy and
Common Law in the Reign of Henry IV', in R. F. Hunnisett and J. B. Post, eds.,
Medieval Legal Records Edited in Memory of C. A. F. Meekings (London, 1978),
342–408; 353–61; Storey in addition provides a reconstruction of the order of events
that draws on other records and accounts. The preamble to a second writ concerning
another proclamation about the rumours dated 18 June states that various religious
and other men who had feloniously, or better traitorously, conspired to incite
insurrection have been executed: 'Licet nuper, publicatis et inaniter praedicatis
nonnullis fabricatis Mendaciis, tam in Civitate nostra Londoniae quam alibi infra
Regnum nostrum Angliae, per Viros Religiosos diversos, et alios, Insurrectionem et
Commotionem Populi eiusdem Regni nostri felonice, ymmo verius proditorie, contra
eorum Ligeantiam nequiter Conspirantes, et ad effectum pro eorum viribus
dampnabiliter deducere Cupientes, Quidam eorum, propriis et publicis sui Reatus
Confessionibus praecedentibus, suisque Demeritis exigentibus in hac parte, Convicti
et Morti adjudicati extiterint, Judiciaque, in hac parte reddita debite fuerint executa',
'Although recently many invented lies were published and foolishly preached, both in
our city of London and elsewhere in our realm of England by various religious and
others, wickedly plotting insurrection and disturbance among the people of our
realm, feloniously and indeed traitorously, contrary to their allegiance, and damnably
desiring, to that end, to lead out their forces, some of them, after public confessions
of their own guilt, as their own faults required, were convicted and condemned to
death, and the sentence rendered was carried out' (*Foedera*, iv: 29–30; 30).

23 *Continuatio Eulogii*, in F. S. Haydon, ed., *Eulogium Historiarum*, 3 vols. (London,
1858–63), iii: 333–421; 389–94. For a general introduction to the importance of the
chronicle see A. Gransden, *Historical Writing in England*, 2 vols. (London, 1982), ii:
158 and n. 5. For the conclusion that the anonymous continuator is a Franciscan at
Canterbury, a favourable opinion of the chronicle's accuracy and contemporaneity
with the events described, and a judicious assessment of the usefulness of the
presumably largely fictional dialogues it frequently includes, see J. I. Catto, 'An
Alleged Great Council of 1374', *English Historical Review*, 82 (1967), 764–71; 764–5.
Storey draws on the chronicle for his account, taking its dialogues between friars and
the king at face value: see 'Clergy and Common Law in the Reign of Henry IV',
353–7. Since I originally wrote this chapter this dialogue has been discussed in two
articles on early Lancastrian writing: see Grady, 'The Lancastrian Gower and the
Limits of Exemplarity', and Strohm, 'The Trouble with Richard: The Reburial of
Richard II and Lancastrian Symbolic Strategy'.

Ricardian loyalist friar's ideals of kingship very similar to that found in the *Upland Series* (391–2):

> Et dixit Rex magistro: 'Isti sunt fatui et idiotae, nec legere sciunt nec intelligunt. Tu deberes sapiens esse, dicis tu quod Rex Ricardus vivit?'
>
> Magister respondit: 'Non dico quod vivit, sed dico si vivit ipse est verus Rex Angliae.'
>
> Et Rex opposuit, dicens: 'Ipse resignavit.'
>
> Et dixit magister: 'Resignavit sed invitus et coactus in carcere, quae resignatio nulla est de jure.'
>
> Cui Rex: 'Ipse resignavit cum bona voluntate.'
>
> Et magister: 'Non resignasset si fuisset liber. Et resignatio facta in carcere non est libera.'
>
> 'Adhuc,' dixit Rex, 'ipse fuit depositus.'
>
> Et magister, per modum conquestus, dixit: 'Dumesset rex vi armorum captus fuit, incarceratus, et regno spoliatus, et vos invasistis coronam.'
>
> Cui Rex: 'Non invasi coronam, sed fui rite electus.'
>
> Magister dixit: 'Electio nulla est, vivente possessore legitimo. Et si mortuus est, per vos mortuus est. Et si per vos mortuus est, perdidistis titulum, et omne jus quod habere potestis ad regnum.'
>
> Cui Rex dixit: 'Per caput istud, tu perdes caput tuum.'
>
> Magister dixit: 'Nunquam dilexistis ecclesiam, sed multum illi detraxastis antequam fuistis Rex, et nunc illam destruetis.'
>
> 'Mentiris,' dixit Rex; 'recede.' (*Continuatio Eulogii, Eulogium Historiarum* iii: 391–2; my paragraphing.)

And the king said to the master: 'These are fools and idiots, not able to read or understand. You ought to be wise, do you say that king Richard lives?'

The master replied: 'I do not say that he lives, but I say that if he lives he is the true king of England.'

And the king opposed him, saying: 'He resigned.'

And the master said: 'He resigned, but unwillingly and constrained in prison, and that sort of resignation is null according to law.'

To which the king: 'He resigned with good will.'

And the master: 'He would not have resigned if he were free. And a resignation made in prison is not free.'

'Still,' said the king, 'he was deposed.'

And the master, in the manner of complaint, said: 'While he was king he was captured by force of arms, imprisoned, and deprived of his realm, and you usurped the crown.'

To which the king: 'I did not usurp the crown, but was elected in accordance with custom.'

The master said: 'Election is null while the lawful possessor is living. And if he was dead, he was dead through you. And if he was dead through you, you lost the title, and every right that you could have to the realm.'

To which the king said: 'By this head, you lose your head.'

The master said: 'You have never loved the church, but often detracted from it before you were king, and now you will destroy it.'

'You lie', said the king, 'depart'.

Henry's contention is that he is the lawful king and rules within the law with the advice of his council and judges, according to the model given prominence in his first parliament and presented by Upland in his Rejoinder. The order of events in the chronicle account of this case reinforces Henry's claim: after Henry's dispute with the friar he asks for counsel from the onlookers before sending the friars for trial by judges at Westminster, and within his dispute with the friar Henry attempts to prove to the friar that he is the lawful king. However, the Franciscan chronicler's sympathies are on the other side: his mode of presenting these events tends to undermine their official import. The immoderate antifraternal outburst by a king's knight in the council held after the dispute, 'Nunquam extinguemus clamorem istum de vita Ricardi nisi fratres extinguantur', 'We will never get rid of this clamour about Richard being alive unless the friars are gotten rid of' (392/16–18), shows that rule according to counsel will not necessarily be just. The friars' replies to the accusations of the justiciary at Westminster (392–3) are reserved, for maximum pathos and impact, for the scaffold (393). And within their dispute, the friar's argument and Henry's reaction to it belie Henry's claims.

For the friar, as for Daw, any attempt to constrain Richard's will cannot be lawful. Henry cannot be the lawful king if he has deposed Richard, and he must have deposed Richard, for the circumstances of Richard's resignation could not have been in accordance with law. The circumstances could not have been lawful, because they involved coercion and constraint: Richard was in prison at the time when he supposedly resigned the crown, and resigning the crown is an act that

Richard would never have performed unless he were made to. Rather than admitting the force of the friar's argument, Henry responds by demonstrating his lawlessness: he resorts to trial and execution on what seem trumped up accusations (390–1).

Although its sympathies lie in the opposite direction, the chronicle episode deploys the same contrast between Ricardian and Lancastrian royalism that gives force to Upland's counterargument. Richard rules by will: any attempt to constrain his will counts as treason on the grounds of accroachment. Henry at least claims to rule by law and according to counsel (though the chronicle account shows how such claims may fail in practice to produce just rule), while the kind of treason that worries him most is that of conspiratorial loyalty to Richard. When Upland accuses Daw and other friars of conspiring, of damning the true, and of raising the false, then, he links Daw to the kinds of activities for which Ricardian loyalist friars were executed for treason in June 1402. And the form of Daw's own accusation of treason against Jack has left him wide open to an accusation of Ricardian loyalism – an accusation that in the climate of the first decade of the fifteenth century delegitimates Daw's reply to Jack, and allows Upland to set up his own opposed claim in its place.

Where it addresses Lancastrian rule, then, the *Upland Series* is very different from Lancastrian courtly writings, both in the way it approaches the topic and in the manner in which it treats it. The approach and mode of argument that the series uses on this question is far more natural to the rest of the questions Jack poses: elsewhere the series is not concerned with the king at all, but with the sort of interclerical arguments that until the late fourteenth century were typically posed with an entirely insouciant attitude, unconcerned with any possibility of wider audience. As has already been amply demonstrated, however, this sort of insouciance had been seriously eroded in the late fourteenth century, even in the 1380s, and especially after 1395, and most especially for vernacular writers. It is very odd that the *Upland Series* resembles interclerical controversial writings circulated amongst clerics in Latin, rather than other extraclergial writings, in its attitude to vernacular audience; all the more so when we consider the larger terms of contestation in the series as a whole. Even while they continue to ignore the possibilities of 'lewed' audience, the participants are much concerned with the leverage they can gain by manipulating the terms of 'lewed' and 'clergie'.

Critics who have given any attention to the Upland Series have tended not to pay sufficient attention to the kind of contest it stages. Often they view all respondents through the lens of one: thus for Heyworth, *Jack Upland*'s style is 'flaccid' because Jack does not, like Daw, write alliterative verse, whereas for Scattergood Jack is less well educated than Daw, still less the Rejoinder, because he does not use Latin quotations.[24] The principle to keep in mind when reading an exchange like the *Upland Series*, however – and it is because of this principle that Jack tends to come off worst according to writers like Heyworth and Scattergood – is that each reply in succession sets out to best what it confronts. Even if the content of each reply is to some extent fixed by the arguments to which it responds, each reply makes its place in the debate by reframing the argument thus far on its own terms, and responding in a manner advantageous to its immediate situation. The ways that each respondent reframes the debate – by switching from prose to verse, by using Latin quotations, by criticizing his opponent's use of authorities, and so on – do not necessarily indicate that he has better command over the new features he has introduced than his predecessors. Instead, they show only that he finds them advantageous as strategies of debate in the circumstances in which he finds himself.

Rather than being inept, ill-educated, and 'flaccid', then, we might observe that if Jack Upland's aim is to provoke 'lewed' or vernacular debate over the issues he raises, as the comment 'jack vpon lond lookith for an answer' appended to *JU*2b observes, then he is wildly successful.[25] The content of at least some of his questions, and of the homiletic frame *JU*2a puts round them, is topical and inflammatory, as Mary and Richard Rouse have shown by explaining links between Jack's question about the friars' habit of locking up books and tension

---

[24] See Heyworth, p. 7 and V. J. Scattergood, *Politics and Poetry in the Fifteenth Century* (London, 1971), 239–45.
[25] This comment follows the text of *Jack Upland* on f. 80. Heyworth includes it in his variants, p. 72, line 411n.

over the accessibility of books in late medieval Oxford,[26] and as I will show by explaining the relationship between the oddly vociferous discussion of the theoretical issue of Christ's mendicancy in the series and contemporary debates at Oxford.[27]

But it is not principally the content of *Jack Upland*'s questions and complaints that brings about its success; more important is the manner in which they are posed. An angry comment appended to *JU*2a illustrates well just why it is that Jack Upland is so provoking:

> Jacke, in þi ianglinge charite þe wantis, for þou pinchist at oure pouce as a parid schrewe. Þis is þe leþerist lessoun þat euer ȝit j herde, of lerid or of lewid, daies of my lijf. Seynt Fraunces curs & al foure ordris come vpon þat fals þeef þat þus þee haþ enformed, for þe pointis of our priuytees he haþ prickid to þ<. . .>, or þou art apostata & proued al þis þi silf.[28]

The combination of Jack's detailed knowledge of the friars' inconsistencies and embarrassments with his naive, wide eyed pose of uplandish 'lewed'ness is hard to bear; it creates a discomfiting uncertainty about whether Jack is a turncoat cleric or an over-informed 'lewed' person. And Jack exploits that uncertainty: in his envoy, for example, he assumes the priestly role as an administrator of confession that is one of the fiercest grounds of contest between friars and their opponents:[29]

> Go now forþ frere & fraiste ȝoure clerkis, & grounde ȝou in Goddis lawe, & ȝeue Iacke an answere, & whanne ȝe asoilen þat I haue seide sadli in truþe, I schal asoile þee of þin ordre & saue þee to heuene. (*JU* 408–11)

The ground for the questions learned clerks will be required to 'solve' remains, as always, Jack's 'lewed' naiveté. Nonetheless Jack implies,

---

[26] R. H. and M. A. Rouse, 'The Franciscans and Books: Lollard Accusations and the Franciscan Response', in A. Hudson and M. Wilks, eds., *From Ockham to Wyclif, Studies in Church History Subsidia* 5 (Oxford, 1987), 369–84.

[27] See below, pp. 162–77.

[28] Heyworth, *Jack Upland*, 137, line 411n. Modern punctuation and capitals added; ampersand retained as in Heyworth's edited text.

[29] For Jack's challenge to friars' assumption of the role of confessor see *JU* 222–3. Jack's strategy is to point out the friars' preference for acting as confessors to the rich, but as Daw points out in his reply, it is much more common for antifraternal writers to mount a broader complaint against the friars' confessional practices, as for example Fitzralph does in the *Defensio curatorum*.

exploiting the double meaning of 'asoile', that he is more of a priest than the friars' clerks, and better qualified to administer confession: when their solutions have forced them to conclude that their practices are indefensible, Jack will 'absolve' them of their oaths.

In reaction to Jack's envoy, Friar Daw repeatedly comments that the answer of a 'lewed' friar is all that the questions need: '. . . it nediþ not to sharpen oure clerkes,/ For Frere Dawe is scharpe ynowȝ for al sich enditinge'.[30] Daw firmly classifies Jack as a lay husbandman able to get help only from his parish priest, much though that priest's learning will probably be equally insufficient: 'Iakke, if þou vndirstonde no Latyn, go to þi paroche prest,/ And blundir ȝe boþe wiþ Goddis grace, marren ȝe wolen ful yuele'.[31] Jack's source of information is 'fourmures' for whom, as Daw presents it in his envoy, Jack is little more than an errand boy:

> Now fare forþe to þi fourmures, & Iak, þou hem telle
> Þe mater of oure talkynge & loke how hem likiþ;
> And if hem þinke not þi sawis sufficientli assoilid,
> Lat hem senden aȝen, it shal be amendid:
> (*FDR* 923–6)

However, to counter Jack's argument Daw must deploy at least as much learning as the 'fourmures' he claims gave Jack his ideas. Indeed, even while he claims to be 'as lewid . . . as þou' (*FDR* 211), he chooses the conspicuous display of learning as the ground on which he will surpass Jack, mobilizing Latin quotations from the bible and other authorities and logical terminology in pursuit of his aims.[32] He reiterates and strains even further the paradox of Jack's 'lewed' learning.

While never of course relinquishing its claims to 'lewed'ness, *Upland's Rejoinder* gives at least equally learned counterarguments against Daw – indeed, on occasion he argues so pithily that one suspects

---

[30] *FDR* 927–8. Daw repeatedly classifies himself as 'lewed' or remarks on his low level of learning: see *FDR* 44, 45, 211, 214, 647.

[31] *FDR* 394–5. Daw suggests that Jack is married (*FDR* 450), has a 'knave' (*FDR* 450, 754–63), and keeps animals (*FDR* 451–76).

[32] See *FDR* 210 'dubby' for Latin 'dubio'; 535–6 for an assertion about predestination; 586 for 'By verre contradiccion þou concludist þi silf'; 689 for the scholastic use of 'suppose'; 799 for 'alle siche ȝonge impossibilitees folowen þerof'; 816–21 for a syllogistic argument on God's omnipotence.

a setup. When Daw uses the example of the woman who touched Christ's robe and was healed to suggest that Christ's clothes even if not friars' habits had some intrinsic power, for example, Upland scornfully dismisses his argument: 'For Crist said it hym self, þe vertu passid fro me' – the power has passed *from me*, that is, not from my robe – 'And here þou maist see I knowe a "b" fro a bole fote,/ For I cacche þee in lesynges þat þou laist on þe gospel' (254–6; punctuation modified). Upland's more accurate quotation neatly overturns Daw's example so that it supports his own point. However, on the whole – and it is possible to see the difference even here, where one line of substantive argument is accompanied by two disputing who is learned and who is lying – on the whole in the exchange between Daw and *Upland's Rejoinder* the ground of battle has shifted. More important than the questions and answers themselves now are the *ad hominem* arguments that surround them, and that focus attention on the terms according to which one or the other participant merits being called 'lewed' or clerical.

Upland does not, like Daw himself, attempt to defuse his opponent's claim to be both 'lewed' and 'clergie' by assigning him to one or the other term. Instead, he counterattacks by suggesting that he himself inhabits both terms as well, and in a better sense. Friar Daw's arguments and manner of speech are 'lewed' not in the sense of virtuous and penetratingly direct simplicity, but in that they are unskilled and stupid: Daw is a blabberer and blind leader (71), he barks at the moon like an old dog (88–9), his words are not grounded in holy writ (147–51), his reasons are blunt and his similitudes and solutions not worth the devil's dirt (197–203), and his argument is that of an ape (219). Further, Daw's denial that he has 'clergie' is quite correct, but in a different sense than he thinks. Daw is a clerk in status, Upland stresses,[33] but not in a more important sense:

> Þou saist þou knowist no lettre here, as if þou wer noo clerke;
> To take a clerke as it shuld be, after his vndirstondyng,
> þan sayst þou here more trwly þan in any oþer place.
> Clerk is als meche to mene as of þe sort of God,

---

[33] Upland calls Daw a clerk in the status-bound sense at *UR* 245: 'I meruel þat þou a clerk blaberst þus blyndely.'

And so þou preuist þi self non suche if þou loke riȝt,
Bot a liere apostata with alle his oþer pointes.
(*UR* 114–19)

According to the 'hi vndirstondyng' of the term 'clerk', Daw is by his own admission apostate.

It is very surprising that any friar should participate in a vernacular contest with a writer who presents himself as 'lewed' yet possessed of 'clergie'. Late medieval friars do complain about attacks on their practices, and do compose counterarguments against their opponents. But even when their opponents have written in English they give their replies in Latin; and they avoid laying the debate before a lay audience, even to the point of transferring their side of the argument to a different, more restricted venue. Woodford's reply to Jack's questions, in a Latin treatise extant in only one copy that seems to have remained within the Franciscan convent in London, is much more typical. As examples of the friars' more usual mode of rebuttal we might also instance the fraternal reaction to Fitzralph's London sermons: rather than answering with public sermons of their own, delivered in English even if written in Latin, they appeal Fitzralph to the papal court, and compose Latin objections against the defence he is required to present there (to which objections Fitzralph responds in turn) then subsequently treatises that counter Fitzralph's defence and responses.[34] Similarly, in Oxford in the late 1380s to early 1390s the Carmelite friar Richard Maidstone replies to Ashwardby's vernacular antimendicant sermons given before the laity with a set of scholastic Latin lectures given within the university.[35]

If we take it at face value, *Friar Daw's Reply* is the only extant piece of antiWycliffite polemic written in the vernacular and by (or so it claims) a cleric. The Dominican friar who has ostensibly written it is the only friar, as far as we know, who voices an antiWycliffite, would-be

---

[34] On the widely disseminated version of Fitzralph's defence the *Defensio curatorum* see further ch. 3, pp. 93–100, where Trevisa's English translation is discussed. On the subsequent objections and responses, see below, pp. 169–74.

[35] We know of Ashwardby's sermons only through Maidstone. Even if the sharp contrast between audiences is Maidstone's fabrication more than factual report, it is significant that Maidstone's account reverses the usual extraclergial strategy of gaining rhetorical advantage, restricting his audience rather than extending it. On Maidstone's replies see below, pp. 176–7.

royalist, fraternal position in English; and what is more, who chooses, in contrast to *Jack Upland*'s prose (and perhaps in reaction to Jack's loosely alliterative envoy[36]), to write in alliterative verse, an idiom with longstanding associations with religious writing, but also by the late fourteenth century strongly associated with anticlerical social complaint in the *Piers Plowman* tradition.[37]

There are, of course, plenty of fraternal voices in extant vernacular texts; many works hostile to the friars voice a fraternal point of view for the sake of argument. We might instance the Friar's and Summoner's Tales in the *Canterbury Tales*, Will's encounters with the two friars and with the Master of Divinity in *Piers Plowman*, *Piers the Plowman's Crede*, the Lollard dialogue between a secular clerk and a friar (which claims to record a genuine encounter staged before the duke of Gloucester), or the paired poems 'The Layman's Complaint' and 'The Friar's Answer'. But one reason why we should be inclined to view Friar Daw as perhaps more genuine (or at the very least more genuinely an exponent of the arguments he voices) than these friars is immediately apparent through comparison with the last, and shortest, of these examples. The paired poems, 'The Layman's Complaint' and 'The Friar's Answer', are copied in the same early fifteenth century hand onto the flyleaf of a fourteenth century manuscript of the *Pore Caitif*.[38] Like the version of *Jack Upland* that Daw answers – like, indeed, the academic debate from about 1350 onward – both poems are inclusive in stance, addressing all orders of friars: 'Be þou berfot, be þou schod' in 'The Layman's Complaint' includes the customary attire of all orders, as does 'Wheþer [the friar's habit] be russet, black, or white' in 'The Friar's Answer'.[39] And the poems share several topics with the *Upland*

---

[36] *Jack Upland*'s envoy is quoted above, p. 154.

[37] For a survey of varieties of alliterative writing in late medieval England see D. Pearsall, *Old and Middle English Poetry* (London, 1977), 150–85. I would tend to lay more emphasis than Pearsall does on the wide influence and public importance of the *Piers Plowman* tradition, but his survey of the varying importance of alliterative writing from the tenth century forward admirably disperses the partisan nationalism of previous accounts.

[38] Cambridge, St John's College 195. I cite R. H. Robbins' edition, from *Historical Poems of the XIVth and XVth Centuries* (New York, 1959), 166–8.

[39] On lines 2 and 23 respectively. On the inclusive tendency of the academic debate after Fitzralph see J. D. Dawson, 'Richard FitzRalph and the Fourteenth-Century Poverty Controversies', *Journal of Ecclesiastical History* 34 (1983), 315–44; 332–3 (on Fitzralph),

Series. But 'The Friar's Answer' leads with its chin in a way that Daw's *Reply* does not:

THE FRIAR'S ANSWER

Allas! what schul we freris do,
    Now lewed men kun holy writ?
Alle abowte wherre I go
    Þei aposen me of it.

Þen wondriþ me þat it is so
    How lewed men kun alle writ.
Sertenly we be vn-do
    But if we mo amende it.

I trowe þe deuel browȝt it aboute
    To write þe gospel in englishe,
ffor lewed men ben nowe so stowt
    Þat þei ȝeuen vs neyþer fleche ne fishe.

When I come into a schope
    for to say 'in principio',
Þei bidine me, 'goo forþ, lewed poppe!'
    & worche & win my siluer so!

Yf y sae hit longoþ not
    ffor prestis to worche where þei go,
Þei leggen for hem holi writ
    And sein þat seint polle did soo.

Þan þe loken on my nabete
    & sein, 'forsoþe, withoutton oþes,
Whether it be russet, black, or white,
    It is worþe alle oure werynge cloþes.'

I saye 'I, not for me,
    bot for them þat haue none.'
Þei seyne, 'þou hauist to or þre;
    ȝeuen hem þat nedith þerof oone.'

Þus oure desseytis bene aspiede
    In þis maner & mani moo;
fewe men bedden vs abyde
    but hey fast þat we were goo.

and Walsh, 'The *De Vita Evangelica* of Geoffrey of Hardeby (*c.* 1385),' ii, 77–8 (on Hardeby's opponents).

> If it goo forþe in þis maner
> It wole done us myche gyle
> Men schul funde unneþe a frere
> In englonde wiþin a whille.

The summation in the second last stanza here – 'Þus oure desseytis
bene aspiede' – would tip off anyone who might try to read the poem
as a straightforward fraternal complaint. But even without it, it is
impossible to take seriously a friar who complains, in English, that he
fears laymen will cease to support friars now that the bible is available
in English, still less one who provides in English a series of rebuttals for
laymen to use against his arguments.[40]

Although Daw uses English, his arguments do not undercut themselves as those of 'The Friar's Answer' do: instead, they form a comprehensive and detailed response to Jack's challenge, much though some
of them turn out to be rather easily susceptible to counterattack. And
whereas the medium of 'The Friar's Answer' sorts oddly with its
message, Friar Daw provides, even makes much of, his rationale for
breaking with fraternal custom and writing in English. He asserts that
Jack's questions should not be dignified with a response at a higher
level:

> But Iak þou3 þi questions semen to þee wyse,
> 3it li3tly a lewid man maye leyen hem a water;
> For summe ben lewid, summe ben shrewid, summe falsly supposid,
> And þerfore shal no maistir ne no man of scole
> Be vexid wiþ þy maters but a lewid frere
> Þat men callen Frere Daw Topias, as lewid as a leke.
> (*FDR* 40–5)

The answer of a 'lewed' friar is all, in Daw's view, that Jack's ill-
informed questions deserve.

Still, Friar Daw's claim to 'lewedness' in the sense of stupidity and
lack of education courts our skepticism. Much though Daw distances
himself from Latin tradition by writing vernacular alliterative poetry,
he makes extensive use of conventions, as well as arguments, extant in
the body of Latin scholastic material in circulation among clerics. He

---

[40] For a different assessment of the relationship between 'The Friar's Answer' and *Friar
Daw's Reply* see Dean, *Six Ecclesiastical Satires*, 146.

begins in the mode of social complaint, quoting 'Who shal graunten to myn eyen a strong streme of teres', 'Quis dabit meo capiti fontem lacrimarum', an opening taken from Jeremiah 9:1, and also used by Bernard, Pecham, Fitzralph, a poem on the execution of Richard Scrope, and Lydgate.[41] He cites the canonist Henry of Segusia on the six types of heresy.[42] And his remarks on the Eucharist quote verbatim but without acknowledgement from Aquinas's Eucharistic hymn.[43]

All these examples are relatively easy to explain. We do not even need to posit an extraordinarily high level of education, or access to a particular source, for the writer who uses them: the lachrymose posture of complaint is common, Henry of Segusia's views on heresy might well appear in commonplace books on canon law, and the whole point of Aquinas's hymn is to render his formulation of the doctrine of the Eucharist easily memorized and widely available. But one argument Daw gives is rather more difficult to account for. Daw himself clearly feels that he has employed knowledge inconsistent with his persona at this point: directly after giving the argument we are about to examine he adds,

---

41 This opening to complaint is also used by John Pecham in his *De Perfectione Evangelica*, a late thirteenth century defence of Franciscan poverty and mendicancy, and by an anonymous Latin poem protesting at the manner of Richard Scrope's execution for treason in 1405. Heyworth (pp. 137–8) quotes the Jeremiah passage and notes Lydgate ('Quis Dabit Meo Capiti Fontem Lacrimarum' in H. N. MacCracken, ed., *The Minor Poems of John Lydgate* (London, 1911), part 1, 324–9; 324) and the poem 'On The Execution of Richard Scrope, Archbishop of York', in T. Wright, ed., *Political Poems and Songs*, 2 vols. (London, 1859–61), ii: 114–18; 114; Pecham's use of it appears in A. G. Little, ed., 'Selections from Pecham's *Tractatus Pauperis* or *De Perfectione Evangelica*', *British Society of Franciscan Studies* 2 (1910), 13–90; 21; and Fitzralph cites a meditation by Bernard in *Quia in proposicione nuper facta* (see below, pp. 172–4).

42 See *FDR* 645–72.

43 See *FDR* 853–64. Heyworth notes and describes in detail parallels with the hymn by Aquinas 'Lauda Sion salvatorem', in F. J. E. Raby, ed., *The Oxford Book of Mediaeval Latin Verse* (Oxford, 1959), 398–400. Heyworth does not note that Daw includes further details in his exposition on Eucharistic doctrine that render Daw's theory incompatible with Aquinas's: like Wyclif, Aquinas refused to accept that substance was annihilated in transubstantiation, but Daw adds to what Heyworth calls his *cento* on 'Lauda Sion salvatorem' the two lines 'Þer leeueþ not of þe breed but oonli þe licnesse, / Which þat abidiþ þerinne noon substeyned substans' (*FDR* 860–1; punctuation modified), making of Aquinas's hymn a standard, well-known anti-Wycliffite position.

Iak, haue no merueyle þat y speke Latyn,
For oones I was a manciple at Mertoun Halle,
& þere y lernede Latyn bi roote of clerkes.
(*FDR* 724–6)

The Latin quotations and explanations given in Daw's answer to this question pose more of a threat than any of his other answers to his claim to 'lewedness': his explanation of how he, a 'lewid frere', can give this argument seems an embarrassed afterthought rather than (as it is often presented) a straightforward factual explanation by Daw of his status and position.

Indeed, the question itself casts doubt on Jack's 'lewed' status as well. In a break with the sort of directly practical *faux naif* questions he typically asks, Jack's question addresses the theoretical issue of Christ's poverty and mendicancy:

Frere, whi sclaundre ȝe falsli Crist lord of alle creaturis, þat he beggid his owne good as ȝe don oþer mennes good, siþ he had no nede þerto on þat wise? (*JU* 272–4)

Jack attempts to make this question look more relevant to lay concerns by suggesting that the fraternal claim *slanders* Christ; thus that the claim itself is not only something he wants to dispute, but an offence against public order. The friars' slander, according to Jack, is to claim that Christ begged when he had no need to do so (because he had universal lordship); if Christ had begged without need, then he would have acted hypocritically in suggesting that he was needy when in fact he was not. However, Jack's attempt to give this accusation the sort of immediate relevance to the laity found, for example, in his questions on the friars' lack of interest in burying the poor or their tendency to build churches in preference to dispensing alms, cannot disguise that Jack has made a detour into a topic of scholastic theory that surely interests only those clerics who use it as a basis for their mendicant and antimendicant arguments.

Further, all Jack's respondents follow along without protest: despite this topic's lack of interest for the ostensibly 'lewed' participants, it provokes a copious Latinate response not only from Woodford, as we would fully expect, but from Daw and Upland's Rejoinder 1, and even, in his first contribution to the debate, from Upland's Rejoinder 2.

Since the full series of replies has never been printed together in full, I include them here for the convenience of the reader:

JACK UPLAND

Frere, whi sclaundre ȝe falsli Crist lord of alle creaturis, þat he beggid his owne good as ȝe don oþer mennes good, siþ he had no nede þerto on þat wise? (272–4)

WOODFORD *RESPONSIONES*

Hic respondeo et dico quod Magister Iohannes Wyclif, cuius discipulus tu es, quaerit istam quaestionem in primo capitulo libri quem fecit *De religione* ubi plane concedit quod Christus mendicavit et fuit mendicus. Item in eodem capitulo concedit quod beatus Paulus mendicavit et similiter alii apostoli, Christi discipuli. Si bene respexisses librum Magistri tui non fecisses quaestionem istam.

Item dico quod ita certum est et verum sicut evangelium quod Christus quantum ad humanitatem assumptam fuit pauper et vixit eleemosyna. Et sive dicas talem mendicum sive non, non est curandum, quia aliqui in ista materia disputant de terminis magis quam de materia reali. Nam quidam doctores dicunt illam esse mendicitatem quam alii dicunt paupertatem, et sic fit disputatio magis de terminis quam realitate.

Verumtamen **doctores antiqui ac etiam novi** illum versum Psalmi: 'persecutus est hominem inopem et mendicum' (Ps 108: 17) exponunt ad litteram de Christo; et similiter alium **versum Psalmi: 'ego autem mendicus sum et pauper'** (Ps 39:18) **de Christo exponunt ad literam. Et sic sacra Scriptura vocat Christum mendicum in sua humanitate et non [est] scandalum imponere Christo quod sacra Scriptura sibi imponit. Stant namque bene simul quod Christus fuit Dominus totius mundi secundum divinitatem suam et servus humilis secundum humanitatem.** Ipse namque humiliter lavit pedes discipulorum suorum dicens in evangelio: 'non veni ministrari sed ministrare.' (Mt 20:28; Mk 10: 45). Et pro ista materia haec pro nunc dicta sufficiant, quia in opere alio de hoc plura intendo dicere. (40ᵃ Quaestio, 150–1)

Here I reply and say that master John Wyclif, whose disciple you are, posed this question in the first chapter of his book *On Religion*, and there he openly granted that Christ begged and was a mendicant. And in the same chapter he granted that the blessed Paul begged, and also the other apostles, Christ's disciples. If you had considered your master's book properly you would not have asked this question.

But I say that it is certain and true according to the gospel that

Christ, with respect to the humanity he took on, was poor and lived by alms. And whether you call this mendicancy or not does not matter, because the dispute over that point is over terms more than reality. For some doctors call mendicancy what others call poverty, and in this way there is a dispute about terms more than reality.

Nonetheless, doctors both old and new explain this verse of the psalm, 'he was persecuted, the man destitute and mendicant' as referring literally to Christ; and likewise this other psalm verse 'but I am mendicant and a pauper'. And in this way sacred scripture calls Christ a mendicant with respect to his humanity, and it is not a scandal to impute to Christ what scripture imputes to him. For it is logically consistent that Christ was lord of the whole world with respect to his divinity and a humble servant with respect to his humanity. For he humbly washed the feet of his disciples, saying, in the gospel: 'I have not come to be served but to serve.' And enough has now been said on this subject, because in another work I intend to say more about it.

FRIAR DAW'S REPLY

Anoþer mater is meued, þat touchiþ begging þou seist,
Þat we falsly Crist him silf disclaundren, to seie þat he beggid,
Siþ he was lord of al, & al in his demeyns.
But for þis mater Iacke, þou most vndirstonde
Þat Crist in his godhede is lord of alle þingis,
As testimonie of scripture preueþ in many places.
As touching his manheed, he was nedi & pore,
For of his nede spake Dauid in his psalmes:
> *Ego, inquit, mendicus sum et pauper;*
> *et Dominus sollicitus est mei.*

And aftir Austin & Ierom þis word of Crist was seid,
<u>**So þanne þese twey stonden wel to gidere:**</u>
Þat Crist aftir oo kynde was lord of alle,
<u>**And aftir þat oþer nedide to begge.**</u>
For if Crist seie soþ, him silf ne hadde noon harborow
To resten in his owne heed, & steken out þe stormes:
> *Vulpes, inquit, &c., vbi caput suum reclinet.*

And if we shulen ȝeue credence to doctours wordes,
Heere what seiþ Seint Ierom & Seint Bernard also:
> *Caue, inquit Ieronimus, ne mendicante Deo*
> *tuo alienas diuicias augeas. Et Bernardus.*
> *Vt te, Domine, per omnia nostre paupertati*

conformares, quasi vnus in turba pauperum
stipem per hostia mendicabas.
Wherfore þou feynest fonnedli þat oure lord we sclaundre
Or ellis oure holy doctours diden not her deuer.
Iak, haue no merueyle þat y speke Latyn,
For oones I was a manciple at Mertoun Halle,
& þere y lernede Latyn bi roote of clerkes.
(698–726)

UPLAND'S REJOINDER 1
Ȝit, Dawe, þou drawist in many fals prompynges,
For to hirt symple men, bot me neuer a del;
For Crist in his membres beggid ful oft
For synne of þe puple when þai were at mischef,
Bot as suche bolde beggeres in bodily hele,
Begged neuer Crist ne non of his membres.
For Crist þat is truþe, may in no wise
Contrarie him self, ne God þat is his fadir,
For in many places þai damnen suche sturdy beggyng.
And so, Dawe, þou dotest allegyng þe water,
Þe asse, or þe herberowe, for he was lorde of alle.
And so þou mysse takist Ierom, & lyest on Bernarde,
For Alrede his clerke wrote þis reson
Þat þou mysse layst & dokkist it as þe likiþ.
Herfor a clerk saiþ þat euel mot he spede,
Þat beggiþ of þe puple more þan is nede
   Mendax mendicus non est veritatis amicus.
   Nutantes transferantur filij eius et mendicent.
God gif þe grace to knowe how þou art Iudas childe,
Which psalme þou leggist to me as to an euel entent.
(330–49)

UPLAND'S REJOINDER 2
For ȝit þou schuldest be damned more softly in helle
Nutantes transferentur filii &c.
Þou spillest much breþe Daw with legyng of þy tyxtes;
For summe þou legest kenely to a fals entente,
But of oþer þou blundyrst as a blynde buserde,
For þes pore of whom þu spekyst myȝt not helpe hem selfe
But ȝoure prowde losengerse þat runne abowt as snekdrawers
Ben neyþer pore ne febil, & so juge þou how þes to acorde.
(349a–h, or 1–8; modern punctuation and capitals supplied)

What in Daw's contribution needs explaining even more than its embarrassing erudition is that it includes, within the sections printed above in bold type, a very close word-for-word parallel with part of Woodford's reply to the same question. Both replies (cf. the underlined passages) quote Psalm 39:18, citing the authority of the church fathers that it refers to Christ, to show that scripture calls Christ in his humanity a beggar; and both reconcile Christ's mendicancy with his lordship by distinguishing his humanity from his divinity. Daw and Woodford give similar answers, in whole or in part, to seventeen of the thirty-six questions that both cover,[44] but this example is the only precise verbal echo. There is not enough evidence to justify the assertion that Daw knew Woodford's *Responsiones*, or indeed that Woodford knew Daw's text, but on the other hand, the parallel is too close to result from coincidence. Why, where Daw moves closest to scholastic idiom, does he move so very close to Woodford?

For that matter, why is Woodford making this argument? As Catto showed in his thesis focusing on Woodford's early works, in his 1376 *De dominio civili clericorum* Woodford opposes the traditional Franciscan position on the poverty question, affirming Christ's civil dominion.[45] Catto suggests that Woodford's reversal anticipates a more general fraternal impulse in the next decade to seek common ground with possessioner monks in an increasingly anticlerical climate.[46] But here in the *Responsiones* Woodford begins by citing approvingly against his Wycliffite opponent precisely Wyclif's rebuttal, in *De civili dominio*, of Woodford's own previous *De dominio civili clericorum*.[47] Certainly any

---

[44] The answers with significant points of similarity are (using Woodford's numbering) 1–6, 11–13, 15, 18–20, 39, 40, 47, 50; these match in whole or in part with the following lines in *FDR*: 236–70, 351–85, 386–95, 421–76, 739–53, 754–63, 771–88.

[45] Catto, *William Woodford O. F. M.*, 191. Rather than Catto's title, 'Determinatio de civili dominio', I use the title Doyle subsequently gave the work in his edition: see E. Doyle, O.F.M., 'William Woodford's *De Dominio Civili Clericorum* against John Wyclif', *Archivum Franciscanum Historicum* 66 (1973), 49–109.

[46] Catto, *William Woodford*, 191–8.

[47] See the first paragraph of Woodford's reply quoted on p. 183. Wyclif refutes Woodford's arguments in Wyclif, *De civili dominio* iii: 351–iv: 405; Doyle's edition of Woodford's *De dominio civili clericorum* gives detailed cross references. For the identification of Wyclif's work *De religione* with the first three chapters of Wyclif's *De civili dominio* iii and the first two chapters of his *De apostasia* see E. Doyle, O.F.M., 'William Woodford, O.F.M., and John Wyclif's *De Religione*', *Speculum* 52 (1977), 329–36.

scholar is entitled to an about-face on at least one issue in twenty-four years of active writing and teaching, but not without remark.

Upland's rejoinder to Daw raises problems as well: it refers to arguments that Daw does not make. When Upland quotes Psalm 108 at Daw, he behaves as if he is capping Daw's quotation from the same psalm:

> *Nutantes transferantur filij eius et mendicent.*
> God gif þe grace to knowe how þou art Iudas childe,
> Which psalme þou leggist to me as to an euel entent.
> (347–9)

Psalm 108 is customarily applied to Judas's persecution of Christ, whereas Psalm 39, the psalm Daw quotes, never is.[48] But although the two psalms are often quoted together, as they are in Woodford's reply, in arguments designed to prove Christ's mendicancy, Daw made no mention of Psalm 108.[49] Nor did either Daw or Woodford refer to the examples of Christ's mendicancy that Upland dismisses: 'And so, Dawe, þou dotest allegyng þe water, / Þe asse, or þe herberowe, for he was lorde of alle.' These examples are frequently used in scholastic treatments of Christ's poverty, and in vernacular Wycliffite works as well: 'þe water' is the drink Christ asked from the Samaritan woman in John 4:7–30; 'þe asse' appears in Zechariah 9:9, where Christ is 'Ipse pauper et ascendens super asinum', and the 'herberowe' is most often

---

[48] For application of Psalm 108 to Judas see for example Nicholas de Lyra *Postilla super biblia*, 3 vols. (Venice, 1472), ii: 421v (I owe this reference to Meersseman's excellent notes to his edition of Barthelmy.); Thomas of York, *Manus quae contra omnipotentem*, in M. Bierbaum, 'Traktat eines Franziskaners zur Verteidigung der Mendikanten gegen Wilhelm von St Amour vom Jahre 1256/57 Inc: Manus que contra Omnipotentem tenditur', in *Bettelorden und Weltgeistlichkeit an der Universität Paris: Texte und Untersuchungen zum Literarischhen Armuts- und Exemtionsstreit des 13 Jahrhunderts (1255–1272), Franziskanische Studien 2 Beiheft* (1920), 37–168; 91; Barthelmy of Bolsenheim, O. P., *Defensorium*, in G. Meersseman, O. P., 'La Défense des ordres mendiants contre Richard Fitz Ralph, par Barthélmy de Bolsenheim O. P. (1357)', *Archivum Fratrum Praedicatorum* 5 (1935) 124–73; 154; Richard Maidstone, *Protectorium Pauperis*, in A. Williams, '*Protectorium Pauperis*, A Defense of the Begging Friars by Richard of Maidstone, O. Carm. (d. 1396)', *Carmelus* 5 (1958), 132–80; 151–2.

[49] For quotation of both psalms see Barthelmy, *Defensorium*, 154, Maidstone, *Protectorium Pauperis*, 148–52; Geoffrey Hardeby, *De vita evangelica*, in Oxford, Bodleian Library, Digby 113, ff. 1–117v; 43v–44; J. Wyclif, *De civili dominio* iii: 8.

the lodging Christ asks from Zacchaeus in Luke 19.[50] But Daw used none of them. Heyworth's claim that the version of *Upland's Rejoinder* found in Digby 41 is the holograph of that text, copied in full into the margins of precisely the version of Friar Daw's Reply to which it directly responds, would seem much weakened by these mismatches.

Before these difficulties may be untangled, it will be useful to lay out the main strands of the ongoing and voluminous scholastic argument upon which this question and its replies allusively draw. The question of Christ's mendicancy was important as far back as the thirteenth century: citations from Psalms 39 and 108, as well as the 'allegyng' of Christ's requests for water from the Samaritan woman and for lodging from Zacchaeus, all for example appear in fraternal and antifraternal arguments produced in the 1250s.[51] But Jack formulates his question in terms that became current only in the series of fraternal replies and further secular rebuttals that followed Richard Fitzralph's treatment of the issue a century later, in the 1350s. What makes it impossible for Jack that Christ could have begged is Christ's lordship, or *dominium*, over all created things, 'alle creaturis': if Christ holds possession of all things, it is impossible for him to beg from 'his owne good'. It was Fitzralph who had linked Christ's lordship or *dominium* with the issue of Christ's, and the friars', mendicancy; and Daw's and Woodford's replies draw upon the fraternal reaction to Fitzralph's arguments.

Fitzralph treats the theoretical issue of Christ's *dominium* at length in book six of the *De pauperie salvatoris*, drawing out its points of application to the friars in book seven. He has already distinguished civil dominion, which involves rights of possession and use and the exercise of human law, from original or natural dominion, which

---

[50] Heyworth's note on this passage should be disregarded. For scholastic use see, for example, Barthelmy's use of all three, *Defensorium*, 158–9. For Wycliffite use see 'The Sermon of William Taylor', in Hudson, *Two Wycliffite Texts*; on the Samaritan woman, 19/607–20/646 (and see Hudson's comparison in her notes of Taylor's treatment of this example with that of the unprinted Lollard sermon 'Omnis Plantacio', 102, 608n.); on Zaccheus, 20/647–58. The Lollard tract 'De Blasphemia, Contra Fratres' (in Arnold, *Select English Works* iii: 402–29) uses all three examples, 413–15.

[51] See William of St Amour *De periculis novissimorum temporum*, in *Opera Omnia*, (Constance [for Paris], 1632), 17–72; 51–2 for the Samaritan woman and Zacchaeus; and *De Quantitate Eleemosynae Quaestio*, in ibid., 73–80, 78–9, for citation of Psalm 39:18. Thomas of York cites Psalm 108; see n. 48.

entitles one to the possession and use of necessities. Fitzralph claims that Christ as man had no civil dominion; therefore the friars in imitating him should renounce any claim to civil, especially pastoral, jurisdiction and to the possession of goods, and retain only the use of necessities. But on the other hand Christ did have natural dominion, with the result that he had no need to beg, since he had dominion over goods necessary to him; therefore the friars, like Christ, should work rather than beg.[52] In reply to subsequent fraternal arguments, Fitzralph extends this argument in his *Defensio curatorum* in order to explain precisely how gospel references to Christ's begging should be understood. The second of the nine conclusions he defends in this work is 'quod Christus nunquam spontanee mendicauit'. Christ never begged from need, Fitzralph argues, because his original *dominium* prevented this being necessary; but he also never begged *spontanee*, that is, as a free choice despite having the capacity to earn a living, because it would have been hypocritical – not to mention contrary to God's law, the Emperor's law, and his own gospel – for him to beg what he did not need.[53]

Widely disseminated as the *Defensio* was, even this is not the most influential of Fitzralph's Christ-based arguments against mendicancy.[54]

---

[52] This account ignores the complexities of Fitzralph's theory of dominion by grace, irrelevant for present purposes. In addition to the copy of *De pauperie salvatoris* in Oxford, Bodleian Library, Auct F inf. 1.2, ff. 1–83 that I have used, more easily available sources are Poole's edition of the first four and summary table of contents for the final three books in J. Wyclif, *De domino divino*, ed. R. L. Poole (London, 1890), 273–476, 264–72, and the discussions by Dawson, 'Richard FitzRalph', 333–41, F. A. Mathes, O. S. A., 'The Poverty Movement and the Augustinian Hermits', ii, *Anal. Aug.* 32 (1969), 5–116; 16–30, and K. Walsh, 'The *De Vita Evangelica* of Geoffrey Hardeby (*c.* 1385)', i, *Anal. Aug.* 33 (1970), 151–261; 251–4.

[53] Richard Fitzralph, *Defensio curatorum*, in M. Goldast, ed., *Monarchiae S Romani Imperii* . . . , 3 vols. (Frankfurt, 1621), iii: 1391–1410; 1405–7, and see the Middle English translation by Trevisa in A. J. Perry, ed., *Dialogus inter Militem et Clericum, Richard fitzRalph's Sermon: 'Defensio curatorum' and Methodius: þe Bygynnyng of þe World and þe Ende of Worldes' by John Trevisa, vicar of Berkeley* (London, 1925), 80/ 28–87/9. As explained in ch. 3 (p. 96), the second conclusion is treated after the eighth, ninth and first conclusions: ostentatiously reordering his presentation so as to give general public concerns greater prominence, Fitzralph discusses the final two conclusions first and at great length, then returns to treat more briefly the first seven conclusions.

[54] On the dissemination of the *Defensio curatorum* see A. Gwynn, 'The Sermon Diary of Richard Fitzralph', *Proceedings of the Royal Irish Academy* 44 C (1937), 1–57, and

More important still to the fraternal arguments against his position –
perhaps because in them Fitzralph is constrained to reply on fraternal
terms – are Fitzralph's responses to the friars' objections to his *Defensio
curatorum*, entitled from their incipit *Quia in proposicione nuper facta*
and frequently copied with the *Defensio curatorum*.[55] In addition to
many copies circulating in manuscripts of the *Defensio curatorum*,
copies of *Quia in proposicione nuper facta* appear in at least two
miscellaneous *summae* (to use Szittya's term) containing antifraternal
material: Oxford, Bodleian Library, Bodley 784 and London, British
Library, Royal 6 E VI & VII.[56] Although the presence of *Quia in
proposicione nuper facta* has been noted, its content has never, to my
knowledge, received more than a glancing reference.[57] The first of the
friars' objections focuses on Fitzralph's second conclusion:

> Contra articulum seu conclucionem 'Quod Christus nunquam
> spontanee mendicauit' obicitur per illud psalm[um] xxxix 'Ego vero
> mendicus sum et[58] pauper' quod in persona christi literaliter dictum
> asseritur.[59]

> Against the article or conclusion 'That Christ never voluntarily
> begged' an objection is made citing Psalm 39 'But I am a mendicant
> and pauper' which is asserted to refer literally to the person of Christ.

K. Walsh, *A Fourteenth-Century Scholar and Primate: Richard FitzRalph in Oxford,
Avignon and Armagh* (Oxford, 1981), 422–51 (for the work's place in proceedings at
the papal court), and 469–75 (for more on the dissemination of Fitzralph's writings).

[55] In her biography of Fitzralph Walsh seemingly confuses this work with Fitzralph's *De
audientia confessionum*. See K. Walsh, *Richard Fitzralph*; she distinguishes the two on
441, remarking that the *Quia in proposicione nuper facta* was disseminated widely
together with the *Defensio curatorum* (n. 104), but her index and p. 474 refer to *De
audientia* giving it the incipit *Quia in proposicione nuper facta*.

[56] See P. R. Szittya, *The Antifraternal Tradition in Medieval Literature* (Princeton, 1986),
112–22, 291–300.

[57] The work has remained unnoticed except by Szittya, Walsh, Gwynn, and those
manuscript cataloguers who have troubled to distinguish it from the *Defensio
curatorum*. I have so far consulted the copies found in Oxford, Bodleian Library,
Bodley 144, 158, and 784; I plan to publish a separate article examining the work in
greater detail and consulting all available manuscripts.

[58] *Corr.* pa

[59] Abbreviations are silently expanded and modern punctuation and capitalization
supplied in this and all subsequent manuscript transcriptions. All departures from the
readings of Bodley 144, Gwynn's base text for his work on Fitzralph's sermons, will be
detailed in the notes. This is Bodley 144, f. 271v; Fitzralph's reply to the first objection
continues to 273.

The objection goes on to cite and expound at length Peter Lombard's interpretation of Psalm 39:18 as referring to Christ. The eight articles of Fitzralph's reply to this objection elaborate the two points brought forth in the first of them: that the psalm may not properly be interpreted as referring to Christ *in propria persona*, and that the state described by the verse is not that of spontaneous corporeal mendicancy. Instead of Christ, the psalm refers to his members, that is, the Church (a possibility Peter Lombard also includes); and instead of corporeal the psalm means to refer to spiritual mendicancy and poverty; or else the alternative translation 'egenus et pauper' is preferable and refers to a corporeal poverty not severe enough to compel its sufferers to beg.[60]

To his comment in this first reply that Peter Lombard's explanation is untrue and ungrammatical, Fitzralph in his reply to the tenth objection, 'Paulum Apostolum mendicasse a Corintheis et Romanis saltem collectus in sanctos pauperes', 'the apostle Paul begged from the Corinthians, or at least took a collection for the holy poor', adds a dismissal that is less harsh, but because of its elaborate theoretical backing and wider implications far more weighty.[61] This crucial passage has never yet been discussed.[62] But it was disseminated widely in company with the *Defensio*, and Wyclif and Maidstone evidently knew it: indeed, it explains the contention behind Wyclif's statement

---

[60] For the first point see articles 1a, 3, 4, 5, 7; for the second, 1b, 2, 3, 6, 7, 8.

[61] Fitzralph's comments on Peter Lombard appear in his reply to the first objection, article 1 (ff. 271v-272). What I number as the tenth objection covers ff. 275v-277v. The portion of the reply to the tenth objection to be discussed here (Bodley 144, ff. 276rv) expands and explains the first reply, article 7, 'cum iste glosator, scilicet magister sentenciarum, illud *exponat* de christo et aliter de suis membris, nemo potest concludere quod alteram exposicionem *affirmat*', 'when this writer of glosses, that is the master of the Sentences [i.e., Peter Lombard] gives an exposition of that [verse] that relates it to Christ and also to his members, nobody can conclude that he affirms either exposition' (f. 272v, my emphases). I number as a separate objection each point where Fitzralph's argument departs anew from a new proposition put to him by the friars: Bodley 144 includes no numbers, Bodley 158 numbers as I do but labels the argument against Bernard as objection 11 even though there is no new proposition at this point, and Bodley 784 recognizes the beginnings of new sections within the text, but skips some of them in its numbering.

[62] Minnis has briefly examined how Fitzralph in his *Summa de questionibus Armenorum* distinguishes assertors from editors or compilers. But he does not discuss the more complex and detailed theory Fitzralph develops here. (A. J. Minnis, *Medieval Theory of Authorship: Scholastic Literary Attitudes in the Later Middle Ages*, 2nd ed. (Aldershot, 1988), 100–2).

in *De civili dominio* that Bernard 'simpliciter assereret', 'unconditionally asserted' that Christ begged.[63] Taylor summarizes Fitzralph's reply accurately in his 1406 sermon: 'And as to Bernard or Alrede his clerk, answeriþ Ardmakan and seiþ þat it is seid bi maner of meuyng and not bi maner of affermyng': it is said in a manner designed to excite emotion, that is, rather than in a manner that affirms what is said as truth.[64] A contemporary annotator of Bodley 144 labels Fitzralph's explanation 'Nota bene pro auctoritatibus sanctorum', 'Notice this on the authority of the saints': its possible influence on late medieval English theories of authority in general, and in particular on later Wycliffite attitudes to the citation of patristic authorities, is overdue for examination.[65]

In his reply to the friars' tenth objection Fitzralph rehearses and refutes the fraternal argument using 'Bernard' that Daw so elliptically mentions. 'Bernard' (to whom Ailred's sermon on Christ's stay in the temple at twelve years of age is more often attributed) unequivocally refers to Christ as an impoverished beggar in this address: 'Vt te, Domine nostre, per omnia paupertati conformares,[66] quasi vnus in turba pauperum stipem[67] per hostia mendicabas', 'So that you, our lord, should in all things conform to poverty, you begged money as if one among the mass of the poor' (f. 276). Therefore fraternal begging may be justified as a meritorious imitation of Christ. Particularly when this quotation is ascribed to such an authoritative speaker, its description of Christ's mendicant activity is difficult to circumvent or discount. Fitzralph's strategy is to give an elaborate theoretical argument for diminishing its authority.

In the course of showing how the 'Bernard' sermon should be understood, Fitzralph explains that the saints have four ways of speaking: 'aliquando excitatiue, aliquando expositiue, aliquando assertiue sed transcursiue siue inaduertentis, et aliquando assertiue ac probatiue

---

[63] J. Wyclif, *De civili dominio* iii, 8. For Maidstone's reference see below, pp. 176–7.

[64] 'The Sermon of William Taylor', 21/687–9. The comma I have added to remove ambiguity. On Taylor's career and the occasion of the sermon see Hudson's introduction, xiii-xxv.

[65] I plan to investigate the textual tradition and influence of this passage in a separate article; for now, the copies available to me will have to suffice. The marginal annotation in Bodley 144 appears on f. 276.

[66] conformares] confirmares   [67] *Corr.* per omnia.

seu diffinitiue', 'sometimes excitatively, sometimes expositively, sometimes assertively, but in passing over certain matters or along the way, and sometimes assertively and in a probative or definitive manner'.[68] In the three manuscripts of this passage I have so far examined I have already found three versions of this list: in this longest version we can see two locations for eyeskip, over the two words beginning with 'ex' and the two occurrences of 'assertiue'; an abridging tendency might also result from the scribal expectation that after an announcement that four ways are to be listed, no more than four terms should be given. Be that as it may, it is the first two items on the list that concern us here, and that most concern Fitzralph, because as he explains they are the kinds of saintly statements that should not, however authoritative their speakers, be considered fully authoritative.

When a saint speaks 'excitatiue', as Bernard does in the sermon quoted or in his meditation *De compassione beate virginis gloriose* where he asks 'Quis dabit capiti meo aquam et oculis meis ymbrem vt possem[69] flere per diem et noctem donec seruo suo dominus iesus christus appareat', 'Who will give to my head water and to my eyes a well that I may weep day and night until lord Jesus Christ should appear to his servant', his statement is meant to excite himself and others toward devotion (276).[70] But the statement is edifying rather than authoritatively true: 'tale dictum sancti Bernardi aut sancti alterius auctoritatem[71] non habet quoniam neque asseritur neque affirmatur ab ipso et ob hoc ad aliquid[72] probandum frustra et inepte adducitur', 'such a statement by St Bernard or another saint does not have authority since it is neither asserted nor affirmed by him, and thus to adduce it in proving something is useless and inept' (276v).[73] Similarly, when a saint speaks expositively, he explains the meaning of another

---

68 This list is taken from Bodley 158, f. 169; the version in Bodley 144 has been truncated to 'aliquando excitatiue, aliquando assertiue ac probatiue seu diffinitiue' (276) (even though like the other copies this text goes on to discuss expositive and assertive/ transcursive speech at length), while the version in Bodley 784, f. 95 omits 'siue inaduertentis'. A possible explanation follows; confirmation will have to wait until I can examine more manuscripts.

69 possem] possim

70 I cite the longer more descriptive title for the meditation from Bodley 158, f. 169.

71 *Corr.* e.   72 *Corr.* ad.

73 See also 276: 'non intendit quod dicit discutere siue asserere sed edificare', 'he does not intend to discuss or assert what he says, but to edify'.

writer rather than giving the truth as he sees it, and thus once again his statements are not authoritative:

> Vnde ad probandum aliquid esse verum sola exposicio sancti alicuius doctoris videtur fragile argumentum, quamuis ipse quia catholicus, non quia expositor, veritatem scripture defendere teneatur, quia in exponendo non pro defensione scripture sed pro expressione intencionis[74] scribentis laborat, non in hoc intendens intencionis scribentis discutere ueritatem. Vnde videtur quod glosa magistri super illo versiculo psalmi 'Ego vero mendicus sum et pauper', ex quo duas exposiciones expressit, non debet glose aut exponenti tanquam eius auctoritatis seu ab eo assertum ascribi; et ob hoc ad probandum christum fuisse mendicum non satis solide est adductum. (276v)

> And thus to prove something is true, any sainted doctor's exposition alone would seem a fragile argument, although he is held as a catholic, not as an expositor, to defend the truth of scripture; because in giving an exposition he aims at the expression of the intention of the writer, not at the defence of scripture, and does not intend to discuss the truth of the intention of the writer. And thus it seems that the gloss of the master on this verse of the psalm, 'But I am a mendicant and pauper', because he gives two expositions, should not be ascribed to the gloss or expositor as asserted by him or associated with his authority; and thus it is inadequate when adduced to prove that Christ was a mendicant.

The fact that Peter Lombard gives two alternative explanations for Psalm 39:18 shows that he is speaking expositively; thus, his explanation should not be credited with the same sort of authority that would be granted to such an important and respected writer if he were speaking assertively.

If Jack's question employs the terms of Fitzralph's discussion of Christ's mendicancy, while Daw's reply refers to a fraternal argument Fitzralph rehearses in the course of his exposition, two fraternal rebuttals of Fitzralph's reply publicized in the 1380s to 1390s provide close analogues to Daw's and Woodford's answers. Geoffrey Hardeby in his *De Vita Evangelica* attempts, like Daw and Woodford, to

---

[74] intencionis] intencione. Unsurprisingly there are scribal errors in this sentence in both Bodley 144 and 158; Bodley 784 omits all of this passage but a modified version of the first phrase.

reconcile Christ's lordship with his mendicant poverty.[75] In chapter nine Hardeby argues that Christ as man was both rich and poor at once, resolving the contradiction implied by suggesting that Christ and his apostles were 'divitissimi', 'most rich', as concerned their worthiness for possessing temporal goods, but 'pauperrimi', 'most poor' as concerned their actual use of temporal possessions; their riches, therefore, were spiritual, and their poverty corporeal.[76] In chapter eleven Hardeby's sources are strikingly similar to Daw's and Woodford's: after reminding us of Christ's corporeal poverty, Hardeby argues – using Psalm 39:18 and Psalm 108, as well as the passages from Jerome and Bernard that Daw cites – that Christ as man needed to beg because he was subject to human law rather than merely divine law:

> Unde Christus iure divino habens dominium et potestatem super omnia temporalia, eodem titulo mendicare ab hominibus fuisset omnino contra racionem. Sed quia iure humano multa sibi necessaria sua non fuerunt ante mendicacionem, idcirco talia gracie titulo potuit ab hominibus mendicare.[77]

> Since Christ by divine law/right had dominion and power over all temporal things, by the same title for him to beg from men would have been altogether against reason. But because by human law many things were necessary to him that he did not have before begging, thus he could by title of grace beg those things from men.

Because according to human law Christ did not (before begging for them) possess many things that were necessary to him, therefore he could beg those things from human beings.

---

75 On Geoffrey Hardeby, see the thorough study by Walsh, 'The *De Vita Evangelica*', i and ii. There is also useful context and a summary in Mathes, 'The Poverty Movement', ii: 30–48. I have worked from the manuscript copy in Digby 113, ff. 1–117v, but will give crossreferences to passages discussed in Walsh or Mathes where appropriate. For the portion of ch. eleven, 'Utrum Christus huius vite necessaria ab hominibus aliquociens mendicauit', 'Whether Christ sometimes begged the necessities of this life from men' (ff. 43–8), discussed here, see Digby 113, ff. 47–8; Walsh, 'The *De Vita Evangelica*', ii: 21–2; Mathes, 'The Poverty Movement', ii: 37–8.

76 Ch. nine, 'Numquid Christus et eius apostoli quo ad possessiones temporalium fuerunt veri pauperes in hoc mundo', 'Whether Christ and his apostles were true paupers as regards temporal possessions in this world'; see Digby 113, ff. 30–6, esp. 32v, 35v, Walsh, 'The *De Vita Evangelica*', ii: 17–19, Mathes, 'The Poverty Movement', ii: 37 and nn. 129, 130.

77 Digby 113, f. 47; Walsh, 'The *De Vita Evangelica*', ii: 21–2 (she quotes this passage as well, in n. 108); Mathes, 'The Poverty Movement', ii: 37–8.

Richard Maidstone's *Protectorium Pauperis* – a set of academic lectures given at Oxford in the late 1380s to early 1390s in opposition, Maidstone says, to Ashwardby's vernacular sermons before the laity – is similarly very close to the Upland Series in both content and choice of authorities. Maidstone is closer still to just the passages from Fitzralph's *Quia in proposicione nuper facta* we have examined: either Ashwardby relied heavily on Fitzralph, or else Maidstone is at some points more interested in answering Fitzralph than Ashwardby. As Woodford does in the second paragraph of his reply,[78] Maidstone in his second conclusion notes and dismisses the difficulties over the term 'mendicitas' that Fitzralph raised in his reply to the friars' first objection, article 3 (148–52). Maidstone then rehearses and thoroughly refutes Fitzralph's argument in the same reply, article 4, that the verse 'Ego mendicus sum et pauper' cannot refer to Christ because the rest of the psalm does not. In the process Maidstone uses the same quotation from Jerome that Daw and Hardeby cite, but the key text of Maidstone's reply is Psalm 108, and as for Upland's rejoinder, this psalm is useful to Maidstone chiefly because of its customary interpretation as referring to Judas's persecution of Christ: even if his opponent is right to say that one interpretation must always apply to the whole of a psalm, Maidstone argues, Psalm 108 would nonetheless disprove his opponent's contention that Christ never begged, because in that psalm the persecuted figure, whom all agree figures Christ throughout, is *inops* and *mendicus*. Like Daw and Hardeby, once again, Maidstone also uses the quotation from the 'Bernard' homily, in his fifth conclusion. And as before where he cited Jerome and Psalm 108, Maidstone's argument focuses on rehearsing and dismissing Fitzralph's arguments from the *Quia in proposicione nuper facta* (158; cf. Fitzralph's reply to the friars' tenth objection): even if the statement attributed to 'Bernard' is not an assertion but 'ex devotione et pietate opinative tantum', 'only a pious and devout opinion', Maidstone asks, how could piety move Bernard or even Ailred to affirm something heretical or blasphemous?

---

[78] While it seems overwhelmingly likely that Maidstone's argument refers to Fitzralph's *Quia in proposicione nuper facta*, it is possible that Woodford has in mind Fitzralph's *De Pauperie Salvatoris*, which discusses at even greater length the various terms used to describe poverty. The second paragraph of Woodford's reply is quoted in full above, p. 163.

It is impossible to determine whether Daw, or Woodford, or both, used Hardeby or Maidstone in preparing their answers. But the points of close resemblance we find among these arguments show that Daw, like Woodford, is well acquainted with the academic discussion of this question in the 1380s to 90s. Woodford's earlier attempt to assert Christ's civil dominion in *De dominio civili clericorum* looks increasingly like an original and unusual moment in an otherwise consistent fraternal defence rather than a precursor of a general fraternal shift toward a new strategy; it would seem that others did not follow Woodford's lead, and that even he subsequently abandoned his claims and fell in with the standard line. Against the background of that standard line the close resemblance between Daw and Woodford is not so surprising; I have yet to find an argument that makes a distinction with the precise terms they both employ, but virtually every fraternal defence after 1350 copes with the contradiction between Christ's riches and poverty using some distinction between Christ's divinity and humanity.[79] Daw's and Woodford's answers may be located not only solidly within the 150 year old tradition of fraternal and antifraternal polemic, but among its most up-to-date representatives.

Examining the polemic background can also help us to link the Rejoinder in particular, and perhaps by implication Daw, to Oxford. Although Upland's rejoinder harks back to older (though still current) arguments about Christ's mendicancy in its references to Psalm 108, to 'þe water, / Þe asse, [and] þe herberowe', and to Christ's members, I have so far found its correct attribution of the 'Bernard' sermon to Ailred only in works produced at Oxford in the late fourteenth and early fifteenth centuries. Two of these correct attributions, indeed, those of Maidstone and Wyclif, appear in fourteenth century treatises on clerical dominion and poverty produced by scholars associated with Merton, precisely the college with which Daw claimed a shadowy affiliation, while the third appears in the Oxford clerk William Taylor's controversial sermon against clerical possessions.

---

79 Along with the fraternal arguments already cited, cf. Trevisa's attempt to deal with the distinction in his translation of the pseudo-Ockham *Dialogus inter militem et clericem*, ch. 3, pp. 82–7.

Whether or not this specific location of the series might hold up, it may certainly be urged, against Heyworth's view that the series is 'semi-literate' (18), that all the components of the series, even the ones in English, bear the marks of university production. The participants' sketchy and telegraphic references to well-known arguments are the products of allusion to points of debate familiar to all, not (as Heyworth thought) sketchy knowledge. Their claims to 'lewed'ness are focused to a remarkable degree on gaining advantage over one another; although each claims to speak on behalf of a 'lewed' position, none makes any reference to any projected 'lewed' audience other than his interlocutors in debate. As we saw in Daw's and *Upland's Rejoinder's* exchange on treason, even invoking loyalty to the king is important mostly because it is a way to gain advantage in debate; there is no anticipation, let alone apprehension, that the king will read the exchange. Here as elsewhere thoughout the debate, writing in English seems to carry for the participants an immediate association with 'lewed'ness, but no association with its availability to a potential 'lewed' audience, and no concerns with the implications of that availability. For these extraclergial writers, using English is mainly a way to score against their opponents by taking a 'lewed' stance; the 'lewed' persons mentioned, even the king, are little more than vehicles of argument.

This sort of insularity, this failure to consider the obvious implications of the vernacular, is very unusual: the Upland participants show none of the interest in the exemplary quality of their 'lewed' argumentative stance that – as we will see – preoccupied William Thorpe; nor are they concerned about the possible reactions of a universal (let alone a limited) 'lewed' audience, in the way that Dymmok was even though he wrote in Latin. The ostensible participants seem indifferent to those possibilities of vernacular audience that so exercised their contemporaries; indifferent even (or more accurately) to the possibilities of the gesture toward such an audience. Yet (in contrast once again to most extraclergial works) this insular attitude was not shared by those who disseminated the series. *Jack Upland* in particular seems to have found a wide readership – indeed, probably extending to the sort of reader by which it claims to have been written, one critical of the clergy but entirely separate from it.

6

Vernacular argumentation in
The Testimony of William Thorpe

The *Testimony of William Thorpe* presents itself as an account written by Thorpe of his examination before Arundel and three clerks.[1] There is no extant record of such an examination having taken place, and the account is strongly biased in Thorpe's favour.[2] However, patently the text's value is not as a record of actual procedure but as a representation of ideal, even exemplary, steadfastness in adversity; one which some Wycliffites thought worthy of translation, transport to Bohemia, and dissemination and conservation sufficient at least to preserve the text for printed publication in 1530.[3] Like many a martyr or heretic on trial, Thorpe models his present predicament on Christ's passion and his dissenting activity more generally on Christ's mission.[4] Thorpe's steadfastness is not however the silently enduring variety common among martyrs.[5] Instead, Thorpe's 'crucifixion' is through argument:

---

[1] *The Testimony of William Thorpe, 1407,* in Hudson, ed., *Two Wycliffite Texts.* Until recently available only in a modernized version ('The Examination of William Thorpe', in A. W. Pollard, ed., *Fifteenth Century Prose and Verse* (Edinburgh, 1903), i: 97–167), and a facsimile of the 1530 printed edition (*Examinacions Thorpe and Oldcastell* (Antwerp, 1530), facsimile ed. (Amsterdam and Norwood, NJ, 1975)), the *Testimony* has been newly edited from the early fifteenth century Bodley manuscript. Hereafter unless otherwise noted parenthetical references will refer to page and line numbers in the 1993 edition.

[2] This is not, of course, to say that the examination did not in fact occur; see Hudson's comments on the historicity of the text in *Two Wycliffite Texts,* xlv-xlvii.

[3] For details of the Latin and English manuscripts in England and Bohemia and of the early print, see Hudson, *Two Wycliffite Texts,* xxvi-xlv.

[4] For another Wycliffite writer who models his prosecution for heresy on Christ's passion, see Richard Wyche's account of his sufferings in gaol in 'The Trial of Richard Wyche', ed. F. D. Matthew, *English Historical Review* 5 (1890), 530–44. On Thorpe's comparison of his teaching mission with Christ's see especially 45/694–703.

[5] Thorpe does maintain a (verbosely reported) silence between 36/410 and 37/434, but refusal to speak is not on the whole his preferred tactic.

'as a tree leyde vpon anoþer tree ouerthwert on crosse wyse, so weren þe Archebischop and hise þree clerkis alwei contrarie to me and I to hem' (93/2245–7). Thorpe wins through by means of better arguments and more adept manoeuvring: even while claiming not to be 'curious' and 'sotil' like the 'sofestris' he deplores, he makes extensive use of terminology and techniques of argument familiar from medieval academic disputation. In the course of the *Testimony*, he manages to profess his Wycliffite belief in some detail while evading both the charges brought against him and Arundel's demands that he grant or deny orthodox statements.

Thorpe rejects the authority of the institutional clergy of the established church[6] and insists instead on grounding his arguments in the authority of 'clergie' in the sense of 'learning'.[7] The terms he uses to defend Taylor's sermon neatly encapsulate his paradigm of 'clergial' clerical grounding:[8] 'bi þe autorite of Goddis word and bi appreued seyntis and doctours and bi opin resoun þis clerk proude clereli alle þingis þat he þere prechide' (85/1972–7; emphases mine). This trio of authorities deserves some amplification. The authority of the pair 'opin resoun' and 'Goddis word' is approved three times in the *Testimony* and frequently in other Wycliffite writings;[9] it was also noted by their

---

[6] See 51/896–52/917, where Thorpe affirms that he wishes to be governed by 'holi chirche' but then, at Arundel's prompting, admits that in his view 'holi chirche here in erþe' is not the established church. This method of rejecting the church's authority appears frequently in Wycliffite writings; see the list of examples in Hudson's note on this passage (*Two Wycliffite Texts*, 116–17).

[7] On the usage of 'lewed' and 'clergie' see ch. 1, p. 13, and ch. 2 *passim*.

[8] I am accepting Hudson's identification of the 'clerk' Thorpe refers to here as William Taylor and her argument that the sermon by William Taylor in Oxford, Bodleian Library, Douce 53 (printed in *Two Wycliffite Texts* along with the *Testimony*), is the sermon Taylor preached at St Paul's Cross. See Hudson, *The Premature Reformation*, 13–14 and *Two Wycliffite Texts*, xiii.

[9] The pair appears in the *Testimony* at 33/319–20 and 37/430 in addition to the passage quoted above, and it appears elsewhere in Wycliffite texts, to give a few examples, in L. M. Swinburn, ed., *The Lanterne of Liȝt* (London, 1917), 117; the epilogue to a commentary on Matthew printed in M. Deanesly, *The Lollard Bible* (Cambridge, 1920), 457–61, *passim* and especially 458; 'De Pontificum Romanorum Schismate' in Arnold, ed., *Select English Works of John Wyclif*, iii: 242–66; 251; Gradon and Hudson, eds., *English Wycliffite Sermons*, vol. ii, ed. P. Gradon (Oxford, 1988), 86/106–10 and 188/59–70; the dialogue between Reson and Gabbyng (Dublin, Trinity College 245, ff. 153v–160 at f. 159); and the dialogue between Jon and Richerd (Cambridge, Trinity College B.14.50, ff. 35–55 at f. 36v). (There is, of course, some minor variation among these examples in the terms used to denote *resoun* and *scripture*.)

contemporary opponents: 'haec regula est Lollardorum: hoc non habetur ex sacra scriptura, neque ex racione naturali, ergo hoc non est ponendum'.[10] The insistence of Wyclif and Wycliffites on scriptural authority has long been asserted, but not much attention has been paid to the frequency with which Wyclif and many Wycliffites ground their alternative 'clergie' on reason – which by analogy to its scholastic Latin contemporary *ratio* has a wide semantic range from 'capacity for reasoning' through 'rational argument/argumentation' and 'definition' to 'logic'[11] – as well as scripture.[12] While Wyclif had asserted the importance of scripture to reason in the opening of his earliest extant work on logic,[13] in *De veritate sacrae scripturae* he gives a more

10 From one of the tracts against the Lollard Walter Brut's advocacy of women, London, British Library, Harley 31, f. 219 (quoted in Hudson, *Premature Reformation*, 377; Hudson uses it as an example of how the opponents of Wycliffites were aware of Wycliffite insistence on scriptural authority, but does not remark on the pairing of *sacra scriptura* with *racio naturali*).

11 See *MED* s.v. *resoun*. On the exploitation of the full semantic scope of the word *resoun* in *Piers Plowman*, see J. A. Alford, 'The Idea of Reason in *Piers Plowman*', in Kennedy, Waldron, and Wittig, eds., *Medieval English Studies Presented to George Kane*, 199–215.

12 Hudson points out against the prevailing view that Wyclif himself did not hold to *scriptura sola*, but grants that 'it is probably a reasonable summary of many of his followers' attitudes' (*Premature Reformation*, 228). Although she does not discuss Wyclif's followers, G. R. Evans does insist on Wyclif's place within a late medieval trend toward employing logical and philosophical terms and concepts in biblical interpretation: see *The Language and Logic of the Bible: The Road to Reformation* (Cambridge, 1985), chs. 8 and 11; 'Wyclif's *Logic* and Wyclif's Exegesis: The Context' in Walsh and Woods, *The Bible in the Medieval World*, 287–300; and 'Wyclif on Literal and Metaphorical', in *From Ockham to Wyclif*, ed. A. Hudson and M. Wilks, *Studies in Church History Subsidia* 5 (Oxford, 1987), 259–66.

13 Wyclif claims in the proem of his *De logica* to be 'making plain the logic of Holy Scripture' by eschewing pagan references and relying exclusively on biblical proofs: 'Motus sum per quosdam legis dei amicos certum tractatum ad declarandam logicam sacre scripture compilare. Nam videns multos ad logicam transeuntes, qui per illam proposuerant legem dei melius cognovisse, et propter insipidam terminorum mixtionem gentilium in omni probacionem proposicionum propter vacuitatem operis eam deserentes, propono ad acuendum mentes fidelium ponere probaciones proposicionum que debent elici ex scripturis', 'I have been moved by certain friends of the law of God to compile a certain treatise that will explain the logic of sacred scripture. For I see many advancing to the study of logic, who had intended to know the law of God better thereby, and because of the insipid admixture of pagan terms in every proof of a proposition they leave off their study on account of the vacuity of the labour; so as to sharpen the minds of the faithful, I plan to posit proofs of propositions that are taken from the scriptures.' The *De logica* is printed in *Tractatus de logica*, 3 vols., ed. M. H. Dziewicki, Wyclif Society (London, 1893–9), i: 1–74; for the quoted

considered assessment of the relationship between reason and scripture.[14] Although this work has been selectively quoted to prove Wyclif's reliance on *scriptura sola,* through the claim that Wyclif is founding a new 'logic' different in kind than that of the schools, based not in rational argumentation but in scriptural interpretation and 'application of the text to life',[15] it would be more accurate to say that for Wyclif, scripture's logic includes scholastic logic without superseding it. There is no need to dismiss scholastic reasoning, 'que ut plurimum est recta', 'which is for the most part correct', because 'logica Aristotelis . . . sit logica scripture . . . non est sustinenda ut Aristotelis, sed ut scripture sacre, cum ipsa sit autor summus et prima regula, de qua sola sequitur, si quidquam asserit, ergo verum . . . ', 'the logic of Aristotle . . . is the logic of scripture . . . it should be held to not as Aristotle's, but as sacred scripture's, since it itself is the highest authority and first rule, and from it alone can one conclude that if it asserts something, therefore it is true'[16] (47/16–48/23). Educated Wycliffites who employ scholastic techniques of argument appear to have espoused a similar theory: scripture is itself logical, and reason when properly employed arrives at conclusions that accord with and may be illustrated from scripture. They tend in their own writings to prefer arguments based on biblical proofs, and often insist that their opponents ought to use such proofs if they want to produce valid arguments. They also accept, and employ, the 'resouns' of other authorities, as Thorpe's acceptance of Taylor's 'appreued seyntis and doctours' shows and his

passage, see i: 1. W. R. Thomson dates the *De logica* to *c.* 1360 and explains how Dziewicki's three volume edition conflates the *De logica* with two parts of the longer work *Logice Continuacio* dated 1360–3 (*The Latin Writings of John Wyclif,* 4–6); but see J. Wyclif, *Tractatus de universalibus,* ed. I. J. Mueller (Oxford, 1985), xxxv, xxxvii–viii; Mueller redates the second work to the early 1370s and the first more loosely between 1360 and 1368. Wyclif does give scriptural examples in the *De logica,* but in addition he freely makes use of standard logical examples of Socrates sitting, men being in Rome, and so on.

14 J. Wyclif, *De veritate sacre scripture,* 3 vols., ed. R. Buddensieg (London, 1905–7), i. Dated by Thomson, *Latin Writings of John Wyclif,* 55, between late 1377 and the end of 1378.

15 For this comment, see 'John Wyclif from *The Authority of Sacred Scripture*', in D. L. Jeffrey, ed. and trans., *The Law of Love: English Spirituality in the Age of Wyclif* (Grand Rapids, MI, 1988), 332; and for a more general discussion of Wyclif along the same lines, see pp. 30–8 of the introduction to the volume.

16 Wyclif, *De veritate sacre scripture,* ed. Buddensieg, i:47/23–48/6.

own practice corroborates. But these other authorities must survive verification against reason and scripture: 'eny doctrine ['doctors' in the Pollard edition and the *STC* print] discordinge from holi writt' (51/ 912–13) is not to be credited.[17]

Thorpe's grounding, then, is upon 'clergie' rather than the clergy; he approves not the authorities the institutional clergy tell him to believe, but only those that are consistent with reason and scripture. Since 'clergie' remains the ideological basis of the clergy's own authority and the means by which clerics distinguish themselves from the lay population, Thorpe's opponents find his grounding hard to dismiss, even if they may disagree with some of its limitations and emphases.[18] But Thorpe does not merely establish for himself and display to his newly enlarged audience a dissident authority better, because grounded in more authoritative writings and more adept reasoning, than that of the established church. In addition, he extends that dissident authority to non-academics: he includes all members of his audience, regardless of their level of formal education, as interpreters of scripture and even as reasoners – provided, of course, that they are virtuous and have God's grace. And he claims that all properly virtuous interpreters and reasoners have the authority to reject bad interpretation and bad reasoning pronounced by the clerical authorities.

To accomplish this surprisingly egalitarian extension of authority, Thorpe represents his own ability to produce interpretations of scripture and arguments from 'opin resoun' as a result not, or not so much, of his clerical education, but of virtue conferred by grace. Rather than affiliating himself with a prestigious school in order to

---

[17] Authorities whose words Thorpe cites approvingly are included in Hudson's index of proper names: they include Grosseteste, Higden or 'Cistrence', Augustine, pseudo-Chrysostom, and Gregory. Wycliffites tend to approve patristic writers such as Augustine and pseudo-Chrysostom, but to contest with their opponents the interpretation of certain key passages. They frequently refer to a few favourite 'modern' writers, such as Grosseteste and Fitzralph. But they will cite other near contemporaries and even canon law when expedient. Hudson analyses one writer's use of authorities in 'A Wycliffite Scholar of the Early Fifteenth Century', in Walsh and Woods, *The Bible in the Medieval World*, 301–15, and surveys Wycliffite practice in *The Premature Reformation*, 274–5 and 377–82. For a hitherto unnoticed but apparently influential discussion by Fitzralph of the authority to be granted to statements by patristic and more recent writers, see ch. 5, pp. 170–4.

[18] For more detailed discussion of this point see the works listed in nn. 12, 17 above.

assert the superiority of his 'clergie' to Arundel's and the clerks', when at Arundel's prompting he recounts his education (37/437–39/516), Thorpe takes care to emphasize his dissociation from traditional clerical patterns of education: although his parents 'spendiden moche moneye in dyuerse [but unnamed] placis aboute my lore, in entent to haue me a preest of God' (37/438–9), there was constant friction between Thorpe and his patrons because of his disinclination to become a priest. After leaving school he continued learning, but in a mode he presents as studiedly non-institutional: much though the teachers he names are Oxford men closely associated with Wyclif, Thorpe does not name his college and the master under whom he determined, but instead claims to have been 'ofte homli' with his teachers; to have 'comownede wiþ hem long tyme and fele'; and to have chosen 'wil fulli to be enformed bi hem and of hem, and speciali of Wiclef himsilf' (41/577–9).[19]

While Thorpe repeatedly affirms his dependence on grace and the virtue it confers,[20] one passage in particular presents an exemplary demonstration of reasoned interpretation through grace which Thorpe's readers could take note of as evidence of Thorpe's own virtue, and perhaps even emulate themselves. When one of the clerks asks Thorpe to interpret the assertion from Chrysostom that it is a 'synne to swere wele', Thorpe is momentarily confused. As he recounts,

> And certis I was sum deele agast to answere herto, for I hadde not bisyed me to stodie aboute þe witt þerof. But, liftynge vp my mynde to God, I preied him of grace. And anoon I þouȝte how Crist seide to hise disciplis 'Whanne for my name ȝe schulen be brouȝt before iugis, I schal ȝeue to ȝou mouþ and wisedom, þat alle ȝoure aduersaries schulen not aȝenseie.' And tristing feiþfulli to þe word of

---

[19] For biographical details of the teachers and associates Thorpe names, see Hudson's note on this passage (pp. 112–13).

[20] On both occasions when Thorpe appeals to scripture and reason, for example, he links his 'clergial' grounding to grace and virtue. After invoking scripture and reason in his opening protestation, Thorpe adds 'For bi autorite speciali of þese lawes I wole þoruȝ þe grace of God be ooned charitabli to þese lawes' (33/324–34/325). While Arundel and the clerks are for the first time trying to make him swear on the book, Thorpe prays for grace so that he may use his two authorities properly: 'I preiede God for his goodnesse to ȝeue me þanne and alwei grace to speke wiþ a meke and an esy spirit, and, whateuer þing þat I schulde speke, þat I miȝht haue þerto trewe autorite of scripture or open resoun' (36/427–37/430).

Crist, I seide, 'Sere, I knowe wel þat many men and wymmen haue
now so swerynge in custum þat þei knowen not, neiþer wole knowe
þat þei don yuel for to sweren as þei done. But þei gessen and seien
þat þei done wele for to sweren as þei done, þouȝ þei witen wele þat
þei sweren vntreweli. For þei seien now þei mowen bi her swerynge,
þouȝ it be fals, voyde blame or temperal harme whiche þei schulden
haue if þei sworen not þus. Also, sere, manye men and wymmen now
meynteynen strongli þat þei sweren wele, [þouȝ þei neden not to
sweren but bi yuel custum,] whanne þat þing is sooþ þat þei sweren
fore. Also ful many men and wymmen seien now þat it is wele idone
to swere bi creaturis, whanne þei mowen not, as þei seyne, oþer wyse
ben trowid. And also ful many men and wymmen now seyne þat it is
wele idone to swere bi God and bi oure Ladi and bi oþer seyntis, and
so for to haue hem in mynde. But siþ alle þese seyinges ben now
excusaciouns in synne, me þinkiþ, ser, þat þis sentence of Crisostom
mai be allegid skilfulli aȝens alle sich swerers, witnessinge þat alle
þese synnen greuousli, þouȝ þei d[em]e hemsilf to sweren in þis
forseide wyse wele. For it is yuel don and gret synne for to swere
truþe, whan in ony manere a man may excuse him wiþouten ooþ.
(76/1706–77/1730)

Confronted with an unfamiliar text, Thorpe prays for grace. He recalls
a gospel passage in which Christ promises to give his apostles wisdom
which their judges will not dispute. Trusting this promise, he delivers
an interpretation which Arundel duly grants without further argument
(see 77/ 1731–2).

Nor is Thorpe's interpretation merely a mystical effusion, despite the
way it is presented; it hinges on a thoroughly academic explanation of
how the adverb 'well' is being used. Indeed the argument does not
make much sense unless its academic background is understood; it is
anything but a straightforward exposition. Thorpe does not take up the
immediately puzzling aspect of Chrysostom's assertion: that is, if
swearing 'well' is a meritorious act, then how can 'to swear well' be a
sin? It would be easy enough to resolve this obvious question by
distinguishing 'well' meaning 'in a meritorious way' from a sense of
'well' in which moral approval is not necessarily implied, such as
'fluently'; then attributing only the second meaning to Chrysostom.
But there is a logical trap perhaps not immediately apparent to the
modern reader in Arundel's question; a trap into which this explanation
would fall.

In the phrase presented for interpretation, Chrysostom modifies 'swear' with the adverb 'well'. If Thorpe were to allow, in the course of his explanation, that 'well' qualifies 'swear', then he would be admitting that Chrysostom's statement is not a universal categorical proposition.[21] Chrysostom's statement would not then be a universal categorical condemnation of swearing but would refer only to a restricted kind or circumstance of swearing. Thorpe's opponents would then be able to point out that even if Chrysostom were saying that 'to swear' is a sin in the restricted case he is discussing, it is possible (indeed probable, since Chrysostom troubles to modify the verb) that in other circumstances Chrysostom thinks 'to swear' is not a sin. But Chrysostom is one of Thorpe's 'appreued' authorities. Therefore if Thorpe were forced to admit the truth of this (admittedly strained, but logically sound) argument, then he would have to accept that in some circumstances 'to swear' is not a sin – and that is just what Arundel wants.

Another solution Thorpe could have chosen would have been to insist on the larger context of this phrase: Chrysostom is addressing clerics who encourage people to swear, and the sentence from which this phrase comes is 'nunc autem cum sciatis, quia et bene jurare peccatum est', 'but now since you know, because it is also a sin to swear well'.[22] If Thorpe were to insist on including even just the *et*, Arundel's trap would be sprung; if Chrysostom is saying that it is *even* or *also* a sin to swear well, there is not the same implication that another kind of swearing remains which is *not* sinful. The force this sort of insistence on

---

[21] On the various kinds of proposition see Wyclif, *De logica*, in *Tractatus*, i: 15/26–17/21; for a lucid modern introduction, see A. Broadie, *Introduction to Medieval Logic*, 2nd ed. (Oxford, 1993), ch. 3. A universal categorical proposition implies no restrictions, conditions, or qualifications: examples would be 'all swearing is sinful' or 'all cows eat grass'. Here and later on I will use Wyclif's *De logica* to illustrate points of logic. Wyclif's *De logica* is a basic introductory work which provides short, clear explanations shorn of the elaborations and complications present in some other works; like most late fourteenth century textbooks of its type its content is for the most part derivative rather than innovative (on this point see E. J. Ashworth and P. V. Spade, 'Logic in Late Medieval Oxford', in J. I. Catto and R. Evans, eds., *The History of the University of Oxford*, vol. 2 (Oxford, 1992), 35–64; 48). Since Wyclif is the master Thorpe acknowledges, Wyclif's seems the most appropriate textbook to consult, especially since where Wyclif does differ from the mainstream (see, for example, below at nn. 28, 46), his interests and methods seem close to Thorpe's.

[22] Pseudo-Chrysostom, *Opus Imperfectum*, in J. P. Migne, ed., *Joannis Chrysostomi, Opera Omnia*, vol. 6, *Patrologia Graeca*, vol. 56 (Paris, 1862), 611–946, 698.

context could have for a disputant wishing to assert clerical or clergial authority will be appreciated by those who recall Conscience's dispute with Mede in *Piers Plowman* B iii:[23]

> 'I leue wel, lady', quod Conscience, 'þat þi latyn be trewe.
> Ac þow art lik a lady þat radde a lesson ones
> Was *omnia probate*, and þat plesed hire herte
> For þat lyne was no lenger at þe leues ende.
> Hadde she loked þat [left] half and þe leef torned
> She sholde haue founden fel[l]e wordes folwynge þerafter:
> . . .
> Ac yow failed a konnynge clerk þat kouþe þe leef han torned.
> (B iii, 337–42 and 347)

Like other writers who use this argument, Conscience is claiming that his opponent is an inadequate student of 'clergie' who cannot read well on her own, but needs guidance from a better educated clerk. Instead of using this tactic, however, Thorpe bases his solution solely on the puzzlingly contradictory phrase put to him.

In addressing only the phrase 'bene jurare peccatum est' Thorpe exploits another method of asserting 'clergie': he behaves as though he were a respondent in a disputation *de sophismatibus*, a logic exercise conducted in public in which upper level undergraduates, or *sophistae*, would be required to resolve syntactically confusing or apparently illogical statements, or *sophismata*, by subjecting them to grammatical and logical analysis.[24] That is just what Thorpe does; he renders 'to swear well' innocuous by claiming that 'well' modifies 'swear' only in an even more restricted case: when 'swear well' is in indirect discourse, governed by verbs such as 'think', 'believe', 'guess', or 'say' describing

---

[23] As in ch. 2, I use Kane and Donaldson's edition of the B text.

[24] On disputations *de sophismatibus* see J. A. Weisheipl, 'Curriculum of the Faculty of Arts at Oxford in the Early Fourteenth Century', *Mediaeval Studies* 26 (1964), 143–85, esp. 154–6; W. J. Courtenay, *Schools and Scholars in Fourteenth Century England* (Princeton, 1987), 33; P. O. Lewry, 'Grammar, Logic, and Rhetoric', in J. I. Catto, ed., *The History of the University of Oxford*, vol. 1 (Oxford 1984) (hereafter *HUO* i), 401–33, esp. 417; E. D. Sylla, 'The Oxford Calculators' in N. Kretzmann, A. Kenny, and J. Pinborg, eds., *The Cambridge History of Later Medieval Philosophy* (Cambridge, 1982), (hereafter *CHLMP*), 540–63. For analysis of some exponible *sophismata* see N. Kretzmann, 'Syncatoremata, Sophismata, Exponibilia', in *CHLMP*, 211–41. (On the meaning of 'exponible' see below.)

the mental state and/or willed action of the sinner: 'þei *knowen* not, neiþer *wole knowe* þat þei don yuel for to sweren as þei done. But þei *gessen* and *seien* þat þei done wele for to sweren as þei done, þouȝ þei *witen wele* þat þei sweren vntreweli' (my emphases). His discussion relies on subtle distinctions between inward states such as 'knowen', 'wolen knowen', 'gessen', and 'witen', about the context and implications of which I will have more to say later on.[25] But his most immediate concern is to neutralize the phrase presented to him; and his method of doing so employs a technique of analysis prominent in the logic course at Oxford in the latter part of the fourteenth century.

Richard Billingham's *Speculum puerorum* or *De probatione propositionum* was the most influential text in the literature explaining this mode of analysis by means of the *probationes terminorum*.[26] Billingham teaches that complex propositions are 'exponible', 'resoluble' or 'officiable'; they may be 'proven' by one of three different methods of reducing them to basic components whose truth is self-evident. The propositions that concern us here are *officiabiles* propositions.[27] An 'officiable' proposition consists of a *dictum*, or accusative-plus-infinitive construction, governed by an 'official' term, that is, a modal verb or verb describing a mental act. The 'officiable' proposition is analysed, or 'officiated', by spelling out the *officium*, or function, of its official term in relation to its *dictum*. Wyclif's discussion of officiation derives from Billingham's (as most late medieval discussions do), but Wyclif's treatment is unusual in that he focuses almost exclusively on

---

[25] See pp. 204–8.

[26] On strong interest in this method of analysis, and in Billingham in particular, at Oxford from *c.* 1350–1400 see Ashworth and Spade, 'Logic', 48; they discuss Billingham's and other treatises on the *probationes terminorum* at 42–5. Five versions of Billingham's treatise are included in *Some 14th Century Tracts on the Probationes Terminorum*, ed. L. M. de Rijk (Nijmegen, 1982), which includes five versions of the Billingham tract. Recall Wyclif's focus in the opening of his *De logica* upon the *probaciones proposicionum* (see n. 13 above). On the development of Billingham's and other specialized logic treatises from treatises on suppositions, see J. A. Weisheipl, 'Developments in the Arts Curriculum at Oxford in the Early Fourteenth Century', *Mediaeval Studies* 28 (1966), 151–75; 157–61; for a recent survey of research in the various areas of late medieval logic teaching, see Courtenay, *Schools and Scholars*, 234–40.

[27] Useful discussions of 'official' analysis appear in A. Maierù, *Terminologia logica della tarda scholastica* (Rome, 1972), 451–67 and the preface to Paul of Venice, *Logica Magna*, pt. 1. fasc. 7, ed. and trans. P. Clarke (Oxford, 1981), xiii-xviii.

'official' terms describing mental acts.[28] Here is one of Wyclif's examples of officiation:

> scio deum esse
> Ista proposicio est scita a me, 'deus est',
> que primarie significat 'deum esse'.[29]

> I know that God exists
> This proposition is known by me, 'God exists',
> which primarily signifies 'that God exists'.

This is a relatively basic version; texts on the *probationes* sometimes provide much more elaborate specifications of the conditions constituting reliable knowledge.[30] But the truth of each component here can be readily verified: Wyclif knows the proposition 'deus est', and (in his century at least) 'deum esse' is self-evidently true.

In Thorpe's version of Chrysostom's meaning, the terms 'knowen', 'wolen', 'gessen', 'seien', and 'witen' are *termines officiales* governing the *dictum* 'they swear well'.[31] Thorpe's explanation discusses the components that would result from the officiation of his newly created proposition 'they guess and say that they swear well':

> estimant et dicunt (eos) jurare bene
> Ista proposicio est estimata et dicta ab eis, 'jurant bene',
> que primarie significat 'eos jurare bene'.[32]

> They guess and say that they swear well
> This proposition is guessed and said by them, 'they swear well',
> which primarily signifies 'that they swear well'.

---

28 In the *De logica* Wyclif defines 'official' terms as 'specialiter tales qui concernunt actum mentis', 'especially those that concern a mental act' (*Tractatus,* i: 67) 'ut, scire, credere, intelligere, precipere, dubitare, imaginari, appetere', 'for example knowing, believing, understanding, perceiving, doubting, imagining, desiring' (*Tractatus,* i: 7), and includes modal terms only after his discussion of officiation, among terms to which all three sorts of analysis may be applied (*Tractatus,* i: 68).

29 *Tractatus,* i: 67 (punctuation modified).

30 See, for example, the Italian version of Billingham's *Speculum puerorum* printed in de Rijk, ed., *Some 14th Century Tracts,* 113–40.

31 The circumlocutions of 'they swear well' Thorpe provides – 'þei done wele for to sweren as þei done', 'þat it is wele idone to swere', 'hemsilf to sweren in þis forseide wyse wele' – show that he sees the danger in attaching 'well' to 'swear'. But I use the simplest formula here.

32 Here I use the Latin vocabulary of the Latin manuscripts of the *Testimony* Prague, Metropolitan Chapter Library o.29, f. 203 and Vienna, Österreichische National-bibliothek 3936, f. 17v, from the transcription kindly lent to me by Anne Hudson.

It is true that these people guess and say that they swear well, as Thorpe begins his explanation by acknowledging. But despite all their 'excusaciouns in sinne', of which Thorpe details several, the fact remains that the primary significate 'they swear well' is invalid, because their ways of swearing are sinful. And therefore 'þis sentence of Crisostom mai be allegid skilfulli aʒens alle sich swerers, witnessinge þat alle þese synnen greuousli, þouʒ þei d[em]e hemsilf to sweren in þis forseide wyse wele'. Thorpe's reply embeds 'to swear well' in a proposition governed by a *terminus officialis*, and thus avoids conferring upon 'to swear well' status as anything other than a mental act which he in any case immediately labels as mistaken. In representing a reply of which any *sophista* might be proud as divinely inspired, Thorpe finds the narrow ground where he can present an explanation so 'opin' in its 'resoun' that the archbishop who opposes him will accept it without further argument, yet still present himself as an apostolic defender of the faith who is ultimately validated by God's grace rather than his own 'stodie'.

Thorpe's position on that narrow ground appears precarious when, in reply to Arundel's attempt to pin him down to a heretical statement about the Eucharist, Thorpe condemns 'sofestris' and their methods in the strongest of terms:

> Ser, as I vndirstonde it is al oon to graunte, eiþer bileue, þat þere dwelliþ no substaunce of breed and to graunte, or to bileue, þat þis moost worþi sacrament of Cristis owne bodi is an accident wiþouten soget. But, ser, forþi þat ʒoure axinge passiþ myn vndirstondinge, I dar neiþer denye it ne graunte it, for it is scole-mater aboute whiche I neuer bisied me for to knowe in. And þerfor I committe þis terme *accidentem sine subiecto* to þo clerkis which deliten hem so in curious and so sotil sofestrie, þat þei mouen ofte so defficult materis and straunge, and waden and wandren so in hem fro argument into argument wiþ *pro* and *contra* to þe tyme þat þei witen not ofte where þei ben neiþer vndirstonden clerli hemsilf. But þe schame þat þese prowde sofestris haue to ʒelden hem to men and bifore men makiþ hem ofte folis and to ben concludid schamefulli bifore God. (55/ 1026–38)

By attacking methods he himself uses Thorpe would appear to lay himself open to a charge of hypocrisy. Beyond his claims that his ability is rooted not in scholastic training but in virtue conferred by grace, it seems that Thorpe also means to distance himself from the *kind* of

'scole-mater' some 'clerkis' indulge in: although in the course of the
Testimony he shows – shows off, even – his ability as a disputant, he
implies here that *his* ability is manifested differently than theirs. In a
dispute where his opponents set the terms of the argument and frame
every issue, the difference cannot of course be great. But Thorpe may
succeed in establishing it in the most densely technical part of his
defence, where he confronts the clerks and explains the rationale
behind the model of virtuous ability he has presented.

Directly after the exemplary interpretation of Chrysostom which
silences Arundel, the clerks challenge Thorpe once again about his
refusal to swear on the mass book (78/1753–80/1826). Thorpe's confrontation with them is also a confrontation between conflicting
methods of using academic terminology in the vernacular. The clerks
use academic language to flaunt the authority which (they apparently
think) greater knowledge gives them. They try to intimidate Thorpe
into assent: one condescendingly glosses 'equypolent' for him, under
the impression, it seems, that once Thorpe has been acquainted with
the concept he will consent; while the other accuses him of not knowing his 'equyuocaciouns' (78/1754, 80/1811). Thorpe replies with a
barrage of academic terms; in this small section appear the following
direct translations of specialized Latin terms: 'sentence', 'vertue',
'vnperfit', 'pryncipal part', 'propirli', 'sencible', 'effectual(li)', as well as
'equyuocacion' and 'equypolent'. But he uses this barrage to propound
an egalitarian theory of knowledge.

We will examine in a moment how Thorpe's use of academic terms
and techniques contrasts with the clerks' intimidatory style. But first,
in order to locate these conflicting methods within late medieval
vernacular academic usage, it will be worthwhile to pause and consider
the provenance and vernacular uses of the mini-glossary of academic
terms generated in this passage. This selection is a good index to
sources of academic terms used in late medieval vernacular writings.
'Equypolent' derives from a concept important in logic; 'effectual(li)',
'vertue', and 'sencible' are translations of ideas basic to natural science;
and the other terms are tools of exposition and argumentation used
widely in academic prose.

Logic, natural science, and the parlance of argumentation are precisely the academic ground we would expect to be common to men

who had attended university for even a short time in late medieval England,[33] for they were the basis of the university curriculum. In the faculty of arts, where most students studied before proceeding (if at all) to the higher faculties of law, medicine, and theology,[34] students heard lectures on the *libri logicales et naturales* concurrently from the beginning of their studies, and argumentation was a basic tool of instruction.[35] Lectures given by masters included exposition of the text in *quaestio* form, according to which the master would simulate argumentation by posing and answering questions and objections.[36] Students were taught to reason and argue by means of supplementary textbooks (teaching, for instance, rules of inference and ways of opposing and responding) and they were required to attend – and later in their studies to participate in – disputations of various kinds taking place at least once a week.[37]

Words with specialized academic meanings in Latin came to be used in English not only in logical and scientific works, but in other sorts of writing that were being produced by clerks who had completed at least the early years of the university arts curriculum or comparable instruction in some other school. 'Equypolent', the first clerk's contribution, provides a convenient illustration. *(A)equipollens* has a specialized

---

[33] As Courtenay points out, students frequently did not complete a full course leading to a degree (*Schools and Scholars*, 21 and esp. n. 27).

[34] There seems to have been considerable variation in how long students would remain in the faculty of arts before proceeding to the higher faculties; the issue has been discussed most recently by Fletcher, 'The Faculty of Arts', *HUO* i: 369–99; 370–1, and Courtenay, *Schools and Scholars*, 30–6. Although there seems not to have been a formal requirement for a fixed period of study in arts, students would have needed to learn the material covered in the early years of arts study in order to proceed with work at any higher level.

[35] On this point see A. Kenny and J. Pinborg, 'Medieval Philosophical Literature', *CHLMP*, 11–42; esp. 15. For information on university curriculum, teaching methods, and texts, see Lewry, 'Grammar, Logic, and Rhetoric', *passim*; J.M. Fletcher, 'Faculty of Arts', 369–99, *passim*; A. Maierù, *University Training in Medieval Europe*, trans. D. N. Pryds (Leiden, 1994), esp. ch. 5 on methods of teaching logic; Courtenay, *Schools and Scholars*, 30–6; Sylla, 'Oxford Calculators', 542–7; and Weisheipl, 'Curriculum' and 'Developments', *passim*.

[36] On the various sorts of academic lectures see most recently Fletcher, 'Faculty of Arts', 374–8 and Courtenay, *Schools and Scholars*, 32–3.

[37] On supplementary textbooks see Weisheipl, 'Developments', 153–67, and most recently Ashworth and Spade, 'Logic', 48–60; and Lewry, 'Grammar, Logic, and Rhetoric', 406–10. On disputations, see Fletcher, 'Faculty of Arts', 378–92 *passim*; Courtenay, *Schools and Scholars*, 33; Weisheipl, 'Curriculum', 153–5 and 158–60.

usage in logic, for which it may have been coined and with which it was especially associated: equipollent propositions are logically equivalent and interchangeable; it is useful to analyse the equipollence of propositions in order to determine, for example, the effect of double negatives on certain kinds of propositions.[38] The word may also have a specialized usage in scientific writing associated with its other sense, 'equal in power, authority, influence, or capacity'; but until there is a comprehensive study or dictionary of the language of scientific and philosophical writings in this period, it will be impossible to ascertain to what extent *(a)equipollens* used in this sense appeared in late medieval Latin scientific contexts or, indeed, to make any firm statements about the origins and development of either meaning.[39]

With that proviso, it is possible with the aid of the *MED* to provide at least a sketch of developments in the use of 'equypolent' in later Middle English. The word and its derivatives are recorded by the *MED* in works written from *c.* 1412 up to the end of the medieval period. In some contexts the logical or scientific meaning is invoked, but more in order to lend an aura of education than because the complexity of the discussion requires the technical term.[40] Elsewhere uses derived from

---

38 See *Thesaurus Linguae Latinae*, gen. ed. C. O. Brink (Leipzig, 1900–) s.v. 'aequipollens', adj., and *Dictionary of Medieval Latin from British Sources*, prepared by R. E. Latham and (subsequently) D. R. Howlett (Oxford, 1975–) (hereafter *DMLBS*) s.vv. 'aequipollenter', adv. b, 'aequipollentia', n. b, and 'aequipollere', v. b. Wyclif briefly discusses equipollence in his *De logica* (*Tractatus*, i: 22–3). A useful introduction to the theory of equipollence in medieval logic appears in Broadie, *Introduction to Medieval Logic*, 2nd ed., 153–6.

39 The scientific use of this meaning in the seventeenth century by Robert Boyle may point toward a provenance for this term in medieval Latin scientific academic writings; see the *Oxford English Dictionary*, 2nd ed., prepared by J. A. Simpson and E. S. C. Weiner (Oxford, 1989), (hereafter *OED*) s.v. 'equipollent'. The entries for this meaning in the *DMLBS* (s.vv. 'aequipollenter', adv. a, 'aequipollentia', n. a, and 'aequipollere', v. a) are all from legal or legalistic contexts; however, this dictionary does not aim to provide the sort of comprehensive coverage of philosophical and scientific writing that I hope a more specialized work will in future. I would appreciate having any further insights into or examples of the logical and scientific use of '(a)equipollens' brought to my attention.

40 To save space, I use the *MED*'s abbreviated references throughout this discussion. See *MED* s.v. 'equipol', adj. ('The which seyinge in singuler may wel be seid equipolle to a plurelle' c1450 *Pilgr.LM* 64), and *MED* s.v. 'equipolence', n. b ('Late hym study in equipolences, And late lyes and fallaces' a1425 (?a1400) *RRose* 7076), as well as *MED* s.v. 'equipolent', adj. 2 ('Thyne Elementes be made equipollent' c1500 (1471) *Ripley CAlch.* 58a).

the academic ones fall into three broad categories: (1) in Lydgate's aureate style, the word is used to extol poetic excellence, as well as for assessing punishments in the pagan hell;[41] (2) in discussions of governance, various writers use the word with a monitory tone to describe intended or actual violations of proper hierarchy;[42] (3) in devotional or polemical religious contexts, it is used to explain theological concepts involving equivalence and/or interchangeability.[43] In none of these cases is 'equypolent' used because it is the simplest word for the purpose; nor as a straightforward extension of its usage in science or logic or even in legal writing. Rather, 'equypolent' begins to appear in new contexts where it would never have occurred to a Latin writer to use it; contexts, indeed, that are not available, or at the very least do not have the same valence, in Latin. Broadly speaking, 'equypolent' begins to appear in just the sorts of works – aureate poetry, advice-to-princes, and devotional religious writings – where academic terminology is employed in a style rather like that of Thorpe's clerks: where writers are attempting to import intellectual authority for themselves into English, but making little effort to transfer concepts and arguments to a new sphere and a new audience.

In contrast to the clerks' grandiloquent word-dropping, Thorpe uses technical terms to build an exposition. One of the most obviously

---

[41] The famous example is 'Among oure bokis of englische perles / . . . þer is no makyng to his [Chaucer's] equipolent' (a1420) Lydg. *TB* 2.4712; see *MED* s.v. 'equipolent', adj. 2. For the second usage, see for example 'Þe peyne of Yxyon in helle / Or of Manes / . . . Were not egal nor equipolent / To venge mordre' (a1420) Lydg. *TB* 5.1053; see *MED* s.v. 'equipolent', adj. 3.

[42] Two examples: *MED* s.v. 'equipolent', adj. 1 ('They [women] wille wayten been equipollent, / And sumwhat more, vnto hir housbondis' a1450 (c1412) Hoccleve *RP* 5108; 'Ther may no grettir perell growe to a prince, than to have a subgett equepolent to hym selff' (a1475) Fortescue *Gov.E* 130/30).

[43] The word is glossed, as it is in the *Testimony*, in a fifteenth century rule for minoresses: 'A fest double or anoþer feste whiche is equypollent þat is for to vnderstonde, a fest of þe same dignite' (a1500 *Rule Minoresses* 114/18; see *MED* s.v. 'equipolent', adj. 2. It is used to discuss penance in a translation of the *Pilgrimage of the Life of Manhood*: ('Equipollence ther shulde be of penitence' c. 1450 *Pilgr.LM* 190; see *MED* s.v. 'equipolence', n. a), and to explain eternity in a set of lessons on the Dirige ('Mennes dayes . . . in respyte of tyme euermare . . . beth nothyng equipolent' c1450 *LDirige[2]* 340; see *MED* s.v. 'equipolent', adj. 2). There are many similar later examples in religious writings dating from the sixteenth to the nineteenth century: see *OED* s.vv. 'equipollent' A2, A3a,b, 'equipollently', 'equipollency' 1, 'equipollence' 1, 'equipolle'.

academic features of Thorpe's expository method, here and elsewhere, is his use of that basic building block of scholastic argumentation, the distinction. Scholastic counterargument frequently involves distinguishing two or more ways that an important term in the opposing argument may be understood so as to diminish or dismiss the force of that argument. Some methods of distinction appear often enough in counterargument that they may be considered conventional: examples are distinction between what is true of something generally speaking and what is true in a particular case; between what is true at a particular time as opposed to another time or the usual state of affairs; between the sense a verb has when modified by an adverb as opposed to its sense when unmodified or modified otherwise; and between what a term is applied to in precise philosophical usage, *proprie*, as opposed to the common colloquial use of the term, *communiter* or *vulgariter*.[44] Distinctions of this last sort are closely related to another kind used generally in academic expository writing as well as counterargument: academic expositions often proceed by distinguishing then explaining in turn the various senses of a term or expression;[45] and for many terms there is a set of different meanings that are standardly differentiated.

When the second clerk accuses Thorpe of not knowing his 'equyvocaciouns', he is referring to the context in which both sorts of distinctions were apparently taught and discussed: they are listed (in varying amounts of detail) in logic textbooks in the discussion of fallacies, most of them under the heading 'fallacia aequivocacionis'.[46]

---

44 For those familiar with scholastic argumentation these observations need no demonstration. For others, I have provided at least one example of each in my discussion on pp. 184–90, in the discussion that follows here, or on pp. 202–3.

45 For example, Wyclif in his *De composicione hominis* (ed. R. Beer (London, 1884); dated *c.* 1372 by Thomson, *The Latin Writings of John Wyclif*, 36) distinguishes four senses of *homo*: 'pro anima', 'for the soul'; 'pro corpore', 'for the body'; 'pro natura integra', 'for the whole nature'; and 'pro persona vel substancia que est quelibet istarum trium naturarum vel rerum vel eciam omne ens contraccius, quod est aliqua earundem', 'for the person or substance which is any of these three natures or things, or even any being, in a more restricted sense, which is any of those things' (15–18); then he uses this distinction as a principle in his answers to objections throughout the work (e.g., 109–13).

46 Several treatises on fallacies that contain discussions of equivocation are printed in L. M. de Rijk, *Logica Modernorum*, vol. 2, pt 2 (Assen, 1967). E. J. Ashworth gives a comprehensive explanation of theories of equivocation up to Aquinas, extending far beyond their appearance in treatises on fallacies, in 'Analogy and Equivocation in

But far from not knowing his 'equyvocaciouns', Thorpe uses both of these sorts of distinction in his reply. To dismiss the arguments of the clerks he distinguishes between 'effectual' and ineffective accomplishment of an action (79/1799–1801) and between 'vnperfit speche' and speaking 'propirli' (79/1788–9). And he structures his counterargument around the equivocal senses of 'vertue'. These references to 'vertue' appear on pages 78 and 79:

> Þe gospel þat is vertu of Goddis word (1775: Jerome)
> Þe rewme of God is not in word but in vertue (1778–9: I Cor. 4:20)
> Þe vois of þe Lord, þat is his word, is in vertue (1779–80: Ps. 28:4)
> in þe spirit of his mouþ is al þe vertue of hem (1781–2: Ps. 32:6)
> al þe vertue of a tree is in þe roote þerof (1791–2)
> þe godhede of Crist þat is þe vertue of God (1801–2)
> þe gospel þat is þe vertue of Cristis word (1802–3)

And more are implied. 'Vertue' or *virtus* is used in natural science to mean 'power' or 'capacity'; this is the sense in which God's 'vertue' is Christ's divinity, man's 'vertue' is his soul, and a tree's 'vertue' is in its root. Another sense of 'vertue', used in ethical writings and elsewhere, is close to what 'virtue' ordinarily means in modern usage: the correct disposition of man's soul, partly infused by grace and partly acquired by conforming oneself to the living and teaching of Christ. Thorpe exploits both.

Thirteenth-Century Logic: Aquinas in Context', *Mediaeval Studies* 54 (1992), 94–135. Wyclif gives the most basic explanation possible for equivocation in the *De logica*: 'Terminus equivocus est, qui propter raciones diversas significat res diversas, sive ipsa sint diversarum specierum (sicut animal latrabile, marina bellua, et celeste sidus, quorum quodlibet sit iste terminus "canis", secundum diversas raciones specificas), sive sint eiusdem specie', 'An equivocal term is one that according to different definitions signifies different things, whether these are of different types (as barking animal, sea beast, and star, any of which is this term "dog" according to different specific definitions) or whether they are of the same type' (*Tractatus*, i: 4); he eliminates all the complexities developed in the thirteenth-century works printed by de Rijk and discussed by Ashworth. But he seems to have become more interested in equivocation later on, even if his explanation of it does not become more complex; in the *De veritate sacre scripture* he ascribes the principle of equivocation to Augustine and makes it fundamental to his account of scriptural logic (i: 9–10). The clerk's accusation and Thorpe's disproof of it may very well have special significance for Wycliffites: in the *De veritate sacre scripture* Wyclif repeatedly accuses those who misinterpret scripture of not knowing their equivocations (e.g. i: 12/7–10, 14/11–13, 61/15–24, 94/9–17, iii: 165/5–9).

The crucial points in Thorpe's counterargument are the equipollence
in authority between Christ and Christ's word that he draws from the
first clerk's assertion: 'as ʒe seide to me riʒt now, god and his word ben
of oon autorite' (79/1797–8) and the distinction he draws between the
written gospel and the understanding of the gospel: 'þe gospel þat is
vertu of Goddis word is not in þe leues of a book but it is in þe roote of
resoun' (78/1775–6): The 'vertue', i.e. power, of God's word is not in
the book at all, but in man's 'vertue', his soul, the root of his reason or
source of his power of understanding.[47] But proper understanding
comes about only through proper belief in God: 'as þe godhede of Crist
þat is þe vertue of God is knowen [by the vertue] þoruʒ bileue, so {on
the premise that 'Christ' and 'Christ's word' are 'equypolent'} is þe
gospel þat is þe vertue of Cristis word' (79/1801–3).[48] To understand
Christ's word properly in the 'vertue'/soul/root of reason, then, one
must conform to Christ in 'vertue'/virtue. Anyone whose 'vertue'/soul
is not virtuously conformed to God's 'vertue'/Christ, no matter how
learned he or she may be, cannot understand scripture. Thorpe cites
Christ's authority – from the gospel in his 'root of reason', we might
note, since Arundel has taken his book away – to clinch his argument:

> bi autorite of Crist himsilf þe effectual vndirstondyng of Cristis word
> is taken awei from alle hem chefly whiche ben grete lettrid men, and
> presumen to vndirstonden hiʒe þingis and wolen b[en] holde wise
> men, and desiren maistirschipe and hiʒe staate and dignyte, but þei
> wolen not conforme hem to þe lyuynge and techynge of Crist and of
> hise apostlis. (80/1818–23)

This argument might well have been put together using a distinction
collection, a preacher's manual which gives multiple senses of words

47 '. . . a mannys soule, þat may not now here be seen ne touchid with ony sencible
þing, is propirli man' (79/1790–1). Thorpe does not reiterate the word 'vertue' in this
phrase, but it seems clear that he is referring to the standard late medieval doctrine on
the human soul developed from thirteenth century commentaries on Aristotle's *De
anima*. The immaterial, incorruptible (thus, immortal) aspect of the human soul is its
virtus intellectiva, which is the source of the human capacity for understanding
abstractions, though its functions are not confined to those we might regard as those
of the intellect. This notion is not controversial, as far as I have been able to
determine, for Wyclif or Wycliffites.
48 The phrase 'by the vertue' appears only in the 1530 edition of Thorpe's testimony. I
include this phrase because it emphasizes the way Thorpe is turning *vertue* to his
advantage, but its meaning is implicit in the medieval text reconstructed by Hudson
as well; belief, or faith, is a 'vertue'/virtue inhering in man's 'vertue'/soul.

around which a sermon may be constructed.[49] This claim may appear farfetched, and will require some justification. Normally the distinctions employed in philosophical writing would be only distantly related to those found in distinction collections for preachers. Preachers' manuals were compiled by educated writers who were scholastically trained and had access to a number of books (or, at minimum, by those who had access to a number of earlier manuals); thus certain terms for which a set of meanings are standardly distinguished in scholastic exposition would obviously tend to be assigned the same meanings in distinction collections. The entries for these terms would even include examples from scholastic writers as well as the usual patristic and biblical sources. But academic distinctions and those in preachers' manuals were employed in quite different ways and, to a large extent, by distinct groups; the writer of an academic lecture and the parish priest constructing a sermon around senses of *canis* or 'vertue' would have moved in separate spheres and addressed separate audiences.

When the separate spheres and modes of address associated with academic argument and vernacular sermon become less distinct, and methods of academic address begin to appear in vernacular polemical material aimed (ostensibly at the very least) at a lay audience, there are obviously grounds for suspecting that methods of constructing these two kinds of expositions might become more closely associated. But we have better grounds even than these, for the Wycliffites compiled a distinction collection of their own, known as the *Floretum/Rosarium*.

In the study of the Latin and English manuscripts of the *Floretum* and *Rosarium* that accompanies her edition of a selection of articles from the text of the one Middle English manuscript of the *Rosarium*,[50] Christina von Nolcken suggests that the main motivation for the

---

[49] For the development and use of these manuals, see R. H. and M. A. Rouse, '*Statim invenire*: Schools, Preachers, and New Attitudes to the Page', in R. L. Benson and G. Constable, eds., *Renaissance and Renewal in the Twelfth Century* (Cambridge, MA, 1982), 201–25; and *Preachers, Florilegia and Sermons: Studies on the Manipulus Florum of Thomas of Ireland* (Toronto, 1979), esp. 3–42. For their use in the fourteenth century, see C. von Nolcken, 'Some Alphabetical Compendia and How Preachers Used Them in Fourteenth-Century England', *Viator* 12 (1981), 271–88.

[50] C. von Nolcken, *The Middle English Translation of the Rosarium Theologie* (Heidelberg, 1979).

revision from *Floretum* into *Rosarium* was precisely the perceived importance of organizing the entries around distinctions.[51] The *Floretum* entries are listed in alphabetical order, but the contents of each entry are amassed rather than organized; material from each work consulted was added on to each entry in turn, and what distinctions the work includes come from its sources. An elaborate index is required to make the contents accessible. Each *Rosarium* entry, in contrast, is organized around an elaborate and often tendentious distinction between various senses of the word in question.[52] Preachers using the *Rosarium* could easily incorporate the most academic of distinctions into their vernacular sermons: the most striking example von Nolcken has found is a distinction on avarice drawn from Wyclif's *De mandatis* which appears in the *Rosarium* entry on avarice then subsequently at the end of sermon 11 of the *Lollard Sermons*.[53] Although von Nolcken focuses on the *Rosarium's* increased usefulness for preachers constructing sermons,[54] her findings also have wider implications. If it helps preachers to construct sermons when they have an elaborately distinguished entry to work with, then it also helps polemicists. Indeed, along with finding distinctions from the *Rosarium* and even the *Floretum* incorporated into sermons, von Nolcken has also found tracts into which *Rosarium* distinctions are incorporated, and tracts which consist of single *Rosarium* entries copied and circulated separately.[55]

While von Nolcken suggests that Thorpe could have drawn his material on preaching from the *Floretum* entry on 'Predicacio' (36), we may note in addition that for his argument against the clerks Thorpe could have used the entry for 'Vertue' in the Middle English manuscript of the *Rosarium*; when in the course of his explanation Thorpe reels off a list of biblical passages in which the word 'vertue' appears, he gives the impression that he has at some point consulted a reference

---

[51] *Rosarium Theologie*, 20–1.   [52] *Rosarium Theologie*, 25–9.

[53] *Rosarium Theologie*, 37.

[54] Von Nolcken states that preaching is the focus of her interest in the *Rosarium* edition, in 'Some Alphabetical Compendia and How Preachers Used Them in Fourteenth-Century England', *Viator* 12 (1981), 271–88, and also in 'An Unremarked Group of Wycliffite Sermons in Latin', *Modern Philology* 83 (1985–86), 233–49.

[55] *Rosarium Theologie*, 34–7.

work of this sort.[56] The *Rosarium* entry begins by distinguishing 'virtue made and vertue vnmade', naming 'vertue vnmade' as God, then gives the three sorts of 'vertu made' as '[1] naturall ^(kyndely)^, and [2] intelectuale or vnderstandyng, and [3] morale ^(manly)^'; it explains 'morale' virtue in part as 'ane habite, þat is to sey a roted qualite . . . ' Although Thorpe does not make the same initial distinction between created and uncreated virtue, the categories given in the *Rosarium* match up well with his: 'vertue vnmade' corresponds to his 'vertue of God', 'vertue naturall' to the tree's 'vertue', 'vertue intelectuale' to the 'vertue' in the 'roote of resoun', and 'vertue morale' to the 'roted qualite' through which the gospel may be 'effectualli' understood. However, since none of Thorpe's biblical references match those given in the *Rosarium*; and given that as in scholastic contexts, the distinctions made on particular words tended to be fairly standard in preachers' manuals much though the examples and presentation might vary, the case remains unproven.[57]

What I am more concerned to stress is the contrast between the kind of attitude to the use of academic words in the vernacular the *Rosarium* represents and that of the clerks. The *Rosarium* entries are designed to be readily comprehensible and transmissible, not to impress and intimidate. Each distinction provides a way of learning and remembering the various senses of a word; in many cases it also teaches why the word is controversial and gives a polemical argument for a Wycliffite position. Academic words become a vehicle for the dissemination of concepts and arguments; there could not be a greater contrast to the clerks' attempts to use them as bludgeons of assent.

It must be conceded that Thorpe's 'exposition' on vertue does not provide as great a contrast, or at least not in the same way; it does not have the clear structure and comprehensibility of the *Rosarium* entry. His argument looks more like a set of enigmatic puns than the usual sort of academic distinction. What his presentation certainly does is to

---

[56] Cambridge, Gonville and Caius College 354/581, f. 131, s.v. 'uertue'; not included in von Nolcken's edition. Material between carets in the following quotation is written above the line in the same or a similar hand in the manuscript; abbreviations are silently expanded and modern punctuation supplied. No importance need be attached to the variant spellings of 'vertue'.

[57] On the uniformity in content of preachers' manuals, see von Nolcken, 'Some Alphabetical Compendia', 272.

mark out a style qualitatively different from that of 'scole-mater', even
if that style can be characterized by a hostile listener as being instead
'ful derk mater and vnsauery' (79/1804). Enigmatic utterances may of
course derive power for those who understand them, and menace for
those who do not, from their very obscurity: a special group who
'knows the code' may divine the import on that basis.[58] Anyone who
knows the *Rosarium* distinction on 'vertue' also holds the key to
Thorpe's answer, even if they cannot follow him every step of the way.
But whether or not Thorpe's exposition on 'vertue' might advocate
egalitarian comprehension in its style, it certainly does so in its
sentiments.

By imputing the 'unperfit speche' that 'men usen' to the clerks –and
thus using the standard scholastic tactic of discarding a 'common' or
'vulgar' way of understanding an expression – Thorpe is throwing the
clerks' condescension back in their teeth. But rather than simply
joining the clerks in dismissing 'common' understanding, in the
argument he constructs around the equivocal senses of 'vertue' Thorpe
transmits intellectual authority to the less educated but virtuous men
and women he imagines as the newly extended audience for his and
other writers' vernacular polemical works. When he denies authority
to anyone without 'vertue' in his 'vertue', no matter how knowledge-
able that person may be, Thorpe implicitly extends authority to
everyone virtuous. He does not dismiss academic argument altogether,
but rather subordinates it to an alternative religious authority
grounded principally in virtue. Yet the egalitarian implications of
Thorpe's theory stretch back to their academic source as well as out to
everyone else.

Later Thorpe follows out the implications of his 'vertue' argument
to enlist all virtuous people as his fellow supporters of William Taylor
against Alkerton:

---

[58] R. F. Green and A. Hudson each suggest, for example, that the cryptic and allusive
letters attributed to John Ball in Knighton's and Walsingham's accounts of the
Peasants' Revolt contain 'veiled' or 'coded' references comprehensible to participants
in the revolt; the chroniclers' inclusion of the letters testifies, I think, to their
perceived menace. (R. F. Green, 'John Ball's Letters: Literary History and Historical
Literature', in Hanawalt, ed., *Chaucer's England*, 176–200, esp. 188–90; and Hudson,
'*Piers Plowman* and the Peasants' Revolt'.) The letters are edited in an appendix to
Green's article.

Sere, I gesse certeynly þat þere was no man ne womman þat hatide verily synne and louede vertues, heerynge þe sermoun [of þe clerk of Oxenford and also Alkirtouns sermoun], þat ne þei seiden eiþer my3te iustly seien þat Alkirtoun repreuede þe clerke vntrewli, and sclaundride him wrongfully and vncharitabli, [as I seide to hym in Watlynge strete]. For no doute if þe lyuynge and techinge of Crist cheuely and of his apostlis be trewe, no liif þat loueþ God and his lawe wole blame ony sentence þat þe clerk prechide þan þere . . . (85/ 1967–77)

Thorpe does not suggest that Taylor's sermon was entirely free of academic terms, or that it ought to have been – indeed, by saying that Taylor 'prouede clereli' using the authorities Thorpe himself accepts, Thorpe implies that Taylor's sermon has affiliations similar to his own. Rather, in order to enlist new and potentially favourable adjudicators in addition to the academics who are already on his side, Thorpe is proposing a kind of egalitarianism in virtuous understanding which would allow any virtuous listener who loves God and his law to recognize the clerk's arguments as good, no matter how little formal education the listener might have or how complex those arguments might be.

If Thorpe puts his academic knowledge to use, or even on display, in his exchanges with the clerks, it is in his exchanges with Arundel that he shows to best advantage his skill at evasion. In response to Arundel's attempts to induce Thorpe either to grant without qualification that he will obey the ordinances of Holy Church, or to deny the church's tenets outright so that he may be condemned, Thorpe uses every delaying tactic he can muster. On some occasions he withholds assent, saying that he does not have the necessary knowledge, as here: 'siþ *I knowe not* þat Goddis lawe appreueþ it {the doctrine on the Eucharist brought in by Thomas Aquinas}, in þis mater *I dar not graunte. But vttirli I denye to make* þis freris sentence or ony oþer sich *my bileue*, do wiþ me, God, what þou wolt' (56/1050–2, my emphases). Strictly speaking, Thorpe is not denying the 'freris sentence' here any more than he is granting it; rather, he says, in the absence of the knowledge he would need to judge its truth, he is refusing to affirm it as his belief.

In other places, Thorpe distinguishes different meanings in Arundel's statements as a way to avoid denying them; for example, in reply

to Arundel's assertion that those who have recanted Lollardy have
become wise much though Lollards might think them fools, Thorpe
equivocates:

> Ser, I gesse wel þat þese men and such oþere ben now *wise men as to
> þis world,* but as her wordis sowneden sumtyme, and her werkis
> schewiden outward, it was licly to many men þat þei hadden eer[n]is
> of þe *wisdam of God* and þei schulden haue deserued myche grace of
> God to haue saued her owne soulis and manye oþer mennes if þei
> hadden perseyuered feithfulli . . . (39–40/522–7; my emphases)

Rather than contradicting Arundel directly, Thorpe distinguishes two
sorts of wisdom and imputes to the recanters the lesser of the two.

Whenever he can, Thorpe avoids being backed into the sort of
situation where he might have to either grant or deny. He takes every
opportunity to question Arundel instead, in an attempt to get him to
do the granting and denying. For the most part Arundel is too wary to
be drawn out.[59] But Thorpe's tactic succeeds brilliantly right at the end
of the *Testimony*, when Arundel has charged Thorpe 'tarie þou me now
no lenger; graunte to do þis þat I haue seide to þee now here schortly,
eiþir denyen it vtterli' (86/2023–4). In reply, Thorpe successfully
engages Arundel in a whole series of questions:

> And I seide to þe Archebischop, 'Owen we, sere, to bileuen þat
> Iesu Crist was and is very God and verry man?'
> And þe Archebischop seide, 'ʒhe'.
> And I seide, 'Sere, owen we to bileue þat al Cristis lyuynge and his
> techinge was trewe in euery poynt?'
> And he seide, 'ʒhe'.
> And I seide, 'Sere, owen we to bileue þat þe lyuynge and þe
> techynge of þe apostlis of Crist and of alle þe prophetis ben trewe,
> whiche ben writun in þe bible for þe helþe and saluacioun of alle
> Goddis peple?'
> And he seide, 'ʒhe'.
> And I seide, 'Sere, owen alle cristen men and wymmen, aftir her
> kunnynge and her power, for to conforme alle her lyuynge to þe
> lyuynge and techynge of Crist specialy, and also to þe lyuynge and to

---

59 See, for example, their discussion of the Eucharist, where Thorpe attempts to question
Arundel about the distinction (if any) between 'form', 'kind', and 'substance' (53/
970–54/990). Here neither Arundel nor Thorpe answers the other: each recognizes
the other's strategy and sidesteps his question.

þe techinge of his apostlis and of hise profetis, in alle þingis þat ben plesynge to God and edificacioun of his chirche?'

And he seide, 'ȝhe'.

And I seide, 'Sere, owiþ þe doctrine, þe heestis eiþer þe counseil of ony liif to be accept eiþer obeied vnto, no but þis doctrine, þese heestis and þis counseil moun ben groundid in Christis lyuynge and techinge speciali, eiþer in þe lyuynge and techinge of hise apostlis or of hise prophetis?'

And þe Archebischop seide to me, 'Oþer doctrine owiþ not to be accept, neiþer we owen to obeie to ony mannys heeste or counseile, [no but we mowen perseyue þat þis heeste or counseil] acordiþ wiþ þe lyuynge and techinge of Crist, and of hise apostlis and prophetis'.

And I seide, 'Ser, is not al þe lore, þe heest[is] and þe counseilis of holy chirche meenes and hel[e]ful remedies to knowe and to withstonde þe priuy suggestiouns and þe aperte temptaciouns of þe fende, and also hel[e]ful meenes and remedies to haten and fleen pride, and alle oþer dedly synnes and þe braunchis of hem, and souereyn meenes to purchace grace for to wiþstonde and ouercome alle fleischly lustis and mouyngis?'

And þe Archebischop seide, 'ȝhis'.

And I seide, 'Sere, whateuer þing ȝe or ony oþer liif biddiþ eiþer counseiliþ me to do acording to þis forseid lore, aftir my kunnynge and my power, þoruȝ þe helpe of God I wole mekeli of alle myn herte obeie þerto.' (86/2025–87/2062)

By asking these questions, Thorpe leads Arundel to agree with him about a body of 'forseid lore'. It is then hardly consistent for Arundel to continue to insist that Thorpe may not qualify his obedience according to that same 'lore'. As Arundel storms out of the room after this exchange, he is demonstrating that his principles are contradictory: his ecclesiastical imperative to make Thorpe submit unconditionally to the authority of 'holy chirche' is in conflict with the logical implications of his religious beliefs.

The manoeuvrings I have detailed show Thorpe's aptitude in evasion. It is worth considering whether this skill, like his abilities in argument and counterargument, is derived from and designed to display his alternative Wycliffite 'clergie'. Other than in his care to avoid granting or denying, we have already seen evidence of Thorpe's interest in carefully differentiating between mental attitudes to propositions during his interpretation of Chrysostom; the discrimination evident in the ways he couches his own assertions – 'I gesse wel', 'I knowe wel', 'I wote wel' – indicates that his interest is more than superficial. Indeed, it is a preoccupation in several other Wycliffite texts as well. Aston has already noted that Thorpe's refusal to grant or deny Arundel's question on the Eucharist – 'I dar neiþer denye it ne graunte it, for it is scolemater. . .'[60] – closely resembles the exemplary refusal to grant or deny the same question given in the Wycliffite tract 'De Blasphemia'.[61] But there remains more to be said about mental attitudes taken up by Wycliffites, and indeed by Wyclif himself, in these and several other texts.

The discussion of mental attitudes in 'De Blasphemia' does not confine itself to the subject of the Eucharist, but is more general in its scope, and even has a theoretical dimension. It recommends that for matters outside the scope of belief, 'we [ne] shulde graunte hom, ne denye hom, ne dowte hom; bot suppose hom, gesse hom, or hope hom',[62] provided there is no contrary evidence. It then discusses three cases where one ought to suppose or hope: when asked whether in a particular instance 'this bread' is God's body, when asked if one is ordained to be saved, and when asked about the remanence of substance after transubstantiation.[63] The most detailed explanation of this theory I have encountered in a Wycliffite text occurs in the dialogue between Reson and Gabbyng,[64] where Reson in replying to Gabbyng's challenge of his caution against believing uncertain things lays out four

---

[60] The passage is quoted in full on p. 190.

[61] Aston, 'Wycliffe and the Vernacular', in Aston, *Faith and Fire*, 66 and n. 99.

[62] 'De Blasphemia' in Arnold, ed., *Select English Works*, iii: 402–29; 426; my emendation. Note that the English Wycliffite tract titled 'De Blasphemia' is not the same text as Wyclif's *De Blasphemia*.

[63] 'De Blasphemia', 426–7.

[64] Dublin, Trinity College 245, ff. 153v–160. As Hudson was the first to point out ('A Lollard Quaternion', in *Lollards and Their Books*, 193–200; 196), this dialogue is a simplified, abridged translation of the first twelve chapters of Wyclif's *Dialogus*. However, the problem of what relation the 'Dialogue between Reson and Gabbyng' bears to whatever shorter or longer versions of Wyclif's *Dialogus* may have been accessible to the translator is greatly complicated by the lack of a critical edition of the *Dialogus*. I plan to pursue the issue in a separate article. See J. Wyclif, *Dialogus*, ed. A. W. Pollard (London, 1886), 24/6–18, for one Latin version of the vernacular exposition quoted here. On the current state of scholarship on the variant versions of the *Dialogus*, see Thomson, *Latin Writings of John Wyclif*, 268–70.

attitudes and briefly outlines the circumstances under which each
should be maintained:

> þer ben foure answeris to spechis. Summe worde men graunten for
> þei witen þat it is soþe before God, as ben poynts of beleeve and oþur
> treuþis þat we seene. Summe wordis men denyen for þei witen þat
> þei ben false as ben wordis contrarie to þo þat we han grauntid for þe
> first truþe. þer ben on þe þridde maner summe wordis þat we douten
> wheþer þei ben soþe or no for contrarie evydens þat we han. But þere
> ben onþe fourt maner summe wordis þat we supposen to be soþe or
> ellis false aftur evydens þat we han. (f.160v)

Laying aside Wyclif's more technical discussions of mental acts in his
early *De logica, Logice continuatio,* and *De actibus anime,*[65] Wyclif
discusses what mental acts and what responses are appropriate to
matters inside and outside belief in several of his later works. A fourfold
scheme of mental acts in *De dotacione ecclesie* closely resembles that in
the vernacular dialogue just cited: 'isti quattuor actus sunt distincti,
scilicet scire, credere, reputare vel supponere et dubitare', 'these four
actions are different, namely knowing, believing, considering or supposing, and doubting'.[66] A more detailed discussion in the *Trialogus*
focuses, like the dialogue, on responses, and shows an even closer
resemblance. '*Phronesis*' explains:

> Verumtamen quia istud non est fides, non oportet quod credatur ab
> ecclesia, sed quod probabiliter supponatur. Nec oportet quod ambi-

---

[65] As already discussed, Wyclif pays unusually close attention to mental acts in his
discussion of officiation in the *De logica.* In the *Logice continuatio* his discussion
centres on issues prominent in treatises *de scire et dubitare* (for an introduction to and
example of such treatises see Paul of Venice, *Logica Magna,* pt 1, fasc. 7, ed. and trans.
P. Clarke) and treatises on obligations (on which see further below). The *De actibus
anime* investigates the nature of mental acts rather than interesting itself in which acts
are appropriate in what circumstances. (Wyclif, *De actibus anime,* in M. H. Dziewicki,
ed. *Miscellanea philosophica* (London, 1902), i: 1–127; dated *c.* 1365 by Thomson,
Latin Writings of John Wyclif, 8 and 1369 by Mueller, in Wyclif, *Tractatus de
universalibus,* xxxvii.) These early discussions are by no means irrelevant to Wyclif's
later views – Wyclif brings up matters discussed in the *Logice continuatio* and *De
actibus anime* in the *De veritate sacre scriptura* while explaining what attitude to
maintain toward uncertain matters (*De veritate sacre scripture* ii: 88/2–16) – but the
topic must await thorough investigation elsewhere.

[66] Printed as a supplement to the *Trialogus* in Wyclif, *Trialogus,* ed. G. Lechler (Oxford,
1869); the passage cited is on p. 412 (*De dotacione ecclesie,* 2). Thomson, *Latin Writings
of John Wyclif,* 83, dates the work to late 1382.

gatur, cum multa sunt proponenda vianti quae nec debet dubitare
nec concedere nec negare, ut proposito mihi, quod sum praedesti-
natus, aut de peccante graviter, quod erit damnatus propter hoc
quod erit finaliter obstinatus, nec talia concedo nec nego nec dubito,
sed reputo unam partem. Et sic visa hostia adoro ipsam conditiona-
liter, et omnimode deadoro corpus Domini, quod est sursum. Et sic
responsio ad istas sex argutias potest esse medium ad tollendum
consimilia argumenta.[67]

Nonetheless, because that is not faith, it is not necessary that it
should be believed by the church, but that it should be supposed as
probable. Both sides of the question need not be given the same
weight, since many things are proposed to someone in this earthly
life which he ought neither to doubt, nor to grant, nor deny; as for
example if it is proposed to me that I am predestined, or, as concerns
a grave sinner, that he will be damned because in the end he will be
obstinate in sin; for such things I neither grant nor deny nor doubt,
but consider one side more likely than the other. And in this way,
when I see the host I adore it conditionally, and in every way adore
the body of the Lord which is above. And thus the reply to these six
difficulties can be the means toward solving similar arguments.

There are several comments in the *De veritate sacre scripture* on
reputative or suppositional knowledge, but since Wyclif is most of all
concerned in that work to explain what things may be infallibly known
through scripture and reason, none of them pursues the matter at
length.[68] Two vernacular Wycliffite texts do, however, elaborate the
description of what sort of things should be supposed or hoped. The
tract 'The Church and Her Members' exhorts 'Holde we us in bondis
of bileve, þat stondiþ in general wordis and in condicionel wordis, and
juge we not here folili.'[69] In general terms, without descending to
discuss particular cases, we know by belief that 'ech membre of þe fend
is dampned', but 'we witen not where *we* ben membris of holi
Churche'.[70] Nonetheless each man should hope and suppose that he is:
'we mai seie bi supposal, þat we gesse þat it is so'.[71] The 'Tractatus de

---

67 *Trialogus*, 281/1–11; Thomson, *Latin Writings of John Wyclif*, 79, dates the work to late
  1382 or early 1383.
68 See *De veritate sacre scripture* ii: 16/10–19, 87/20–88/16; iii: 74/6.
69 'The Church and her Members' in Arnold, ed., *Select English Works*, iii: 338–65; 344.
70 'The Church and her Members', 339; emphasis mine.
71 'The Church and her Members', 344.

Pseudo-Freris' recommends the same modes of speech as a way to avoid falsehood in accusations against friars, although without distinguishing so carefully between conditional or general speech and supposing or guessing: 'many men speken generalliche of here synne, & leuen to descende to persones lest þei medlen fals wiþ soþ. & þus þei speken bi condicioun, or supposyng, or gessyng, þat ȝif freris don þus cristen men schulden be war wiþ hem'.[72] And in the dialogue between 'Jon' and 'Richerd', careful distinction of attitudes becomes a tool of argument when 'Jon' catches up 'Richerd' for leaping from a conditional proposition to a suppositional assertion: 'I graunt wele þei mai . . . But schame ȝou of þis resoun, þat if it mai be so þan it is so and schal be supposed. For be þe same skil, iche frere schulde be a fende and þer order schulde be dampned. For al þis mai be.'[73]

This topic deserves further investigation. But these examples already suggest that there is a reasonably coherent and actively promoted doctrine among Wycliffites about what mental attitudes should be taken to matters lying outside what belongs to belief on the grounds of holy writ and open reason. Netter's retort that the doctrine on the Eucharist is known 'non reputative, sed vere', 'not as something to consider probable, but as true' provides further evidence that the scheme was put into use against orthodox opponents.[74] Further, this doctrine appears to rely on training in scholastic logic, both in its caution about remaining with conditional and general statements and in its interest in mental attitudes which were, as explained in my discussion of the analysis of 'officiable' propositions, of considerable interest to contemporary schoolmen and to Wyclif in particular.

It remains, however, to examine how Thorpe's sensitive discrimination between mental attitudes and his facility in making distinctions are of use to him in his efforts to avoid granting and denying propositions. It will help us to address this topic if we examine one more aspect of logic training. Arundel and Thorpe's last exchange in particular, and the context of an imperative to grant or deny proposi-

---

[72] 'Tractatus de Pseudo-Freris' in Matthew, ed., *The English Works of Wyclif Hitherto Unprinted*, 296–324; 297.
[73] Cambridge, Trinity College B.14.50, f. 47.
[74] T. Netter, *Doctrinale Antiquitatum Fidei Catholicae Ecclesiae*, 3 vols., ed. F. B. Blanciotti (Venice, 1757–9; repr. Farnborough, 1967), ii: col. 95E.

tions put to him within a limited period of time[75] in which Thorpe's other evasive moves appear, resemble a particular kind of disputation in which students engaged known as an 'obligation'.

The 'obligation' is an exercise in which one participant (*opponens*) proposes complex or incomplex statements to the other (*respondens*). At the outset the *respondens* agrees to an alteration in normal truth conditions proposed to him by the *opponens*: he agrees to consider an initial statement (*positum*) that is possible but not necessarily true at the time of the obligation, *as* necessarily true or false during the course of the obligation. The *opponens* then puts a series of further statements to the *respondens*, who is obliged to deny any statements pertaining (*pertinens*) to the *obligatio* and inconsistent with it, even if these might be considered true under normal circumstances, and grant any statements pertaining to the *obligatio* such that their contradictories would be inconsistent with it, even if in normal circumstances such statements would be considered untrue. Statements proposed during the obligation which do not pertain to the *obligatio* are treated as they would be normally. The *respondens* is limited to a narrow range of responses; he may grant (*concedo*), deny (*nego*), say the statement is uncertain because there is insufficient information to grant or deny it (*dubito*),[76] or distinguish (*distinguo*) parts or senses of the statement then grant or deny those. Within a set period of time, the *opponens* attempts to force the *respondens* to give a reply inconsistent with the *obligatio*, or inconsistent with ordinary truth other than when the *obligatio* requires it.[77] Here, in

---

[75] See Arundel's and the clerks' comments that time is limited at 34/349, 42/612, 52/921–2, 61/1220–1, 74/1621–8, 77/1733, 86/2005–9, and 86/2023.

[76] Although this circumlocution is awkward, the translation 'doubt' is inadequate. In the specialized terminology of obligation '*dubito*' indicates a neutral indecision and covers all varieties of uncertainty, whereas in twentieth-century usage (and, as we have seen, in Wycliffite theory), 'doubt' implies denial. See P. Clarke's comments in Paul of Venice, *Logica Magna*, pt 1, fasc. 7, ed. and trans. P. Clarke, xix–xx.

[77] I give a simple account of '*positum*' obligation here, similar to the one Wyclif gives in the last chapter of his *De logica* (*Tractatus*, i: 69–74). Dziewicki (*Tractatus*, i: xxvii–xxx) and Evans (*Road to Reformation*, 126–7) have summarized Wyclif's treatment of obligations; E. J. Ashworth places it in the context of other mid- to late fourteenth century treatises in 'English *Obligationes* Texts after Roger Swyneshed: The Tracts Beginning "Obligatio est quaedam ars"', in *The Rise of British Logic*, ed. P. O. Lewry (Toronto, 1983), 309–33; 313–16. Several other obligations treatises have been edited in recent years: those readily available include L. M. de Rijk, 'Some Thirteenth Century Tracts on the Game of Obligation', *Vivarium* 12 (1974), 94–123; 13 (1975),

my translation and schematic summary, is one of the examples Wyclif gives:[78]

opponens   **respondens**

Positum: 'No proposition is posited to you.'

                     Admitted and granted.

2 Some proposition is posited to you.

                     Denied (inconsistent with obligation).

3 (a) This proposition is posited to you,

   (b) and this proposition is some proposition

   (c) therefore some proposition is posited to you.

                     Consequencia granted (i.e., acknowledges that the form of the argument is sound).

                     Major premise (a) denied.

4 Contra:

   (a) I posit to you this proposition,

   (b) therefore this proposition is posited to you.

                     Consequencia granted.

                     Antecedens (a) denied, because *in isto casu*, in this obligation, in which no proposition is posited to you, it follows that nobody posits a proposition to you.

As this example may suggest, generally the philosophical content of obligations is trivial: naturally enough, since they start from a statement which while possible is not necessarily true, these exercises do not prove anything. They focus instead on testing (usually to destruction) the internal consistency and the cogency of arguments. How they were

---

22–54; and 14 (1976), 26–49; P. V. Spade, 'Richard Lavenham's *Obligationes*: Edition and Comments', *Rivista critica della storica filosofica* 33 (1978), 225–42; P. V. Spade, 'Robert Fland's *Obligationes*: An Edition', *Mediaeval Studies* 42 (1980), 41–60; P. V. Spade, 'Roger Swyneshed's *Obligationes:* Edition and Comments', *Archives d'histoire doctrinale et litteraire du Moyen Age* 44 (1977), 243–85; N. Kretzmann and E. Stump, 'The Anonymous *De Arte Obligatoria* in Merton College U.S. 306', in *Medieval Semantics and Metaphysics*, ed. E. P. Bos (Nijmegen, 1985), 239–80; Paul of Venice, *Logica Magna*, pt. 2, fasc. 8, ed. and trans. E. J. Ashworth (Oxford, 1988). Theories developed in these treatises about what kinds of responses were legitimate or most effective are fascinating, but I cannot pursue them here; the best brief introductions are in E. J. Ashworth's introduction to the *Logica Magna*, pt 2, fasc. 8, ed. and trans. E. J. Ashworth, and in the articles by E. Stump and P. V. Spade entitled 'Obligations' in *CHLMP*, 315–41.

[78] For Wyclif's more discursive Latin version see the *De logica* (*Tractatus,* i: 72).

used – whether mainly to train students in producing consistent arguments, or whether to explore problems in the philosophy of language or counterfactual logic – is a topic of some controversy.[79] We do know that obligations were taught as part of the course in logic in the arts faculty, and thus that students who remained at university even for as little as two years would have been familiar with the terminology and mode of argument of obligations, and would very probably have participated in them. It has been suggested that the specialized usages of words like *concedo* and *nego* and the rules of conduct developed in obligations 'spilled over' into other areas of philosophy;[80] I would suggest that the terminology and techniques of obligation spilled over into the vernacular as well.

The fourteenth century poem the 'Song of Nego' reveals that some vernacular readers and writers knew the terminology of obligation:

> For whoso can lite, hath sone i-do,
> Anone he drawith to *nego*.
> Now o clerk seiith *nego*;
> And that other *dubito*
> Seiith another *concedo*;
> and another *obligo*,
> *Verum falsum* sette therto;
> Than is al the lore i-do.[81]

---

[79] E. J. Ashworth's introduction to Paul of Venice, *Logica Magna*, pt. 2, fasc. 8, ed. and trans. E. J. Ashworth, xiii–xiv provides a balanced assessment of theories about the purposes and uses of obligations; the other editions named are also a valuable source of commentary, as are the recent articles by E. Stump and P. V. Spade cited by Ashworth.

[80] See P. V. Spade, 'Obligations: B', in *CHLMP*, 335–341; 341.

[81] From London, British Library, Harley 913, f. 58v. This manuscript, known as the Kildare manuscript, was compiled by Franciscans in Ireland *c.* 1330 and contains a mixture of Latin and vernacular materials. Several of the English items are of a satirical cast. For the most recent description of the English contents and a bibliography of studies upon the manuscript, see M. Laing, *Catalogue of Sources for a Linguistic Atlas of Early Medieval English* (Cambridge, 1993), 90–1. A. G. Rigg discusses some of the Latin contents in *A History of Anglo-Latin Literature, 1066–1422* (Cambridge, 1992), 304–7. The poem cited is available in two editions: T. Wright, ed., *The Political Songs of England* (London, 1839), 210–11, and W. Heuser, *Die Kildare-Gedichte: Die ältesten Mittelenglischen Denkmäler in Anglo-Irischer Überlieferung* (Bonn, 1904), 139–40; I cite lines 15–22 from Wright. The poem's attitude to scholastic argument has been occasionally and briefly remarked, but the specific link to obligations terminology has never been noticed.

As is obvious, this poem associates obligation terminology firmly with 'scole-mater', to which its attitude is similar to Thorpe's. Arundel's retort against Thorpe's criticism of 'scole-mater' – Thorpe's criticism could itself be construed to describe obligations, among other sorts of disputation – may be a similarly joking dismissal of obligations terminology. When Arundel allows 'I purpose not to *oblische* þe to þe sotil argumentis of clerkis, siþ þou art vnable herto' (55/1039), he certainly means *oblische* in the sense of legal or ethical commitment. But the word's appearance in close conjunction with 'sotil argumentes' and with Thorpe's description may point toward a wry pun.

Beyond joking use of terminology, however, obligations techniques would seem to have some wider influence as well. There is little to go on in most of the vernacular Wycliffite texts that discuss what attitudes should be taken in responding to challenges, since most of these texts merely recommend responses rather than putting them to use in argument.[82] In the *Testimony*, however, it is clear that both Thorpe and Arundel are acutely aware of the advantage to be gained by constraining one's opponent to grant or deny a proposition – and of the perils of being so constrained. Arundel and Thorpe's final exchange does not have the logical rigour of the obligations each might have participated in at Oxford. Nor is it a direct imitation of obligation exercises. But the mode in which it proceeds is suggestive. What Thorpe forces Arundel to acknowledge is, precisely, the inconsistency between the additional obligation to church authority that Arundel is trying to impose on him and the 'lore' and the methods of argument that Arundel also professes to accept. This is exactly the inconsistency in Arundel's clergial grounding that he is least willing to acknowledge; indeed, that occasions the *Testimony* and permits it to continue for as long as it does. Arundel's assumption from the beginning has been that by means of his own 'clergie' it will be possible for him to persuade Thorpe to submit to the institutional clergy; their final exchange shows just why his attempts will never be successful.

The reader of the *Testimony* is meant to enjoy watching Thorpe top

---

[82] The four Wycliffite dialogues are of course an exception, and in conjunction with my edition of them I plan a wider ranging study of polemic and didactic dialogues in Latin and the vernacular from 1100–1500 which will, in part, examine modes of argument in Wycliffite and other dialogues.

the clerks and beat Arundel at his own game. But he or she is never meant to forget that these techniques of argumentation are Thorpe's game as well, not even when Thorpe condemns clerks for their 'curious and so sotil sofestrie'. By setting up an alternative authority for argument grounded in 'vertue' rather than 'stodie', Thorpe apparently thinks he has established his difference from the waders and wanderers from argument to argument whom he has criticized. His idea, it seems, is that there can be a community of belief in which academic argument is not ruled out, but subordinated to grace; where anyone, no matter how little educated, can have intellectual authority by virtue of their 'vertue'.

It must be acknowledged that Thorpe's *Testimony* is remarkably successful in reconciling the requirements of lay and educated appeal; it is perhaps the Wycliffite text that manages this difficult balancing act best. And thus until now we have been taking Thorpe at his word when he offers intellectual authority to the 'lewed'. But we should consider just how far Thorpe really opens the argument to the virtuous but less educated members of his audience. According to the model of interpretation Thorpe has proposed, his virtuous audience should be as capable as he; once they apply their 'vertue', scripture will be plain and reason open. That is why he enlists them as authorities. But a telling elision on Thorpe's part reveals the problem for any educated writer who claims to lay his arguments open to lay judgement.

Because for Thorpe scripture is plain and reason open to the virtuous, he does not leave a space for any unexpected opinions his new audience might want to present. He is so certain of their reply that he does not feel the need to include it: 'I gesse certeynly þat þere was no man ne womman þat hatide verily synne and louede vertues, heerynge þe sermoun of þe clerk of Oxenford and also Alkirtouns sermoun, þat ne þei seiden eiþer myȝht iustly seien þat Alkirtoun repreuede þe clerk vntrewli, and sclaundride him wrongfully and vncharitabli', he confidently asserts (85/1967–71). But on no occasion, here or elsewhere, does he actually elicit their opinion; he never expresses any doubt that it is the same as his own. Indeed, if we consider for a moment, it becomes plain that in this confident assertion, it is the audience's assent that *qualifies* its members as virtuous: if they do *not* agree that Alkerton reproved the clerk untruly, then that reveals only that they do not hate sin and love virtue. Thorpe obliges the new authorities he enlists against Repyngdon to answer in one particular way just as thoroughly as he obliges Arundel. Or perhaps even more thoroughly; he constrains them into granting and denying according to his script *even as* he invites their participation.

It remains that the model the *Testimony of William Thorpe* offers its readers for establishing their authority as reasoners and interpreters of scripture has more far-reaching implications than Thorpe seems to have realized. Once he has conferred authority upon the 'lewed', he cannot take back their *vertue* so easily; and it may even turn out that he has taught them more about argumentation than he expected. In Thorpe's position, these kinds of potential implication are of little concern: his situation in the enclosed chamber where his examination takes place is so dire that any 'opening' whatever to a larger audience is likely to work to his advantage. In the first decade of the the fifteenth century, the institution of the death penalty for heresy and of strict sanctions upon the dissemination of 'clergie' mean that any possibility of wider dissemination is more stringently foreclosed than ever before. Yet it is in these circumstances, it seems, that any lay audience, noble or common, becomes all the more desirable – and that in dissident writings 'clergie' is made all the more genuinely accessible.

In a sense, the problem of access to the sort of 'clergie' examined in this study is eventually solved by history: it is because writings like Thorpe's *Testimony*, Jack Upland's questions, Wyclif's 'Petition', *Piers Plowman*, Fitzralph's *Defensio curatorum*, and the *Dialogus inter militem et clericem* were there for later polemicists to adopt and promote as their precursors that they eventually became available to something like the breadth and scope of audiences they initially projected – in the service of a new set of representations that reconstructed their initial audience in its own aspirational image.[83]

---

[83] Later adaptations of extraclergial works of course lie beyond the scope of the present study. But the interested reader might recall the nineteenth century title attached to the 'Petition', 'A Petition to King and Parliament' (ch. 1, p. 8); the later dissemination of *Upland*, the *Defensio curatorum*, and the *Dialogus inter militem et clericem* in the service of antifraternal, antireligious, and antipapal polemic (see ch. 5, pp. 135–8, 169–70, ch. 3, p. 79); Thorpe's later incarnations in Fox's *Book of Martyrs* and elsewhere as a Protestant martyr (see p. 179 and n. 1, and Hudson, *Two Wycliffite*

Those who later publish medieval 'clergie' seek the validation of historical precedent: showing that earlier polemicists share your views is a motive for studying and re-presenting the history of dissent that persists to the present day. In addition, although the problem of popular access to controversy can be figured around the activities of an extraclergial translator only briefly, the rhetorical pose of extraclergie retains its attraction: the claim to stand outside institutional structures, courting martyrdom to deliver truth guaranteed to grace and immediately recognizable (to all virtuous readers at any rate) as superior to the received dogma, remains and remains still a powerful tool for self-authorization.

What history does leave behind to a large extent, though, is the allure of the terminology and techniques of argument used by highly educated later medieval English clerics to convey controversial ideas. Disinvested of intellectual capital by the very changes in clerical roles and functions that extraclergial writers anticipate and exploit so as to present themselves in marginal positions, 'clergie' in this sense largely ceases to function as a currency of authoritative discourse. As a result, 'clergie' is no longer subject to forgery, to illicit use, and to all the anxieties about unqualified judgement that those possibilities raise. Although it is as opaque as ever (and perhaps more so) to much of its readership, academic language – of this sort at any rate – is no longer a reason for confining materials from publication: it has been rendered innocuous by the same developments that briefly made it seem dangerous.

Texts, xxvi–lix); and *Piers Plowman*'s later presentation as a pioneering Protestant text (see A. Hudson, 'Epilogue: The Legacy of *Piers Plowman*', in Alford, ed., *A Companion to 'Piers Plowman'*, 251–66).

The dating of the *Upland Series*

Definitive new conclusions on the dating of the *Upland Series* must await the broader recontextualization that a new edition will be able to provide. There is, however, strong evidence for overturning Heyworth's datings and proposing an alternative hypothesis.[1]

At the very least the version of *Jack Upland* to which Woodford replies must have been written before Woodford replied to it: the set of sixty-five questions in Latin must therefore have been written by the early 1390s, or even, if we trust (as Eric Doyle does not) Woodford's statement that he wrote his reply in 1385, by the early 1380s. It is entirely possible that both vernacular and Latin versions were available when Woodford wrote, and even that a vernacular version may have preceded the Latin version: Woodford might, like Dymmok and Maidstone, have translated his opponent's arguments before replying to them.[2] All the extant versions of *Jack Upland* must obviously postdate Fitzralph's antifraternal writings of the 1350s, and as chapter five has shown, the work's closest ideological ties are with vernacular Wycliffite writings of the late fourteenth century, as well as the larger extraclergial trend, in which Wycliffite texts are such an important component, toward providing sustained complex argumentation in the vernacular coupled with provocative claims to untutored

---

[1] Several scholars have shared with me their doubts about Heyworth's datings; indeed, this has been the normal reaction to my announcement that I am working on the text. I thank in particular Andrew Hope, who gave me a copy of his unpublished 'Note on the Dating of the Upland Controversy', and Helen Barr, who talked with me about *Mum and the Sothsegger* and lent me a portion of her thesis (see H. Barr, *A Study of 'Mum and the Sothsegger' in its Political and Literary Contexts*, 2 vols., unpubd D. Phil thesis, University of Oxford, 1988, i: 29–32) that has not yet been published elsewhere, in which she discusses both *Mum* and *Upland*. For an introduction to the components of the *Upland Series* see ch. 5, pp. 135–8.

[2] On Dymmok's translation, see ch. 4, pp. 104–5; on Maidstone's, see ch. 5, pp. 157, 176.

simplicity.[3] It seems most probable, then, that the versions of *Jack Upland* available to us were produced or revised in the early 1380s to early 1390s. There could have been earlier, shorter versions: Wendy Scase has suggested that *Jack Upland* mimics the form of earlier lists of polemic questions in Latin.[4] Although I have occasionally seen a polemic author gather a number of arguments against his position together before answering, however, I have never seen a list as long as Jack's, or indeed one that remains provocatively unanswered in the way that Jack's does. In my view *Jack Upland* as we have it is a late fourteenth century formal innovation.

Friar Daw on the evidence of its closest polemic ties alone would seem to belong to the period between 1388, when accroachment became tantamount to treason, and 1399, when it ceased to be: the fraternal replies Daw most strongly resembles were publicized between 1385 and 1392, and so fit with this dating as well.[5] But there are further complications. Daw's treason argument would have been most credible before 1399.[6] But reasons why this Ricardian accusation might have been used after 1399 can be proposed. The writer might indeed have Ricardian sympathies rather like those of the *Continuatio Eulogii* – much though a vernacular rebuttal might seem a particularly bad place to air them.[7] Or this exchange might be our best proof that Daw's reply is yet another constructed fraternal voice like that of 'The Friar's Answer' – even if one more sympathetically conceived, and less thoroughly undermined or refuted, than any other.[8] If I am right that we do not have the full text of either or both of Daw's reply or Upland's rejoinder,[9] then this may account for the imbalance of debate between these two texts and help to render this last possibility more likely.

The reason why these possibilities are even worth considering is that there is one more topical allusion in the *Upland Series* that has not yet been discussed, and that may place Daw after 1399. In the course of his counter-argument on taxation, Daw alludes to recent taxation of the friars:

---

[3] See ch. 5, esp. pp. 153–68.

[4] Scase gives one example, and that a list of answered rather than unanswered questions: Bonaventure's *Opusculum XIII*, answers to forty-nine questions against friars. (W. Scase, *'Piers Plowman' and the New Anticlericalism* (Cambridge, 1989), 25 n. 48.) This is by far the longest list of answered questions I have met with.

[5] See ch. 5, pp. 142–6 on accroachment, and pp. 174–6 for fraternal replies similar to Daw's.

[6] See ch. 5, p. 152.

[7] On the *Continuatio Eulogii*, printed in F. S. Haydon, ed., *Eulogium Historiarum*, 3 vols. (London, 1858–63), iii: 333–421, see ch. 5, pp. 148–52, esp. n. 23.

[8] On 'The Friar's Answer' see ch. 5, pp. 158–60.

[9] For this suggestion see ch. 5, pp. 167–8.

But now is þe compleynt of Ieremye trewe,
Þe prince of prouynces sugette is vndir tribute.
Not for þanne þe comun lawe may wel suffren
Þat presthode mot paye but bi assent of prelatis,
Freli of her owne wille, no þing constreynede.
And þus prelatis & persouns aftir her state,
Ben stended to paien what þat nede askiþ,
But neiþir freres ne anuellers saue now late.
(497–504)

Heyworth lists the occasions within the relevant timeframe on which friars were taxed as 1371, 1404, 1419, and 1429: he concludes that the allusion must be to 1419 (10–12). But as Barr and Hope have both noted, if as Heyworth suggests Daw's reference is to an *unprecedented* tax, the longest and therefore most appropriate gap is that between 1371 and 1404; since the other arguments Heyworth gives to guide us toward a later date do not hold up, they view this as the most likely possibility.[10]

We should note in addition that the *style* of Daw's topical reference is far different. Upland's rejoinder uses 'now late' to refer to a specific, well-known recent instance. Daw's reference to 'now late' is in the mode of social complaint: 'now' is the upside down, unstable world of nowadays; the reference need be neither precisely pinpointed nor quite so recent, especially perhaps for friars who might well have a long memory of a tax they strongly resented. If Daw is writing in the 1380s, therefore, I do not think that it is impossible that he could be referring to the tax of 1371, or to some more recent reminder of it in the form of a financial constraint of some kind upon the friars' activities. It is of course also possible that Daw is writing soon after 1404; perhaps in this case we must consider reasons why a friar or indeed a Wycliffite might have written *Friar Daw's Reply* at this slightly later date. Another possibility is that Daw's reply could have been revised and updated slightly at around the time that *Upland's Rejoinder* was written; this would account for both Daw's close ties to the polemic of the 1380s and 90s and the possible reference to 1404.

Whatever the precise details of composition and revision of *Friar Daw's Reply*, it seems clear that *Upland's Rejoinder* must have been written soon after 1402. Heyworth thought that Upland's date needed to be set far forward, for if Daw called 1404 'now late', then any date after Daw finished writing would be too late for Upland to call 1402 'now late' (10). But as Helen Barr has shown, the writer of *Mum and the Sothsegger* refers to the

---

[10] See n. 1 for Barr and Hope's unpublished work.

1402 hangings as a recent notable event when writing at some point between 1406 and 1410, topping fraternal arguments against Lollards by pointing out the consequences of the friars' own misplaced loyalties in much the same way that Upland does:

> For furst folowid freres Lollardz manieres,
> And sith hath be shewed the same on thaym-self,
> That thaire lesingz haue lad thaym to lolle by the necke;
> At Tibourne for traison y-twyght vp thay were.
> (417–20)

First friars persecuted or pursued Lollards for their manner of living, and now friars have received the same treatment themselves; their lies (as the rumours are called in the proclamations) have led to them being hanged for treason.[11] There seems no reason to suppose that another writer from much the same background and milieu could not regard the executions as a recent event for the same length of time. Indeed, the friars' executions seem likely to have been unforgettable to many for quite some time: two proclamations, three public executions, a grisly ceremony with the master of theology's head, public disputes, mention in several chronicles, and two mentions in Wycliffite poems would seem likely (even if, or perhaps especially because, some of those events are in some respects fictional) to cause accusations against friars of conspiratorial loyalty to Richard to retain their force at least until 1410.[12]

Finally, the paleographic evidence that upholds Heyworth's best argument for his later datings may be dismissed by citing the authority of Professor Ian Doyle, who has stated, *assertiue* I am sure,[13] that the Harley and Digby manuscripts Heyworth dates to 1450 should instead be dated to the first quarter of the fifteenth century.[14] Even if Heyworth is right

---

[11] For the rumours termed lies see ch. 5, p. 148 and n. 22. For Barr's discussion see n. 1.

[12] For the proclamations see *Foedera . . .* , 3rd ed., vol. 4, ed. T. Rymer (London, 1740; reprinted Farnborough, Hants., 1967), 29–30; see also *Calendar of Close Rolls*, vol. 30, 1399–1402 (London, 1927), 570. All the events mentioned here are recounted in the *Continuatio Eulogii*, 389–94; in addition to the *Continuatio Eulogii*, the hangings are mentioned in Walsingham's *Chronica Maiora* (printed as *Annales Ricardi Secundi et Henrici Quarti* in *Johannis de Trokelowe et Anon Chronica et Annales*, ed. H. T. Riley (London, 1866), 155–420; 339–41) and *Historia Anglicana*, 2 vols., ed. H. T. Riley (London, 1864), ii: 250, and in Usk's chronicle, *Chronicon Adae de Usk A. D. 1377–1421*, ed. E. M. Thompson, 2nd ed. (London, 1904), 255.

[13] See ch. 5, pp. 172–4 for the usage of 'assertiue' here.

[14] A. I. Doyle, 'The Manuscripts', in D. A. Lawton, ed., *Middle English Alliterative Poetry* (Cambridge, 1982), 88–100; 98 and n. 44.

that the copy of *UR* in Digby 41 is the holograph,[15] by Doyle's new dating for Digby 41 the manuscript's date is compatible with my dating of the text.

[15] For my explanation of why I think Heyworth may be incorrect, see ch. 5, pp. 167–8.

Works Cited

MANUSCRIPTS

Aberystwyth, National Library of Wales 733B
Baltimore, Walters Art Gallery W 144
Brno, University Library Mk. 28
Cambridge
    Corpus Christi College 156
    Corpus Christi College 283
    Corpus Christi College 296
    Gonville and Caius College 354/581
    Jesus College Q B 9
    St John's College 115
    St John's College 160
    St John's College 195
    Trinity College B.14.50
    Trinity College R.3.14
    Trinity Hall 17
Cambridge University Library Ee 2 17
Cambridge University Library Ff.6.2
Cambridge University Library Ii.4.3
Dublin
    Trinity College D.4.12
    Trinity College 244
    Trinity College 245
Durham University Library, Cosin V.I.9
Florence, *Bibl. Laurent. Flor. Plut. xix cod. xxxiii*
Liverpool University Library F.4.8
London
    British Library, Cotton Nero D VIII
    British Library, Cotton Otho C.xvi
    British Library, Cotton Titus D.v
    British Library, Egerton 2820
    British Library, Harley 31

British Library, Harley 875
British Library, Harley 913
British Library, Harley 6041
British Library, Harley 6641
British Library, Reg. 6 E III
British Library, Royal 6 B V
British Library, Royal 6 E VI and VII
British Library, Royal 15 E VI
Lincoln's Inn 150
Sion College, Arc. L. 40.2/L. 26
Society of Antiquaries 687
New York
  Pierpont Morgan Library M 818
  Pierpont Morgan Library 122
Oxford
  Bodleian Library, Ashmole 1468
  Bodleian Library, Auct. F inf. 1.2
  Bodleian Library, Bodley 144
  Bodleian Library, Bodley 158
  Bodleian Library, Bodley 234
  Bodleian Library, Bodley 703
  Bodleian Library, Bodley 784
  Bodleian Library, Bodley 851
  Bodleian Library, Digby 41
  Bodleian Library, Digby 113
  Bodleian Library, Digby 145
  Bodleian Library, Digby 188
  Bodleian Library, Digby 233
  Bodleian Library, Douce 53
  Bodleian Library, Douce 323
  Bodleian Library, English Poetry a.1
  Bodleian Library, Lat. th. e. 30
  Bodleian Library, Laud Misc 702
  Bodleian Library, Rawlinson G 40
  Bodleian Library, Rawlinson Poet. 137
  Jesus College 36
  University College 45
Paris, Bibliothèque Nationale, fonds lat. 3381
Prague, Metropolitan Chapter Library 0.29
San Marino, Huntingdon Library HM 114
Vienna, Österreichische Nationalbibliothek 3936

Works cited

PRIMARY PRINTED SOURCES

Works without a single known author are alphabetized by title when the title is original or longstanding, and by editor when it is not. Authors without surnames are alphabetized by their first names.

Annales. See Walsingham. *Chronica Maiora.*

Aquinas, T. S. *Tho super Ethica Sancti doctoris Thome de aquino in decem libros ethicorum Aristotelis profundissima commentaria cum triplici textus translatione antiqua videlicet Leonardi aretini nec non J. argyropili.* Venice, 1563.

Arnold, T., ed. *Select English Works of John Wyclif.* 3 vols. Oxford, 1869–71.

Barr, H., ed. *The Piers Plowman Tradition.* London, 1993.

Barthelmy of Bolsenheim, O. P. *Defensorium.* In G. Meersseman, O. P., 'La Défense des ordres mendiants contre Richard Fitz Ralph, par Barthélmy de Bolsenheim O. P. (1357)'. *Archivum Fratrum Praedicatorum* 5 (1935), 124–73.

Calendar of Close Rolls. London, 1902– . Vol. 29, 1366–99. London, 1927. Vol. 30, 1399–1402. London, 1927.

Calendar of Entries in the Papal Registers Relating to Great Britain and Ireland, Papal Letters. Vol. 4. Ed. W. H. Bliss *et al.* London, 1902.

Chaucer, G. *The Riverside Chaucer.* Gen. ed. L. D. Benson, 3rd ed. Oxford, 1988 (1987).

Pseudo-Chrysostom. *Opus Imperfectum.* In J. P. Migne, ed. *Joannis Chrysostomi, Opera Omnia.* Vol. 6. *Patrologia Graeca,* vol. 56. Paris, 1862, cols. 611–946.

Cigman, G, ed. *Lollard Sermons.* London, 1989.

Continuatio Eulogii. In F. S. Haydon, ed. *Eulogium Historiarum.* 3 vols. London, 1858–63, iii: 333–421.

de Rijk, L. M., ed. *Logica Modernorum.* Assen, 1967. Vol. 2, pt 2.

'Some Thirteenth Century Tracts on the Game of Obligation'. *Vivarium* 12 (1974), 94–123; 13 (1975), 22–54; 14 (1976), 26–49.

Some 14th Century Tracts on the Probationes Terminorum. Nijmegen, 1982.

Dean, J. M., ed. *Six Ecclesiastical Satires.* Kalamazoo, MI, 1991.

Dymmok, R. *Liber contra duodecim errores et hereses Lollardorum.* Ed. H. S. Cronin. London, 1922.

Erickson, N. N., ed. and trans. 'A Dispute Between a Priest and a Knight'. *Proceedings of the American Philosophical Society* 111 (1967), 288–309.

Examinacions Thorpe and Oldcastell. Antwerp, 1530. Facsimile ed. Amsterdam and Norwood, NJ, 1975.

Fasciculi Zizianorum Magistri Johannis Wyclif Cum Tritico. Ed. W. W. Shirley. London, 1858.

Fitzralph, R. *Defensio Curatorum.* In M. Goldast, ed. *Monarchiae S Romani Imperii* . . . , 3 vols. Frankfurt, 1621, iii: 1391–1410.

De Pauperie Salvatoris, selections. See Wyclif, ed. Poole. 1890.

Foedera, conventiones, literae, et cuiuscungue generis acta publica, inter reges Angliae, 3rd ed. 10 vols. Vol. 4, ed. T. Rymer. London, 1740; reprinted Farnborough, Hants., 1967.

Getz, F. M., ed. *Healing and Society in Medieval England: A Middle English*

Translation of the Pharmaceutical Writings of Gilbertus Anglicus. Madison, WI, 1991.

Gradon, P. and A. Hudson, eds. *English Wycliffite Sermons.* 5 vols. Oxford, 1983–96. Vol. 2. ed. P. Gradon. Oxford, 1988.

Heuser, W. *Die Kildare-Gedichte: Die ältesten Mittelenglischen Denkmäler in Anglo-Irischer Überlieferung.* Bonn, 1904.

Heyworth, P. L., ed. *Jack Upland, Friar Daw's Reply, and Upland's Rejoinder.* Oxford, 1968.

Higden, R. *Polychronicon.* 9 vols. Ed. C. Babington and J. R. Lumby. London, 1865–86. Vol. 6, ed. J. R. Lumby. London, 1876.

Hoccleve, T. *Regement of Princes.* Ed. F. J. Furnivall. London, 1897.

Hudson, A., ed. *English Wycliffite Sermons.* See Gradon.

Selections from English Wycliffite Writings. Cambridge, 1978.

Two Wycliffite Texts: The Sermon of William Taylor 1406. The Testimony of William Thorpe 1407. EETS 301. Oxford, 1993.

Hugh of St Victor. *De sacramentis Christianae fidei.* In J. P. Migne, ed. *Patrologia Latina,* vol. 76. Paris, 1854, cols. 173–618.

Jeffrey, D. L., ed. and trans. *The Law of Love: English Spirituality in the Age of Wyclif.* Grand Rapids, MI, 1988.

Keiser, G. R. *The Middle English 'Boke of Stones': the Southern Version.* Brussels, 1984.

Knighton, H. *Knighton's Chronicle, 1337–1396.* Ed. and trans. G. H. Martin. Oxford, 1995.

Kretzmann, N., and E. Stump, eds. 'The Anonymous *De Arte Obligatoria* in Merton College U.S. 306'. In E. P. Bos, ed. *Medieval Semantics and Metaphysics.* Nijmegen, 1985, 239–80.

Langland, W. See *Piers Plowman.*

The Lanterne of Liȝt. Ed. L. M. Swinburn. London, 1917.

Lydgate, J. *The Minor Poems of John Lydgate.* Ed. H. N. MacCracken. London, 1911, pt. 1.

Maidstone, R. *Determinacio.* In V. Edden. 'The Debate Between Maidstone and Ashwardby'. *Carmelus* 34 (1987), 113–34.

Protectorium Pauperis. In A. Williams. '*Protectorium Pauperis,* A Defense of the Begging Friars by Richard of Maidstone, O. Carm. (d. 1396)'. *Carmelus* 5 (1958), 132–80.

Matheson, L. M., ed. *Popular and Practical Science of Medieval England.* East Lansing, MI, 1994.

Matthew, F. D., ed. *The English Works of Wyclif Hitherto Unprinted.* EETS o.s. 74. London, 1880; 2nd rev. ed. 1902.

Metham, J. *Physiognomy.* In H. Craig, ed. *The Works of John Metham.* London, 1916.

Netter, T. *Doctrinale Antiquitatum Fidei Catholicae Ecclesiae.* 3 vols. Ed. F. B. Blanciotti. Venice, 1757–9; repr. Farnborough, 1967.

Nicholas de Lyra. *Postilla super biblia,* 3 vols. Venice, 1472.

Works cited

Paul of Venice. *Logica Magna*. Ed. and trans. P. Clarke. Oxford, 1981, pt 1, fasc. 7.

Logica Magna. Ed. and trans. E. J. Ashworth. Oxford, 1988, pt 1, fasc.8.

Pecham, John. *De Perfectione Evangelica*, selections. In A. G. Little, ed. 'Selections from Pecham's *Tractatus Pauperis* or *De Perfectione Evangelica*'. *British Society of Franciscan Studies* 2 (1910), 13–90.

Perry, A. J., ed. *Dialogus inter Militem et Clericem, Richard fitzRalph's Sermon: 'Defensio Curatorum' and Methodius: 'þe Bygynnyng of þe World and þe Ende of Worldes' by John Trevisa, vicar of Berkeley*. London, 1925.

Piers Plowman: The A Version. Ed. G. Kane. London, 1960.

Piers Plowman: The B Version. Ed. G. Kane and E. T. Donaldson. London, 1988 (1975).

The Vision of Piers Plowman: A Complete Edition of the B-Text. Ed. A. V. C. Schmidt. London, 1987 (1978).

Piers Plowman by William Langland: An Edition of the C-Text. Ed D. Pearsall. Berkeley, 1982 (1978).

Piers Plowman: The Z Version. Ed. A. G. Rigg and C. Brewer. Toronto, 1983.

Pollard, A. W., ed. 'The Examination of William Thorpe'. In *Fifteenth Century Prose and Verse*. Edinburgh, 1903, 97–167.

Raby, F. J. E., ed. *The Oxford Book of Mediaeval Latin Verse*. Oxford, 1959.

Robbins, R. H., ed. *Historical Poems of the XIVth and XVth Centuries*. New York, 1959.

Rotuli Parliamentorum iii. Ed. J. Strachey. London, 1767–77.

Sayles, G. O., ed. *Select Cases in the Court of King's Bench*. Vols. 1–7 to date. London, 1971, vii.

Simmons, T. F., and H. E. Nolloth, eds. *The Lay Folks' Catechism*. London, 1901.

Skeat, W. W. *Chaucerian and Other Pieces*. Oxford, 1897.

Spade, P. V. 'Roger Swyneshed's *Obligationes*: Edition and Comments'. *Archives d'histoire doctrinale et litteraire du Moyen Age* 44 (1977), 243–85.

'Richard Lavenham's *Obligationes*: Edition and Comments'. *Rivista critica della storica filosofica* 33 (1978), 225–42.

'Robert Fland's *Obligationes*: An Edition'. *Mediaeval Studies* 42 (1980), 41–60.

Statutes of the Realm. 10 vols. London, 1810–28.

Storey, R. L., ed. For the article in which records of the trials of Franciscan friars are included see Secondary Printed Sources.

Taylor, W. See Hudson, ed. 1993.

Thomas of York. *Manus quae contra omnipotentem*. In M. Bierbaum. 'Traktat eines Franziskaners zur Verteidigung der Mendikanten gegen Wilhelm von St Amour vom Jahre 1256/57 Inc: Manus que contra Omnipotentem tenditur'. In *Betttelorden und Weltgeistlichkeit an der Universität Paris: Texte und Untersuchungen zum Literarishchen Armuts- und Exemtionsstreit des 13 Jahrhunderts (1255–1272)*. *Franziskanische Studien* 2 Beiheft (1920), 37–168.

Thorpe, W. See Hudson, ed. 1993.

Trevisa, J. See Perry, ed.

Trevisa, J., trans. Bartholomeus Anglicus. *De proprietatibus rerum*. Ed. M. C.

Works cited

Seymour *et al*. *On the Properties of Things: John Trevisa's translation of Bartholo-maeus Anglicus De Proprietatibus Rerum. A Critical Text*. 3 vols. Oxford, 1975–88.

Giles of Rome. *De Regimine Principum. The Governance of Kings and Princes: John Trevisa's Middle English Translation of the 'De regimine principum' of Aegidius Romanus*. Ed. D. C. Fowler, C. Briggs, and P. Remley. Forthcoming.

Usk, A. *Chronicon Adae de Usk A. D. 1377–1421*. Ed. E. M. Thompson. 2nd ed. London, 1904.

Walsingham, J. *Historica Anglicana*. 2 vols. Ed. H. T. Riley. London, 1864.

Chronica Maiora. Printed as *Annales Ricardi Secundi et Henrici Quarti* in *Johannis de Trokelowe et Anon Chronica et Annales*. Ed. H. T. Riley. London, 1866, 155–420.

William of St Amour. *Opera Omnia*. Constance (for Paris), 1632.

Woodford, William, O.F.M. *De Dominio Civili Clericorum*. In E. Doyle, O.F.M. 'William Woodford's *De Dominio Civili Clericorum* against John Wyclif'. *Archivum Franciscanum Historicum* 66 (1973), 49–109.

Responsiones. In E. Doyle, O.F.M. 'William Woodford, O.F.M. (c.1330–c.1400): His Life and Works, Together with a Study and Edition of his "Responsiones Contra Wiclevum et Lollardos"'. *Franciscan Studies* 43 (1983), 17–187.

Wright, T., ed. *The Political Songs of England*. London, 1839.

Political Poems and Songs. 2 vols. London, 1859–61.

Wyche, R. 'The Trial of Richard Wyche'. Ed. F. D. Matthew. *English Historical Review* 5 (1890), 530–44.

Wyclif, J. *Trialogus*. Ed. G. Lechler. Oxford, 1869.

De composicione hominis. Ed. R. Beer. London, 1884.

De civili dominio. 4 vols. Vol. 1 ed. R. L. Poole. London, 1885. Vols. 2, 3, and 4 ed. J. Loserth. London, 1900, 1903, 1904.

De ecclesia. Ed. J. Loserth. London, 1886.

Dialogus. Ed. A. W. Pollard. London, 1886.

De domino divino. Ed. R. L. Poole. London, 1890. Includes books 1–4 of R. Fitzralph, *De Pauperie Salvatoris*.

De blasphemia. Ed. M. H. Dziewicki. London, 1893.

Tractatus de logica. 3 vols. Ed. M. H. Dziewicki. London, 1893–9.

De actibus anime. In M. H. Dziewicki, ed. *Miscellanea philosophica*. 2 vols. London, 1902, i.

De veritate sacre scripture. 3 vols. Ed. R. Buddensieg. London, 1905–7.

De potestate pape. Ed. J. Loserth. London, 1907.

'Determinacio ad argumenta Wilhelmi Vyrinham'. In *Opera Minora*. Ed. J. Loserth. London, 1913, 415–30.

Peticio ad regem et parliamentum. I. H. Stein, ed. 'The Latin Text of Wyclif's Complaint'. *Speculum* 7 (1932), 87–94.

Tractatus de universalibus. Ed. I. J. Mueller. Oxford, 1985.

Works cited

SECONDARY PRINTED SOURCES

If in a given entry an article is said to appear in a book cited by editor and date, then the book will be found cited in full under the editor's name.

Alexander, J. J. G. 'Painting and Manuscript Illumination for Royal Patrons in the Later Middle Ages'. In Scattergood and Sherbourne, eds., 1983, 141–62.

Alford, J. A. 'The Idea of Reason in *Piers Plowman*'. In Kennedy, Waldron, and Wittig, eds., 1988, 199–215.

Alford, J. A., ed. *A Companion to 'Piers Plowman'*. Berkeley, CA, 1988.

Ashworth, E. J. 'English *Obligationes* Texts after Roger Swyneshed: The Tracts Beginning "Obligatio est quaedam ars"'. In P. O. Lewry, ed. *The Rise of British Logic*. Toronto, 1983, 309–33.

'Analogy and Equivocation in Thirteenth-Century Logic: Aquinas in Context'. *Mediaeval Studies* 54 (1992), 94–135.

Ashworth, E. J., and P. V. Spade. 'Logic in Late Medieval Oxford'. In Catto and Evans, eds., 1992, 35–64.

Aston, M. 'Lollardy and Literacy'. In Aston, 1984, 193–217.

'Lollardy and Sedition, 1381–1431'. In Aston, 1984, 1–47.

Lollards and Reformers: Images and Literacy in Late Medieval Religion. London, 1984.

Faith and Fire: Popular and Unpopular Religion 1350–1600. London, 1993.

'Bishops and Heresy: The Defence of the Faith'. In Aston, 1993, 73–93.

'"Caim's Castles": Poverty, Politics, and Disendowment'. In Aston, 1993, 95–131.

'Wycliffe and the Vernacular'. In Aston, 1993, 27–72.

Baldwin, A. P. *The Theme of Government in 'Piers Plowman'*. Woodbridge, Suffolk, 1981.

Barr, H. *A Study of 'Mum and the Sothsegger' in its Political and Literary Contexts*. 2 vols. Unpubd. D. Phil. thesis, University of Oxford, 1988.

Signes and Sothe: Language in the 'Piers Plowman' Tradition. Woodbridge, Suffolk, 1994.

Bellamy, J. G. *The Law of Treason in England in the Later Middle Ages*. Cambridge, 1970.

Bennett, M. J. 'The Court of Richard II and the Promotion of Literature'. In Hanawalt, ed., 1992, 3–20.

Bloomfield, M. W. 'Was William Langland a Benedictine Monk?'. *Modern Language Quarterly* 4 (1943), 57–61.

Bowers, J. M. '*Piers Plowman* and the Police: Notes Toward a History of the Wycliffite Langland'. *The Yearbook of Langland Studies* 6 (1992), 1–50.

'*Pearl* in its Royal Setting: Ricardian Poetry Revisited'. *Studies in the Age of Chaucer* 17 (1995), 111–55.

'*Piers Plowman*'s William Langland: Editing the Text, Writing the Author's Life'. *The Yearbook of Langland Studies* 9 (1995), 65–90.

Briggs, C. F. 'Manuscripts of Giles of Rome's *De Regimine Principum* in England, 1300–1500: A Handlist'. *Scriptorium* 47 (1993), 60–73.

'The Manuscript as Witness: Editing Trevisa's *De regimine principum* Translation', *Medieval Perspectives* 11 (1996), 42–52.

Broadie, A. *Introduction to Medieval Logic*, 2nd ed. Oxford, 1993.

Burrow, J. A. 'The Action of Langland's Second Vision'. *Essays in Criticism* 15 (1965), 247–68. Reprinted in Burrow, 1984, 79–101.

'The Audience of *Piers Plowman*'. Revised version in Burrow, 1984, 102–16.

Essays on Medieval Literature. Oxford, 1984.

Busa, R., *et al.*, eds. *Index Thomisticus Sancti Thomae Aquinatis Operum Omnium indices et concordantiae*. Italy, 1975.

Carruthers [Schroeder], M. 'The Character of Conscience in *Piers Plowman*'. *Studies in Philology* 67 (1970), 13–30.

The Search for St Truth: A Study of Meaning in 'Piers Plowman'. Evanston, 1973.

Catto, J. I. 'An Alleged Great Council of 1374'. *English Historical Review* 82 (1967), 764–71.

William Woodford O. F. M. (c. 1330–c. 1397). Unpubd. D. Phil. thesis, University of Oxford, 1969.

Catto, J. I., ed. *The History of the University of Oxford*. Vol. 1. Oxford, 1984.

Catto, J. I., and R. Evans, eds. *The History of the University of Oxford*. Vol. 2. Oxford, 1992.

Clanchy, M. T. *From Memory to Written Record*, 2nd ed. Oxford, 1993.

Clopper, L. M. 'Need Men and Women Labor? Langland's Wanderer and the Labor Ordinances'. In Hanawalt, ed., 1992, 110–29.

Coleman, J. 'The Science of Politics and Late Medieval Academic Debate'. In Copeland, ed., 1996, 181–214.

Copeland, R., ed. *Criticism and Dissent in the Middle Ages*. Cambridge, 1996.

Courtenay, W. J. *Schools and Scholars in Fourteenth Century England*. Princeton, 1987.

Crane, S. 'The Writing Lesson of 1381'. In Hanawalt, ed., 1992, 201–21.

Dawson, J. D. 'Richard FitzRalph and the Fourteenth-Century Poverty Controversies'. *Journal of Ecclesiastical History* 34 (1983), 315–44.

Deanesly, M. *The Lollard Bible*. Cambridge, 1920.

Del Punta, F., and C. Luna. *Aegidii Romani Opera Omnia*. Catalogo dei manoscritti [di Egidio Romano]. Vols. 1–12 to date. Rome, 1993, xii.

Dictionary of Medieval Latin from British Sources. Prepared by R. E. Latham and (subsequently) D. R. Howlett. Oxford, 1975– .

Dictionary of National Biography. Ed. L. Stephen and S. Lee. Oxford, 1917.

Dillon, (no initials) and W. H. S. Hope, eds. 'Inventory of Goods Belonging to Thomas Duke of Gloucester'. *Archaeological Journal* 54 (1897), 275–308.

Donaldson, E. T. *The C text and Its Poet*. New Haven, 1949.

Doyle, A. I. 'The Manuscripts'. In Lawton, ed., 1982, 88–100.

'English Books In and Out of Court from Edward III to Henry VII'. In Scattergood and Sherbourne, eds., 1983, 163–81.

Doyle, E., O.F.M. 'William Woodford, O.F.M., and John Wyclif's *De Religione*'. *Speculum* 52 (1977), 329–36.

Eberle, P. J. 'The Politics of Courtly Style at the Court of Richard II'. In G. S. Burgess *et al.*, eds. *The Spirit of the Court*. Dover, NH, 1985, 168–78.

Edwards, A. S. G. 'John Trevisa'. In A. S. G. Edwards, ed. *Middle English Prose: A Critical Guide to Major Authors and Genres*. New Brunswick, NJ, 1984, 133–46.

Emden, A. B. *A Biographical Register of the University of Oxford to A.D. 1500.* 3 vols. Oxford, 1957–9.

Evans, G. R. *The Language and Logic of the Bible: The Road to Reformation.* Cambridge, 1985.

'Wyclif's *Logic* and Wyclif's Exegesis: the Context'. In Walsh and Wood, eds., 1985, 287–300.

'Wyclif on Literal and Metaphorical'. In Hudson and Wilks, eds., 1987, 259–66.

Fisher, J. H. 'Chancery and the Emergence of Standard Written English in the Fifteenth Century'. *Speculum* 52 (1977), 870–99.

'A Language Policy for Lancastrian England'. *Publications of the Modern Language Association of America* 107 (1992), 1168–80.

Fletcher, A. J. 'The Social Trinity of *Piers Plowman*'. *Review of English Studies*, n.s. 44, no. 175 (1993), 343–61.

Fletcher, J. M. 'The Faculty of Arts'. In Catto, ed., 1984, 369–99.

Fowler, D. C. 'John Trevisa and the English Bible'. *Modern Philology* 58 (1960–1), 81–98.

Piers the Plowman: Literary Relations of the A and B Texts. Seattle, 1961.

The Bible in Early English Literature. Seattle, 1976.

John Trevisa. Aldershot, 1993.

The Life and Times of John Trevisa, Medieval Scholar. Seattle, 1995.

Galloway, A. '*Piers Plowman* and the Schools'. *The Yearbook of Langland Studies* 6 (1992), 89–107.

'Gower in his Most Learned Role and the Peasants' Revolt of 1381'. *Mediaevalia* 16 (1993), 329–47.

'The Rhetoric of Riddling in Late-Medieval England: The "Oxford" Riddles, the *Secretum philosophorum*, and the Riddles in *Piers Plowman*'. *Speculum* 70 (1995), 68–105.

Given-Wilson, C. *The Royal Household and the King's Affinity: Service, Politics and Finance in England 1360–1413.* London, 1986.

Godden, M. 'Plowmen and Hermits in Langland's *Piers Plowman*'. *Review of English Studies*, n.s. 35, no. 138 (1984), 129–63.

The Making of 'Piers Plowman'. London, 1990.

Grady, F. 'The Lancastrian Gower and the Limits of Exemplarity'. *Speculum* 70 (1995), 552–75.

Gransden, A. *Historical Writing in England*, 2 vols. London, 1982, ii.

Green, R. F. *Poets and Princepleasers: Literature and the English Court in the Late Middle Ages.* Toronto, 1980.

'John Ball's Letters: Literary History and Historical Literature'. In Hanawalt, ed., 1992, 176–200.

Gwynn, A. 'The Sermon Diary of Richard Fitzralph'. *Proceedings of the Royal Irish Academy* 44 C (1937), 1–57.

Hanawalt, B. A., ed. *Chaucer's England: Literature in Historical Context.* Minneapolis, 1992, 176–200.

Hanna III, R. 'Sir Thomas Berkeley and his Patronage'. *Speculum* 64 (1989), 878–916.

'The Difficulty of Ricardian Prose Translation: The Case of the Lollards'. *Modern Language Quarterly* 51 (1990), 319–40.

'Two Lollard Codices and Lollard Book-Production'. *Studies in Bibliography* 43 (1990), 49–62. Reprinted in Hanna, 1996, 48–59.

'MS Bodley 851 and the Dissemination of *Piers Plowman*'. *The Yearbook of Langland Studies* 7 (1993), 14–25. Reprinted in Hanna, 1996, 195–202.

William Langland. Aldershot, 1993.

'Meddling With Makings: Will's Work'. In A. J. Minnis, ed. *Late Medieval Religious Texts and their Transmission. Essays in Honour of A. J. Doyle*. Woodbridge, Suffolk, 1994, 85–94.

'On the Versions of Piers Plowman'. In Hanna, 1996, 203–43.

Pursuing History: Middle English Manuscripts and Their Texts. Stanford, 1996.

Harvey, M. *Solutions to the Schism: A Study of Some English Attitudes 1378 to 1409*. St Ottilien, 1983.

Harwood, B. J. *'Piers Plowman' and the Problem of Belief*. Toronto, 1992.

Helmholz, R. H. *Select Cases on Defamation to 1600*. London, 1985.

Heyworth, P. L. 'The Earliest Black-Letter Editions of *Jack Upland*'. *Huntingdon Library Quarterly* 30 (1967), 307–14.

Hudson, A. 'A Lollard Quaternion'. *Review of English Studies*, n.s. 22 (1971), 451–65. Reprinted in Hudson, 1985, 193–200.

'The Debate on Bible Translation, Oxford 1401'. *English Historical Review* 90 (1975), 1–18.

'A Neglected Wycliffite Text'. *Journal of Ecclesiastical History* 29 (1978), 257–79. Reprinted in Hudson, 1985, 43–65.

'A Lollard Sect Vocabulary?'. In M. Benskin and M. L. Samuels, eds. *So meny people longages and tonges: Philological Essays in Scots and Medieval English presented to Angus McIntosh*. Edinburgh, 1981, 15–30. Reprinted in Hudson, 1985, 165–80.

'Lollardy: The English Heresy?' *Studies in Church History* 18 (1982), 261–83. Reprinted in Hudson, 1985, 141–63.

'"No Newe Thyng": The Printing of Medieval Texts in the Early Reformation Period'. In D. Gray and E. G. Stanley, eds. *Middle English Studies presented to Norman Davis*. Oxford, 1983, 153–74. Reprinted in Hudson, 1985, 227–48.

Lollards and Their Books. London, 1985.

'A Wycliffite Scholar of the Early Fifteenth Century'. In Walsh and Wood, eds., 1985, 301–15.

'Wyclif and the English Language'. In A. Kenny, ed. *Wyclif in His Times*. Oxford, 1986, 85–103.

The Premature Reformation: Wycliffite Texts and Lollard History. Oxford, 1988.

'Epilogue: The Legacy of *Piers Plowman*'. In Alford, ed., 1988, 251–66.

'*Piers Plowman* and the Peasants' Revolt: A Problem Revisited'. *The Yearbook of Langland Studies* 8 (1994), 85–106.

'William Taylor's 1406 Sermon: A Postscript'. *Medium Aevum* 64 (1995), 100–6.

Hudson, A., and M. Wilks, eds. *From Ockham to Wyclif. Studies in Church History Subsidia* 5. Oxford, 1987.

Hunt, S. A. *An Edition of Tracts in Favour of Scriptural Translation and of Some Texts connected with Lollard Vernacular Biblical Scholarship*. 2 vols. Unpubd. D. Phil. thesis, University of Oxford, 1996.

Jones, W. R. 'The English Church and Royal Propaganda During the Hundred Years War'. *Journal of British Studies* 19 (1979), 18–30.

Jusserand, J. J., and J. M. Manly. Articles reprinted in *The 'Piers Plowman' Controversy*. London, 1910.

Justice, S. 'The Genres of *Piers Plowman*'. *Viator* 19 (1988), 291–306.

Writing and Rebellion: England in 1381. Berkeley, CA, 1994.

'Inquisition, Speech, and Writing: A Case from Medieval Norwich'. *Representations* 48 (1994), 1–29. Reprinted in Copeland, ed., 1996, 289–322.

Kane, G. *Piers Plowman: The Evidence for Authorship*. London, 1965.

'The Autobiographical Fallacy in Chaucer and Langland Studies'. R. W. Chambers Memorial Lecture, 1965. University College, London. Printed in G. Kane. *Chaucer and Langland: Historical and Textual Approaches*. London, 1989, 1–14.

Kellogg, A. L. 'Langland and the "Canes Muti"'. In R. Kirk and C. F. Main, eds. *Essays in Literary History Presented to J. Milton French*. New York, 1955, 25–35.

Kennedy, E. D., R. Waldron, and J. S. Wittig, eds. *Medieval English Studies Presented to George Kane*. Woodbridge, Suffolk, 1988.

Kenny, A., and J. Pinborg. 'Medieval Philosophical Literature'. In Kretzmann, Kenny, and Pinborg, eds., 1982, 11–42.

Kerby-Fulton, K. *Reformist Apocalypticism and 'Piers Plowman'*. Cambridge, 1990.

Kretzmann, N. 'Syncatoremata, Sophismata, Exponibilia'. In Kretzmann, Kenny, and Pinborg, eds, 1982, 211–41.

Kretzmann, N., A. Kenny, and J. Pinborg, eds. *The Cambridge History of Late Medieval Philosophy*. Cambridge, 1982.

Laing, M. *Catalogue of Sources for a Linguistic Atlas of Early Medieval English*. Cambridge, 1993.

Latham, R. E. *Revised Medieval Latin Word-List From British and Irish Sources*. London, 1965.

Lawton, D. 'Dullness and the Fifteenth Century'. *English Literary History* 54 (1987), 761–99.

'The Subject of *Piers Plowman*'. *The Yearbook of Langland Studies* 1 (1987), 1–30.

Lawton, D., ed. *Middle English Alliterative Poetry and its Literary Background*. Woodbridge, Suffolk, 1982.

Lawton, L. 'The Illustration of Late Medieval Secular Texts, with Special Reference to Lydgate's *Troy Book*'. In D. Pearsall, ed. *Manuscripts and Readers in Fifteenth Century England*. Woodbridge, Suffolk, 1983, 41–69.

Lewry, P. O. 'Grammar, Logic, and Rhetoric'. In Catto, ed., 1984, 401–33.

McFarlane, K. B. *Lancastrian Kings and Lollard Knights*. Oxford, 1972.

McHardy, A. K. 'Liturgy and Propaganda in the Diocese of Lincoln during the Hundred Years War'. *Studies in Church History* 18 (1981), 215–27.

McNiven, P. *Heresy and Politics in the Reign of Henry IV: The Burning of John Badby*. Woodbridge, Suffolk, 1987.

Maierù, A. *Terminologia logica della tarda scholastica*. Rome, 1972.

University Training in Medieval Europe. Trans. D. N. Pryds. Leiden, 1994.

Manly, J. M. See Jusserand.

Mann, J. *Chaucer and Medieval Estates Satire*. Cambridge, 1973.

'The Power of the Alphabet: A Reassessment of the Relation between the A and the B Versions of *Piers Plowman*'. *The Yearbook of Langland Studies* 8 (1994), 21–50.

Mathes, F. A., O.S.A. 'The Poverty Movement and the Augustinian Hermits'. pt ii. *Analecta Augustiniana* 32 (1969), 5–116.

Middle English Dictionary. Ed. H. Kurath *et al*. Ann Arbor, MI, 1954– .

Middleton, A. 'The Idea of Public Poetry in the Reign of Richard II'. *Speculum* 53 (1978), 94–114.

'Narration and the Invention of Experience: Episodic Form in *Piers Plowman*'. In L. D. Benson and S. Wenzel, eds. *The Wisdom of Poetry: Essays in Early English Literature in Honor of Morton W. Bloomfield*. Kalamazoo, 1982, 91–122.

'The Audience and Public of *Piers Plowman*'. In Lawton, ed., 1982, 101–23.

'Introduction: The Critical Heritage'. In Alford, ed., 1988, 1–25.

'Making a Good End: John But as a Reader of *Piers Plowman*'. In Kennedy, Waldron, and Wittig, eds., 1988, 243–66.

'William Langland's "Kynde Name": Authorial Signature and Social Identity in Late Fourteenth-Century England'. In Patterson, ed., 1990, 15–82.

'Acts of Vagrancy'. Forthcoming.

Miethke, J. 'Zur Einführung'. In J. Miethke and A. Bühler, eds. *Das Publikum politischer Theorie im 14. Jahrhundert*. Munich, 1992, 1–23.

Minnis, A. J. 'Langland's Ymaginatif and Late-Medieval Theories of Imagination'. *Comparative Criticism* 3 (1981), 71–103.

Medieval Theory of Authorship: Scholastic Literary Attitudes in the Later Middle Ages, 2nd ed. Aldershot, 1988.

Orme, N. 'The Education of the Courtier'. In Scattergood and Sherbourne, eds., 1983, 63–85.

Oxford English Dictionary, 2nd ed. Prepared by J. A. Simpson and E. S. C. Weiner. Oxford, 1989.

Pächt, O., and J. J. G. Alexander. *Illuminated Manuscripts in the Bodleian Library, Oxford*. 3 vols. Oxford, 1966–73.

Pantin, W. A. *The English Church in the Fourteenth Century*. Toronto, 1980 (Cambridge, 1955).

Patterson, L., ed. *Literary Practice and Social Change in Britain, 1380–1530*. Berkeley, 1990, 216–47.

Pearsall, D. *Old and Middle English Poetry*. London, 1977.

'The "Ilchester" Manuscript of *Piers Plowman*'. *Neuphilologische Mitteilungen* 82 (1981), 181–93.

An Annotated Critical Bibliography of Langland. New York, 1990.

'Hoccleve's *Regement of Princes*: The Poetics of Royal Self-Representation'. *Speculum* 69 (1994), 386–410.

Richardson, H. G. 'Heresy and the Lay Power Under Richard II'. *English Historical Review* 51 (1936), 1–28.

Rigg, A. G. *A History of Anglo-Latin Literature, 1066–1422*. Cambridge, 1992.

Roskell, J. *The History of Parliament: The House of Commons 1386–1421*. 4 vols. Stroud, 1992.

Ross, C. D. 'Forfeiture for Treason in the Reign of Richard II'. *English Historical Review* 71 (1956), 560–75.

Rouse, R. H. and M. A. *Preachers, Florilegia and Sermons: Studies on the Manipulus Florum of Thomas of Ireland*. Toronto, 1979.

'*Statim invenire*: Schools, Preachers, and New Attitudes to the Page'. In R. L. Benson and G. Constable, eds. *Renaissance and Renewal in the Twelfth Century*. Cambridge, MA, 1982, 201–25.

'The Franciscans and Books: Lollard Accusations and the Franciscan Response'. In Hudson and Wilks, eds., 1987, 369–84.

Russell, G. H., and V. Nathan. 'A *Piers Plowman* Manuscript in the Huntingdon Library'. *Huntingdon Library Quarterly* 26 (1963), 119–30.

Scanlon, L. 'The King's Two Voices: Narrative and Power in Hoccleve's *Regement of Princes*'. In Patterson, ed., 1990, 216–47.

Scase, W. *'Piers Plowman' and the New Anticlericalism*. Cambridge, 1989.

Scattergood, V. J. *Politics and Poetry in the Fifteenth Century*. London, 1971.

Scattergood, V. J., and J. W. Sherbourne, eds. *English Court Culture in the Later Middle Ages*. London, 1983.

Schroeder, M. See Carruthers.

Simpson, J. 'From Reason to Affective Knowledge: Modes of Thought and Poetic Form in *Piers Plowman*'. *Medium Aevum* 55 (1986), 1–23.

'*Piers Plowman*': An Introduction to the B-Text*. London, 1990.

Spade, P. V. 'Obligations: B'. In Kretzmann, Kenny, and Pinborg, eds., 1982, 335–41.

Spencer, H. L. *English Preaching in the Late Middle Ages*. Oxford, 1993.

Stein, I. H. 'The Wyclif Manuscript in Florence'. *Speculum* 5 (1930), 95–7.

Storey, R. L. 'Clergy and Common Law in the Reign of Henry IV'. In R. F. Hunnisett and J. B. Post, eds. *Medieval Legal Records Edited in Memory of C. A. F. Meekings*. London, 1978, 342–408.

Strohm, P. '"A Revelle!": Chronicle Evidence and the Rebel Voice'. In *Hochon's Arrow: The Social Imagination of Fourteenth-Century Texts*. Princeton, 1992, 33–56.

'Chaucer's Lollard Joke: History and the Textual Unconscious'. *Studies in the Age of Chaucer* 17 (1995), 23–42.

'The Trouble with Richard: The Reburial of Richard II and Lancastrian Symbolic Strategy'. *Speculum* 71 (1996), 87–111.

Stump, E. 'Obligations: A'. In Kretzmann, Kenny, and Pinborg, eds., 1982, 315–34.

Swanson, R. N. *Church and Society in Late Medieval England*. Oxford, 1993.

Sylla, E. D. 'The Oxford Calculators'. In Kretzmann, Kenny, and Pinborg, eds., 1982, 540–63.

Szittya, P. R. *The Antifraternal Tradition in Medieval Literature*. Princeton, 1986.

Tachau, K. H. *Vision and Certitude in the Age of Ockham: Optics, Epistemology, and the Foundations of Semantics, 1250–1345.* Leiden, 1988.

Thesaurus Linguae Latinae. Gen. ed. C. O. Brink. Leipzig, 1900–.

Thomson, W. R. *The Latin Writings of John Wyclif: An Annotated Catalogue.* Toronto, 1983.

Thorne, J. R. 'Piers or Will: Confusion of Identity in the Early Reception of *Piers Plowman*'. *Medium Aevum* 60 (1991), 273–84.

Tierney, B. *The Crisis of Church and State 1050–1300.* Toronto, 1988 (New Jersey, 1964).

Tout, T. F. *Chapters in the Administrative History of Medieval England.* 6 vols. Manchester, 1920–33.

Tuck, A. *Richard II and the English Nobility.* London, 1973.

Tuck, J. A. 'Carthusian Monks and Lollard Knights: Religious Attitude at the Court of Richard II'. *Studies in the Age of Chaucer, Proceedings* 1 (1984), 149–61.

von Nolcken, C. *The Middle English Translation of the Rosarium Theologie.* Heidelberg, 1979.

'Some Alphabetical Compendia and How Preachers Used Them in Fourteenth-Century England'. *Viator* 12 (1981), 271–88.

'An Unremarked Group of Wycliffite Sermons in Latin'. *Modern Philology* 83 (1985–6), 233–49.

Waldron, R. 'John Trevisa and the Use of English'. *Proceedings of the British Academy* 74 (1988), 171–202.

'Trevisa's Original Prefaces on Translation: A Critical Edition'. In Kennedy, Waldron, and Wittig, eds., 1988, 285–99.

Walsh, K. 'The *De Vita Evangelica* of Geoffrey of Hardeby (*c.* 1385)'. pt i, *Analecta Augustiniana* 33 (1970), 151–261. pt ii, *Analecta Augustiniana* 34 (1971), 5–83.

A Fourteenth-Century Scholar and Primate: Richard FitzRalph in Oxford, Avignon and Armagh. Oxford, 1981.

Walsh, K., and D. Wood, eds. *The Bible in the Medieval World: Essays in Memory of Beryl Smalley. Studies in Church History Subsidia* 4. Oxford, 1985.

Watson, N. *Richard Rolle and the Invention of Authority.* Cambridge, 1991.

'Censorship and Cultural Change in Late-Medieval England: Vernacular Theology, the Oxford Translation Debate, and Arundel's Constitutions of 1409'. *Speculum* 70 (1995), 822–64.

Weisheipl, J. A. 'Curriculum of the Faculty of Arts at Oxford in the Early Fourteenth Century'. *Mediaeval Studies* 26 (1964), 143–85.

'Developments in the Arts Curriculum at Oxford in the Early Fourteenth Century'. *Mediaeval Studies* 28 (1966), 151–75.

Wilks, M. 'Royal Priesthood: The Origins of Lollardy'. In *The Church in a Changing Society: CIHEC Conference in Uppsala, 1977.* Uppsala, 1978, 63–70.

The Problem of Sovereignty in the Later Middle Ages: The Papal Monarchy with Augustinus Triumphus and the Publicists. Cambridge, 1963.

Wittig, J. S. '*Piers Plowman* B, Passus IX–XII: Elements in the Design of the Inward Journey'. *Traditio* 28, 211–80.

Index

With the exception of citations of the bible and of manuscripts (both of which are listed comprehensively under those headings) sources cited in the notes are not indexed unless some substantive point is made about them there. Works with known authors are indexed under author even if little is said of the author in the text; all anonymous works are indexed under title. Modern authorities are cited as well as original materials, but more selectively, with a focus on those that are extensively discussed or that provide important background information.

Index

CAMBRIDGE STUDIES IN MEDIEVAL LITERATURE